PENGUIN PLAYS

PL40

NEW ENGLISH DRAMATISTS 4

NEW
ENGLISH DRAMATISTS
4

INTRODUCED BY J. W. LAMBERT
EDITED BY TOM MASCHLER

———

YES, AND AFTER
Michael Hastings

THE HAPPY HAVEN
John Arden
in collaboration with Margaretta D'Arcy

FIVE FINGER EXERCISE
Peter Shaffer

PENGUIN BOOKS

Penguin Books Ltd, Harmondsworth, Middlesex
AUSTRALIA: Penguin Books Pty Ltd, 762 Whitehorse Road,
Mitcham, Victoria

—

Yes, and After

First published in Penguin Books 1962
Copyright © Michael Hastings, 1962

—

The Happy Haven

First published in Penguin Books 1962
Copyright © John Arden, 1962

—

Five Finger Exercise

First published Hamish Hamilton 1958
Published in Penguin Books 1962
Copyright © Peter Shaffer, 1958

—

Made and printed in Great Britain
by Cox & Wyman Ltd,
London, Fakenham and Reading

CONTENTS

THE youngest of the three dramatists represented in this volume, Michael Hastings, was also the first in the field. When his first play, DON'T DESTROY ME, was put on at the off-Shaftesbury Avenue (I speak, of course, not geographically but on the analogy of off-Broadway) New Lindsey Theatre in July 1956 he was only eighteen years old. This irrelevancy brought him a good deal of publicity but shifted attention from the play to the writer and certainly hindered any sensible response to the very real qualities of his work. He was at once bracketed with the then newsworthy Angry Young Men, and became the subject, or object, of a journalists' field-day; a disturbing and in no way helpful experience for any writer.

DON'T DESTROY ME was set in a tenement in Brixton, South London, occupied by Jewish families. None of them was very stable, or they would not have been in this warren; and the theme of the play was the disillusion of ardent, bewildered youth amid the manoeuvres – mostly sexual – of tawdry adults. And, despite the partisan hysteria sounded in its title, it did wring a true and touching poetry out of its dunghill aspirations. At the same time Hastings was working on the play published here, YES, AND AFTER, which was given a Sunday-night performance at the Royal Court Theatre.

Once again we are in South London, but this time in a strongly contrasted milieu. The action takes place in a steady policeman's household; steady, that is, in its broad-based social framework, but beset by strange cries from the metropolitan jungle – and thrown utterly off balance by the retreat into wild aloofness of its thirteen-year-old daughter, who may or may not have been indecently assaulted by the vanished lodger. Out of the failures of sympathy and communication inevitable to this state of affairs, Hastings again develops a haunting dramatic poetry. YES, AND AFTER suffered, I have no doubt, from being a little ahead of its time. Had it appeared more recently it would have been recognized for what it is – a piece fully equal in its groping music to Shelagh Delaney's A TASTE OF HONEY and A LION IN LOVE.

*

The work of John Arden brings to the stage intelligence, passion, and craftsmanship. One may have reservations about their successful application here or there, but these qualities are in themselves enough to give Arden's plays not only interest but a certain stature. LIVE LIKE PIGS was almost a naturalistic comedy, but out of the clash between its steady plodders and its wild, rootless wanderers, it struck sparks more fiercely promethean. SERGEANT MUSGRAVE'S DANCE carried the contrast a stage further; between the townsfolk, both oppressors and oppressed, of his nineteenth-century north-country hell and the visionary madness of Musgrave, lies all the difference between the dead and the living.

In THE HAPPY HAVEN this opposition – which lies at the root of all Arden's plays so far – is given another twist. The dead, in this case, are the patients, or inmates, of an old people's home. All, we may note, have been failures in the life they have left behind them; and their mortification is cruelly echoed, at the end of the play, by the procession of stuffed-shirt public figures which comes to visit them. The life force is represented by the young doctor who runs the home – and once again, as with his outcasts in LIVE LIKE PIGS and with Musgrave, Arden has not repressed a panic horror at the essential nature of this vitality. The doctor is by no means a mere variant of the conventional mad scientist. Bascially neither benevolent nor male-volent, he is, however, a man with an *idée fixe* who is also in all other respects commonplace to the point of parody. And at last the old people win a pyrrhic victory over him; always, in Arden's plays, the dead win the battle if not the war.

All Arden's plays contain an element of technical experiment which, variably successful, constitutes a stimulating challenge to producers and actors – to say nothing of audiences. In THE HAPPY HAVEN he takes a stage further his attempts to integrate song into dialogue: as detached Brechtian comments in LIVE LIKE PIGS; as lyrical, ballad-like exaltation in MUSGRAVE; and here as a sharp rhythmic stepping-stone to verbal counterpoint, a short cut which is also an interlude on the big dipper. But his most striking experiment in THE HAPPY HAVEN is his use of masks. Brecht, of course, borrowed this idea from the theatre of the East, but on the whole made little use of it. Arden here uses masks not merely to establish minor types, but to coax through them a type of character acting which does not rely upon facial grimace but requires the actor, given a suitable face, to get right into the character; to act, that is, primarily with his voice and body. The danger here, of course, is that the strangeness of the method prevents us from seeing round it; but this difficulty will not trouble the reader of the play, which is in any case a striking black farce, embodying a powerful idea, a meaningful conflict, and a number of perceptive observations of life.

*

Peter Shaffer has, in a sense, undertaken by far the most difficult task of any of these three dramatists. Almost alone in his generation he has set out to write a straightforward play of personal relationships set firmly in the middle classes. His characters belong to the most vulnerable of all sections of our society, targets of contempt from above, envy from below, and sharp shooting from their own intelligent young: a successful businessman, a wife with cultural trimmings pasted on to a voracious self-absorption, a jolly little daughter, a terribly sensitive son – there is a group which invites derision.

But it does not get it from Shaffer. The version of the play given here is, by the author's preference, that used in New York; its variations from the text played in London are in themselves minor, and don't affect its basic attitude towards its characters, which remains not, certainly, one of contempt; not quite, even, one of respect; but rather one of anxiety. The changes do, however, underline with small touches Shaffer's preoccupation with naturalism of a kind which suggests that he is still very close to his subject.

FIVE FINGER EXERCISE is firmly placed in a strong tradition of

English plays, leading down from Pinero and Granville Barker by way of Noël Coward and THE VORTEX; a tradition in which the clash of generations is not a background to heroic personal disaster but the play's major preoccupation – one characteristic of a flourishing middle-class society in which the children are always leaving their parents behind. Shaffer's treatment of it is remarkable for its full-blooded dramatic power, a welcome refusal to shrink from the theatrical moment.

MICHAEL HASTINGS

Yes, and After

YES, AND AFTER

First produced at the Royal Court Theatre, London, on 9 June 1957, with the following cast:

JEAN	Patricia Lawrence
JIM	Robert Stephens
CAIRY	Heather Sears
DR BROCK	Alan Bates
JACK	Jimmy Carroll
JERRY	Michael Wynne
MARIE	Olivia Irving
TERRY	Graham Pyle
BOB	Anthony Carrick

Directed by John Dexter

AUTHOR'S NOTE

IN Ansky's *The Dybbuk*, a boy and a girl meet for a moment without speaking and fall instantly in love. That same day the boy, Channon, a student, dies. The girl Leah is engaged to an appointed husband she has not yet met. On her wedding day she refuses to marry him, and the spirit of the dead youth Channon speaks from Leah's betrothed mouth. On her father's request the ritual of Chassidism temporarily restores her sanity. The Dybbuk, dead Channon, cannot resist the Rabbi's invocations and grudgingly relents. Leah is expected to go through with the marriage. She cries out for Channon and he appears to her. He explains that, though he has left her body, their souls can yet be joined together. Leah goes to him.

The story of Leah might help the reader to understand Cairy in *Yes, and After*; though the girls' roles are quite different both in character and in action, *the idea* of the plot in *Yes, and After* is not quite as original as it might seem.

M.G.H.

ACT ONE

―――――――――

SCENE ONE

The time is the present.

As the curtain rises the audience can see the ground floor interior of a small house in Stockwell. The front of the stage is taken up by the effect of two rooms, side by side, but there is no wall. On the left, facing, the more respectable furniture shows the mostly unused dining-room. Whereas next to it, on the right, you have a small sitting-room which is used every day, a settee and two arm-chairs and the usual odd things. Behind the sitting-room there is the kitchen, with sideboards and small cupboards. At the far right, at the back, there is a door leading out to the back-garden. In the centre-back of the complete stage stands an old grandfather clock. In the direct centre between the lounge and dining-room there is an automatic radiogram. On the far left again of the stage you can just see the start of the stairs: three steps, then a sharp turn. And still on the left side, facing, directly behind the dining-room, there is the main door out to the front of the house.

Now upstairs. The audience can see a small landing, farther back from the front rooms downstairs. On the left, facing, there is an alcove where the stairs end and then a door, which should lead to a bathroom. And then opposite it, although the audience cannot see it, is the door to Jimmy and Jean's room. Along the landing there could be a small airing cupboard, facing the audience, then Cairy's room. Apart from a frame door, you can see inside the whole room. By the frame door there is her bed, long-ways as the audience looks at it. Somewhere behind is a window facing into the back-garden. To the far right of her room is a small camp-bed, where Terry eventually sleeps.

Also downstairs. Behind the front door, or where the door turns back, there is another door, to a toilet. And beside the back-door, there is a small

15

window to look out on the back-garden. There is a slight air of close-cluttered positioning.

Sunday morning, early.

JIMMY *is making some food by the kitchen table, humming softly to himself, he is fully dressed. After a moment,* JEAN *comes out from her room upstairs, and descends slowly. She wears her dressing-gown as if it is a piece of sacking. Limp from her heavy sweating last night her hair is untidy. Her face – white from exhaustion. She is carrying her dress for the morning, squeezing and rumpling it, as if it is a rag.*

JEAN: . . . Jim . . . Jim . . . Jim . . . are you in the . . . What are you doing? . . . What did you get up for? . . . You're cooking . . . it's too early . . .

JIM: Hungry.

JEAN: . . . What is that – breakfast? Is it breakfast or lunch? Oh, I feel dreadful . . .

JIM: Go back then – I'll bring some tea up.

JEAN [*very heavily, her face crinkling*]: Tea? . . . It's not tea-time, is it?

JIM [*non-committal*]: No –

JEAN [*slumping down on the lounge settee*]: It must be breakfast then. . . . I feel old and sick, after last night. It was a mad-house in here. What are you trying to make over there –?

JIM: Eggs.

JEAN: Doesn't smell like it.

JIM: Do you want anything else?

JEAN: What?

JIM: Take yourself back to bed.

JEAN: I don't want ever to go back to bed! And face last night again. I wish I could never sleep at any time.

JIM: Don't worry, you slept –

JEAN: I couldn't have done. I was awake the whole time. Listening. And her voice – I've never heard in all my life such – how can a girl scream like that? For hours without a break . . . then she jibbers and cries.

JIM: Sit up here, I can serve it then . . .

[*She lifts herself up by the kitchen table; she sits down.*]

JEAN: My legs . . .

JIM: All right – eggs? [*Putting them down before her.*] There was some beef fat for the toast, and jam, no marmalade. You never got any – yesterday.

JEAN: Jim, how can a girl scream like that?

JIM: You asked me that once. Drink your tea. Then go back –

JEAN: I can't sleep any more. I've had enough. As long as I live.

JIM [*drinking*]: . . . I slept.

[*Pause, while they eat.*]

JEAN [*suddenly*]: I'm not untidy. I've got a slip on underneath. It's only – no stockings. I hope Dr Brock doesn't come in and see me like this. Show him I've got bad manners. I'll go up and wash again. After – after – Cairy's washed.

[*Pause again, while* JIM *is reading a paper.*]

JEAN: . . . Jim . . .

JIM [*still reading*]: . . . Uh –

JEAN [*slightly comic, pouting*]: What are you going to do – about her?

JIM [*lost*]: What?

JEAN [*sharp*]: You must be going to do something –

JIM: How do I know?

JEAN: I don't!

JIM: Wait until Brock comes –

JEAN [*up and across to window, then turning*]: That's it. There's too much waiting. Always it's a little too late. Can't you phone them up – at the station?

JIM: It's not the end of the world.

JEAN: It is to me.

JIM [*softly*]: . . . Ooh.

JEAN: It's all so calm with you. Do you know what it's doing to me? – I'm being strangled!

JIM: You can nag louder than she screams at times.

JEAN [*more to herself*]: . . . Waiting for it to happen, and it has happened already. [*To Jim.*] That noise she made. The whole of London must have heard it.

JIM: You can't act quicker than police. If you're a bag of nerves, it's your fault. I'll phone up Brock now, he'll come over and bring you something.

JEAN: I don't want anything. I want something to happen!

JIM: All I know is they'll contact me as soon as they know something. And he can't get very far, not in a few hours. He can't have much money, if he had any – and a couple of days – they'll have him.

JEAN [*over to him*]: Lend me the paper, will you? [*Crosses back.*] . . . You read about the sort of people these things happen to . . . [*Sitting and looking at him.*] . . . Lodger rapes inspector's daughter!

JIM: I hardly knew what went on. One way or the other – between the two.

JEAN: Well?

JIM: You tell me one or two things, when she is sick and he fusses about, that's all I know, until, this –

JEAN: A man should at least understand his character better than I. You've lived with him here long enough. How long has he been here? – Nine months.

JIM: I'm not a psychologist.

JEAN: Couldn't you see it? Now and again in his actions or what he said?

JIM: But you couldn't! [*Up.*] He was here all the time during school holidays, messing around. You even told me – he got in your way. You had far more time than I did, girl.

JEAN: I don't know what to look for.

JIM: Yes, and the great thing about it all – he wouldn't talk with anybody else. Apart from us, here. Outside he was as dumb as a blinking rock. But you never noticed it! . . . He never drank. He never smoked. Played chess the whole time – with himself! . . . Never went out – what do you expect?

JEAN: I didn't ask for it to happen.

JIM: Don't get excited. . . . What was he teaching – arithmetic?

JEAN: Grammar school.

JIM: Yes, that standard. He mixed with every sort of child there is. If he wanted to be queer, he had plenty of opportunity. Long before this. That's what stumps me. I gathered there was nobody on more friendly terms with Cairy – than Johnson. And as quiet and reasonable as anyone. That's the ridiculous side to it. . . . Why?

JEAN: Ask her.

JIM: I give up. [Silence.] . . . [Loud.] If there is any further nonsense with that girl, I'll send her to a boarding school. Didn't she ask for more than she expected?

[Above on the landing, CAIRY comes out from her room, crosses the landing, slowly, then descends, off. She appears very calm and self-collected.]

. . . Didn't he take her out, all over the place? Private parties, picnics, fairs, anything. It was a long – I know what he was doing. He was working up to something. You can see it now, too late.

JEAN: I can't take her everywhere . . . at least he offered . . . he couldn't have been in his right senses – to try.

JIM: He was clever, I'll grant him. He could have planned it so neatly, like counting a man out.

[The telephone rings. JIM rises.]

[At phone.] . . . Yes . . . Yes, I am. . . . In fact, we both are.

JEAN: Who is it?

JIM: It's Jack. She's much better. . . . Yes. . . . And we're both very tired.

JEAN: Who is it?

JIM: It's Jack! No, you're wrong – I only rang your father last night because I felt desperate. I know you're good friends, but I'm tired.

JEAN: Well, what does he want?

JIM: He wants to help if he can . . .

JEAN: What could he do!

JIM: I can't talk to you now, I'll tell you later. . . . No, I'm very sorry,

I know you're loyal. .... I know you want to help. .... It's very generous of you. .... [*Hangs up.*] God help me if he ever becomes a copper!

JEAN: Is that why he hangs round you?

JIM: I don't know. He's kind in his way. When you find a time when you need friends, it's certainly not the time to start looking for them.

JEAN: I've never needed friends before, I wouldn't know. I don't know, not your kind.

JIM: You're full of self-pity!

JEAN: I talk and think as I think fit.

[*She stops short, as* CAIRY *comes on stage in her dressing-gown. She is slim and short, slow moving, a little concubine. They both pause to watch her come forward, tense.* JEAN *crosses, flurried, to Cairy's side.*]

... Darling ... you shouldn't have got up. We could have brought food up. .... How do you feel?

[*No answer,* CAIRY *seems to look through them.*]

JIM: Come over to the table and sit down. ....

JEAN [*to Jim*]: Shall I get porridge ready – I don't quite know what to do.

JIM: No ... not yet. She'll go back to bed.

JEAN [*whispers in Cairy's ear, secretively*]: Cairy, what do you want to do?

[CAIRY *crosses to the window, and stares quietly out.*]

JIM: Well?

JEAN [*appearing shrunken somehow at Cairy's nonchalance*]: Can you eat something now?

JIM [*haltingly*]: Stay in bed then.

JEAN [*weakly*]: Cairy, you can do anything you want. We won't mind. As long as you're happy. [*Smiling.*] It's you. You're important. Today. Nobody – else – matters ...

CAIRY [*pausing – to herself more*]: I want to go out there ...

JIM: What for?

CAIRY: To see the garden.

JIM: And –?

CAIRY: Yes . . .

JEAN [*crossing to Cairy, she holds her shoulders away from her, as if sizing her up*]: Not now darling . . . the doctor says no.

JIM: Have you left anything out there?

JEAN [*to Cairy*]: You're not serious, besides you've only got pyjamas on.

CAIRY [*softly*]: Yes.

JIM: That's your lot then, you can't.

JEAN [*leading her*]: We are your friends, Cairy. We know what is right, and we love you because we do these things. You act as if you are ignoring us completely. We are your parents – you don't want anybody any closer to you. [*Kneels.*] . . . We can talk.

[JEAN *makes to fondle her a little unconsciously.*]

JIM: She's still the same. It's like concussion.

JEAN: That's what he said.

JIM: Can she understand us any of the time? It won't last long – will it?

JEAN: He said a day or two. Ask him again today. He promised to be round about twice a day.

JIM: Should be now.

JEAN: It was funny – he left no medicine. I don't think he even made out a prescription.

JIM [*getting up to light a cigarette by the book stand*]: Not that I know. I say she should be kept in bed.

JEAN [*to Cairy*]: I'll take you back upstairs. You can have a water-bottle, then breakfast. I think it's wrong you should walk about. . . . You understand? You are a little sick, it will blow over.

JIM: I'll see to things, you take her up.

JEAN [*putting her arm round Cairy's shoulders as if protecting her, they move left slowly*]: . . . Ready? . . . [*Over her shoulder.*] I know what would be a good idea. To get some company for her. Why don't you ring up Marie for me. She could quite easily bring young Terry down here. To stay for a few days.

[*They are nearly off when* CAIRY *breaks loose and runs silently across the stage to the scullery door. She shakes the bolted door violently, then stops, pauses, and turns round, her eyes wide, staring into the ceiling.*]

Cairy, come back here! Jim, can't you stop her!

CAIRY: Open it, please!

JEAN [*aloud*]: What in heaven's name for –?

JIM: Cairy, come over here . . . [*To Jean.*] What's out there in the garden?

JEAN [*loud*]: She seems to know more than I.

JIM: Quiet.

CAIRY [*forward*]: Let me see the tree, please . . .

JEAN: You see – there's that tree out there she likes?

JIM: Why?

JEAN: Don't ask me – it's too cold. You come up with me.

JIM [*breaking any tension up, bravado*]: Oh, it's bed for you. [*He half lifts her over to Jean.*]

JEAN [*softly*]: Any time later, darling. [*She pulls her gently by the arm. To Jim.*] If she runs about any more in her bare feet, she will get more than a fever.

CAIRY [*loose again, her eyes tight closed, running blindly into Jim*]: Let me see it – [*Choking.*]

JIM: Now – whoops! Young lady to bed. Or off with your head. And then you'll be dead. [*Bending, he sweeps her up high and then carries her off, laughing. He shouts back, off.*] If we take her too seriously we'll all end up in a mental home.

[*They re-appear on the landing.*]

CAIRY [*softly*]: Let me go out. [*He claps his hand to her mouth.*]

JIM: No more. Perhaps tomorrow. Not now. [*To Jean.*] Will you phone up Marie. About Terry. It's a good idea. Now let's get you to bed, madame.

JEAN: Will they be up?

JIM [*busy*]: Yes.

CAIRY: ... I want to go down there to Henry Johnson. It's our tree. ... Sssh, they're listening. Whisper. Like that ... they can't hear you. But ... it's our own language. Shall we stay out there, tonight, all night, and listen to it creaking, like an old man's back. And it is one.... You laid the leaves down on the garden, it became green for – promises. Odd isn't it? You can use it for anything. Nearly Autumn and it's like a maypole. So – May colours. And then it is black, and cold in the rain. ... And a house and a throne ... can you imagine anything – it can't be? There's no other anywhere ... but you cannot buy it. They don't belong to anybody, do they?

JEAN [*picks up phone by the couch, dials*]: ... Hallo ... dear ... Jean. Yes. I haven't got you out of bed, have I? ... Good, I know what you are. You'd sleep all day if you had the chance. Yes. I know. How did you know? All right, I'll hold on. ... [*To Jim.*] That was Bobby. Did you tell him about Cairy?

JIM: What?

JEAN: I said that was Bob, did you tell him about Cairy?

JIM: I rang him up last night from the station.

JEAN: ... Hallo – yes – Marie? I know, dear. I've been driven crazy, here all night – listening to her. What could I do? ... We'll have to sit tight and wait. ... Honestly all I know is – that he must have attacked her. ... Yes. While I was out. I had to do some shopping. ... Well, yesterday afternoon is the only chance I get to really look around ... and Jimmy was in the station at Streatham. You see ... I know. We had absolute trust in the man. They had the complete run of the house.... From around three to five. I got back, and she was on the floor. She was shaking to bits. I could do nothing with her. And the brute was gone. ... She's completely lost touch with us.

[*Doorbell rings.* JIM *lets in* DR BROCK. *He takes his coat off quietly while* JEAN *finishes. They wait for her. Brock is a very young doctor.*]

... Darling, the Doctor has come. I'll have to be quick.

CAIRY [*soft but clear*]: Mister Johnson – Mister Johnson – Mister Johnson – Mister Johnson – [*fades*] . . .

JEAN: Would you both come over here this afternoon? You and young Terry, and Bob. Really I'd like Terry to stay here, for a day or two, only to keep Cairy company. She's so nervous. . . . You really don't mind? . . . Fine.

JIM: Come on then! We haven't got all day! Once you let these women on a phone –

JEAN: Yes, well bring some things for him, we'll manage all right. . . . Bless you. Two o'clock. Bye . . . we will. [*Puts phone down, turns and gets up to Brock.*] . . . Hallo, Doctor. . . . [*To Jim.*] They'll be here at two o'clock.

JIM: Uh. What's best? Shall I bring Cairy down here – or do you want to see her upstairs?

JEAN: Believe me, you are a welcome visitor. We are both – quite out of our minds. Worrying. I'm sorry about this. I meant to change them before you came.

JIM: I like the way she says 'we'. I'm in good control of myself.

BROCK: You should be. You're in the police, aren't you?

JIM: Don't pass the buck!

JEAN [*more to herself*]: Everything is so untidy. . . .

BROCK [*to her*]: I ignore what you said. It's not your clothes that worry me – it's your health.

JIM: What do you want to do? Go upstairs –?

BROCK: Yes. I think I'll go up.

JIM: I'll show you. [*They move off.*]

JEAN: While you are up there, I can change myself –

JIM [*off*]: What into?

BROCK [*off*]: How was she last night?

JIM: I don't know. I slept like a drunk.

JEAN: Like hell you did! . . .

[*General laughter off, then they re-appear on landing. They cross to Cairy's room.*]

BROCK: I don't think your wife believes you.

JIM: All women are cranky this time of the morning. [*He knocks lightly on Cairy's door.*] Can you guess who this is? Cairy? [*To Brock.*] I can't see the point in trying to speak to her – in her present state. She doesn't even know me. [*Opens door. To Brock.*] Not her. She won't speak to her father. I'm not important enough! I'll leave you two to it. Leave the door open, if you want anything, shout. [*Crosses landing and off, then on again.*]

    [BROCK *closes door.*]

JEAN: I suppose he's staying for lunch?

JIM [*entering*]: Who?

JEAN: He said yesterday – this is the only visit he's got.

JIM: You better ask him when he comes down.

JEAN [*standing centre, putting her dress over the couch, unfastening her dressing-gown, and slipping into her dress*]: He's got nobody at his place to make him a meal. He'll be grateful for a proper one.

    [*The conversation becomes louder upstairs.*]

BROCK: Why didn't you go out with Mum and Dad yesterday, Cairy –?

CAIRY: I've got no father. He was walking under the flower tree and – he vanished. It must have swallowed him, whole. That sounds rather splendid.

BROCK: And Mother?

CAIRY: I don't know. I can't see her. Whenever I'm in a room . . . and I hear them talking . . . and calling her . . . I look round. I see everybody else – but she's never there.

BROCK: Do you hear her?

CAIRY: When they talk to her – Mr Johnson answers back. You do – it's not her voice. I think he speaks for her, as well.

BROCK [*pausing*]: . . . Am I different from the Mr Johnson, say, of yesterday?

CAIRY: You are always the same. Like the tree out there. You can do so many things with it. But it is the same.

BROCK [*hesitant*]: . . . Cairy. Do you forgive me – for yesterday?

CAIRY: Why? What have you done? [*Chuckling.*] That tragic voice. I forgive you – I don't know what for . . .

BROCK: Do you remember what happened yesterday? Do you remember what we did?

CAIRY [*slowly*]: . . . we went out –

BROCK: No.

CAIRY: Down to the park at Herne Hill –

BROCK: No.

CAIRY [*a little flurried*]: We went somewhere, there was the church choir. You knew some of the boys there. Yes, didn't we join in and –

BROCK: You don't want to, do you? Think hard.

CAIRY: Why is it that important?

BROCK: It's very important.

CAIRY: There were so many. Where did we go?

BROCK: I'm not telling.

CAIRY: You take me to such odd places. Far away – they are – so strange. I can't remember them all. Listen – can you hear water gushing away? It flows so naturally. Smooth like music. Didn't we listen to music once at the Albert Hall? I couldn't understand it. There was too much to see. The huge walls and the musicians. And people there – you had no time to listen to the music!

BROCK: Now don't say any more. Until I'm back. I won't be a moment. [*On landing.*] Mrs Mount?

JEAN: Yes?

BROCK: I have her talking quite well, that is something. I don't know what to do with her now. The more she lets off steam, the more she releases herself.

JEAN: Would you like to bring her down here? If she's talking . . . perhaps she would prefer more company.

[*They talk in a semi-whispered tone.*]

BROCK: She's got a mannerism – of blacking out other people and putting Johnson there. What was his christian name?

JEAN: Henry – Henry Johnson.

BROCK: Did she call him Henry?

JEAN: I think so – but she'd never say it in front of us. She was too bright for that. How long will this go on?

BROCK: Can't say, at the moment. She is so moody. Her stomach muscles are rigid, like cardboard. She is straining inside her, she has to break herself of it.

JEAN: She shivers as if she's cold. Does that mean anything? She won't be violent again, will she?

BROCK: Might. I can't tell with these – they try to bring it out themselves. Unconsciously. They can't hold it inside.

JEAN: Bring her down here – I don't like her on her own.

BROCK [going off]: It won't harm her. I don't think she feels lonely. [BROCK at Cairy's door.]

JEAN [down]: He's bringing Cairy down again.

JIM [lounging]: How is she?

JEAN: He's got her talking.

JIM: Don't you think he's a young fellow?

JEAN: He hasn't started long.

BROCK [upstairs]: Cairy, put your things on and come downstairs. We can talk better.

CAIRY: Where are we going?

BROCK: Your Mother and Father are down there – [Hesitant.]

CAIRY: How far –?

BROCK: O.K.? What about your slippers? They're over there. I'll put them on for you. [He gets them, then kneels in front of her.]

CAIRY: Don't touch my feet. They're ticklish.

BROCK: I've got to put them on you.

CAIRY: I like you kneeling down in front of me. It's awfully pleasant. . . . I am about to chop off your head . . . or, you've laid a cloak at my feet – to step over – [She lays her small hand lightly on his hair.] Johnson . . .

BROCK [looking up]: Haven't I got another name?

CAIRY: What?

BROCK: Christian name –

CAIRY [*hesitant again*]: Yes. Henry –

BROCK: That's better. Let's go. [*He pushes her in front of him.*]

CAIRY: You are very tall. Does that – you must feel it up there.

BROCK: What?

CAIRY: Feel the cold!

BROCK [*really embarrassed by the mood she creates*]: I touched you before, didn't I? I put your slippers on – and – held hands – you remember?

CAIRY: I remember.

BROCK [*faltering*]: . . . Cairy, did I ever touch you – there – did I? [*He presses his hand against her breast lightly.*] . . . like that?

CAIRY: . . . I can't –

BROCK: No, not ever –?

CAIRY [*frigid*]: No.

BROCK: Let's go down. We can talk.

CAIRY: What would we do without it?

BROCK: Talk?

CAIRY: I think I'd scratch – to tell people . . .
    [*Both off descending.*]

JIM: What are you going to cook? [*To Jean.*]

JEAN: I didn't say I was.

JIM: What is there?

JEAN: I don't think there's enough . . .
    [*The two come on stage.*]

BROCK: There they are –

CAIRY: Who?

BROCK [*to Jean*]: . . . I think she'll talk now.
    [CAIRY *walks strangely to the kitchen door, her arms hold the posts, and looks through the door.*]

JEAN: Cairy, are you talking to us?

CAIRY [*turning to Brock*]: Please let's go out.

BROCK: Where to?

JIM: That's what I asked.

CAIRY [*almost herself*]: . . . Mr Johnson.

28

BROCK: What's out there?

JIM: A tree.

JEAN: That's their little secret – the flower tree.

BROCK: What would you do if I took you out there?

CAIRY [*vaguely*]: Yes . . .

BROCK: What would you do?

CAIRY: . . . Just laugh. I'd want to laugh out loud until I cry – under it, there is shelter. You'd like it, may I take you – [*She faces round to Brock.*] – your hands. [*Holding out her hands.*] Come on.

BROCK: What is there in just sitting underneath it?

CAIRY: It shelters you. If you say it to yourself – it will. Say you are cold then it will be a bed, or are you an old man? You can be young out there . . .

JEAN: I want to be sick.

BROCK: Perhaps it doesn't want you to go out there.

CAIRY [*startled*]: You're playing with me.

BROCK: Why that tree? Cairy?

CAIRY [*squats*]: Nothing is so natural as that.

BROCK [*softly*]: There are others.

CAIRY: There are not. They are made of people or flesh and wood.

BROCK: Isn't that made of wood?

CAIRY: It's not made of anything. You know? You should know. It's your tree, isn't it,?

BROCK: There's more to it than that.

CAIRY [*loud*]: I want the window opened!

BROCK [*holding her*]: Now quiet!

JEAN [*to Jim*]: Can't he do more than that?

BROCK: Now are you steady, now? No more, Cairy.

CAIRY: Well, it's all over.

BROCK: You're not fit to go out. [*Kneels.*]

CAIRY [*sinking on to floor*]: Don't make me disbelieve you. I can't see without you, I want to wear glasses, and walk with a stick. I was running backwards, with you, I daren't stop. You wouldn't make me stop until I tripped. I don't need my eyes. You can tell me. I don't need ears or tongue, you can tell me, if you say you know everything I need, you do – you do –

[*Pause.*]

JIM: Tell me what to do and I'll do it.

BROCK: I don't know. [*Rises.*]

JEAN: Up now. Get up. Can you hear me? . . . [*To Brock.*] I'm afraid to touch her in case –

JIM: If Bob was here, he'd probably burst out laughing.

BROCK: Let me count up to ten.

JIM: Have you got any medicine for her?

BROCK: I'm afraid to. Whatever I give her. It might break into her nervous system, and that's what I don't want. It might harm her. I don't know – you need a psychoanalyst, not a doctor.

JIM [*to Brock*]: Shouldn't you know all the answers?

BROCK: I'll write out a note for barbitone tablets. You can get them tomorrow. And [*writing*] sprinkle it in milk . . . for her. By then I don't think she'll need them. Shock goes as quickly as it comes. But she might get a slight fever. Hence the tablets.

JIM: Leave her down here?

BROCK: I'm pretty sure she'll need a hot-water bottle. If there is one ready . . .

JEAN [*crossing*]: There's some water left in the kettle . . . yes. She only needs it half full.

JIM: She could bath . . .

BROCK [*sitting her on sofa*]: You feel her hands. They're freezing.

JIM: I'll take her up. [*Crossing to her.*] Up you get. I did this sort of thing when you were half this age. Taking you to bed.

JEAN: It'll be ready in a minute.

JIM [*sits by Cairy on sofa*]: No more shouting. There's nothing to make too much fuss about. Now you stop it.

BROCK: I believe there should be as many people around her – as soon as she can get them. This isn't a doctor's job at all. Not at the present. I can't prescribe anything. It's up to her –

JIM: You talking to me?

BROCK: Well, either of you, it's just how soon she can break it. [*Sitting.*] I suppose the police are on to him. already?

JIM: I've got some of my own boys working on it. There's some down at Brixton as well – giving a hand. That's my brother-in-law, Bob. Before the week's out, the whole local force will be out looking for him.

BROCK: If he's not caught by then, I suppose you'll both want a full report –

JEAN: Well. Of some kind.

JIM [*to Brock*]: What about this afternoon? Are you coming over? Or leave it till tomorrow –

BROCK: I don't think it will be that necessary.

JEAN: Tomorrow then.

BROCK: I'll come in the morning. She'll be all right by then. I'm sure. She's not too young to fight it. Any child of thirteen or fourteen can react subconsciously.

JIM: How soon will you know – if it's bad or not?

BROCK: You don't. Nobody can tell you how soon her nervous system is or is not going to climb back.

JEAN: It might last weeks.

BROCK: Not with a girl like that. She's too young to keep it tight inside her. Children heal quicker, they forget and they grow.

JIM: Now if I was a kid of thirteen or so, and some bloody old man attacked me, I just couldn't get myself tied up like that. And have her crazy fits. I'd take it quite different. You know – I wouldn't mope over it.

JEAN: If you were thirteen, you wouldn't have the sense to think things – like that. She's not lived as long as you have – has she?

JIM: As I said –

BROCK: I follow you. But it would not be likely that you, personally, would ever get into that position. That's not important. What is – the fact that Cairy has that indisposition. When you were that age were you liable to be raped by the lodger?

JIM: I very much doubt it.

BROCK: So do I. I can't imagine you having much sex-appeal at that age. I bet you were a little tyke – shouting down streets, and tying cats to dustbin lids.

JIM: About Cairy, I'm worried. Suppose – I don't want to bother her with it. But where does she go from here? When it's all over and she settles down . . .

BROCK: Yes –

JIM: . . . at school amongst the other kids what will happen? Suppose she gets a kink against men, she might change completely –

BROCK: If I know children, there's nothing to worry over.

JIM: . . . I can't see it like that. She was always nervous, before he came. She's easily frightened. She's the type of child you can imagine reading poems to herself, and daydreaming –

BROCK: Never! Children appear to be hurt deeply. They can cry their heads off. It's nothing. It's an exuberance.

JIM: She won't forget him – not that quick.

BROCK: She will.

JIM: The man intoxicated the girl! Every little word he said, she noted it down in her head. [*To Jean.*] You can tell him that, can't you? . . . She doted on him.

BROCK: Maybe.

JIM: You see you don't know as much as I do even!

BROCK: Obviously. But whoever knows the most – either side, that's unimportant. This is a matter of chance – and I back her to pull through.

JEAN: He must have hypnotized her, I think.

BROCK: By my reckoning he must have hypnotized you two too.

JIM: What is your Christian name?

BROCK: Owen.

JEAN: Doctor Owen Brock.

BROCK: It's Welsh. I know you both quite well, in a way, but we've never had a real chance to get together.

JIM: Right! The farther we are from you the better.

BROCK: I don't think anybody really likes a doctor in the house.

32

JIM: I don't believe in shouting for one as soon as someone's got a cold – the smallest thing.

BROCK: ... if you knew how many pensioners bother me with the most trivial complaints. They're the only type that really need me. I think they're lonely. They live in small rooms, one foot in the grave and one half out – it terrifies you that there are so many.

JEAN: Poor things.

BROCK: A doctor's a one-man band. Everything – everybody.

JIM: You're quite a youngster for this job. It's a lot to take on.

BROCK: Honestly, I think it's too big. I'm depended on for far too many things. People rely on you, and it's life or death often. They put so much faith into you – you let them down, and you're nothing. They never bring that faith back again.

JEAN: How old are you?

BROCK: Twenty-seven. That's nine years' training.

JIM: After I'd been nine years in the Force all I'd made was a sergeant. I tell you, the locals had less faith in me than in a stray cat!

BROCK [up]: Well, this is where I came in ...

JEAN: There's no hurry to go.

BROCK: You've got more people coming – I think I'll get out of your way.

JEAN: Really.

BROCK: No. I'll push along.

JIM: You don't have to.

BROCK: Oh yes. In any case, I'll be here tomorrow. [Moving away to put on his coat.] I don't want to impose upon you – the more you keep me out of work, the happier you will be.

JIM: No. We were only kidding.

BROCK [turning round]: I'll disappear then – thanks for everything, you know? – ring me if you want –

JEAN [up]: But we'd love you to stay. There are too many lonely bachelors as it is. Are you lonely?

BROCK: With all those patients of mine?

JEAN: They're not the real thing –

VOICE [*off*]: Jim! Jim!

JIM: Did you hear? [*Listening.*]

JEAN: Where?

JIM: In the garden?

JEAN: No.

JIM [*looking through the back window curtain*]: I heard something . . .

JACK [*off – a broad coarse voice*]: Hi – Jim?

JIM: It's those two young fellows from over the flats.

JEAN: Which two?

JIM: Jack and his mate – what's his name.

JEAN: Oh – they're not coming in here –

JIM: What?

JEAN: They're the last couple I want to meet now.

BROCK: Who are they?

JIM: A couple of teds who talk of joining the Force.

BROCK: Why?

JEAN: Because – there's only one reason why they come in here and that's to get a free drink off Jim.

BROCK: I only asked as I thought they might help Cairy. Are they friends of hers?

JEAN [*firmly*]: No!

JIM: That's the kind of conversation women make nowadays! [*Winking.*]

JEAN [*around*]: They think Jim's a hero.

BROCK: Are they friends of Mr Johnson?

JIM: Never! They're nice kids – I helped them once when they were in a spot of bother.

BROCK: Tell me – how normal was this man?

JIM: He was normal.

JEAN: He was not.

JIM [*to Jean*]: You're not listening to the trend of the conversation!

JEAN: Everything about him was abnormal, everything about him was –

JIM: What I mean is – he was normal in an abnormal sort of way.

JEAN [*to Jim*]: What?

JIM: I mean he wasn't normally abnormal. If you see what I mean.

JEAN: No. I don't!

BROCK [*to Jim*]: Why do you like those lads out there?

JIM: Well, they're nothing to do with you, are they? I have a little bit in common with them –

JEAN [*sneering*]: What have you got in common?

JIM: They said they wanted to join the police, didn't they?

JEAN [*stamping her feet*]: Oh for God's sake! You're more like a child than Cairy.

JIM: Why am I?

JEAN [*to Brock*]: They're just a pair of juvenile delinquents, Jim once tried to straighten out. He'd made a promise to their father.

JACK [*off*]: Jim . . .

JIM: Aw – let them in, girl!

BROCK: Shall I go?

JEAN: If you don't I will! I don't like rough types.

JERRY [*off*]: Hey – Cairy!

JEAN: They sometimes used to play with Cairy – but they're too old now for that sort of thing. It's all girls now –

JACK [*sharply-off*]: Cairy!

JEAN: They want to come around to tell us how sad they are because Jim rang their Dad and told him what had happened. He was too desperate to think of anyone else to tell.

JIM: He and I play billiards regular like up Coldharbour Lane.

JEAN: I notice how he never invites me along.

JIM: You can't play billiards.

JEAN: I can try.

JIM: It's men only.

JACK [*off*]: Can we come in?

CAIRY [*sitting up*]: Who is that? [*Not loudly.*]

JACK [*pushing open the kitchen door*]: Hallo – Jim.

CAIRY: Listen – to the tree, talking, oh we can all hear it if we try hard enough . . . listen.

JEAN: You see! You see what happens. She's getting excited.

BROCK: No, don't do that.

JEAN [*she glares round*]: Whose side are you on?

JACK: Hallo, Cairy love, not so well today?

JEAN [*turning away bitterly*]: Who listens to me anyway?

CAIRY: . . . Isn't this our little secret . . .

    [JERRY *and* JACK *edge inside the door staring at Cairy in absolute fascination.*]

JIM: Well – don't just stand there!

JEAN [*reluctantly*]: Hallo Jack – Hallo Jerry.

CAIRY: This would be our tree, you see, and this is – and this is . . .

JIM [*to Brock*]: Speak to her then.

BROCK: She doesn't need me to, she makes up her own answers.

JEAN: You're not very helpful.

BROCK: I have better things to do than to play games with Cairy here; I'd like to find out how to get to the bottom of it.

JERRY: Are we in the way?

JEAN: Yes.

JIM: No.

CAIRY: I love the tree, Mr Johnson.

JACK: Can we talk to her?

CAIRY [*sitting up*]: Oh yes.

JEAN [*to Brock*]: Now what do you do?

BROCK: Listen to her.

JEAN: Is that all?

BROCK: You'll learn more by listening to her and watching what she does than by talking.

CAIRY: Please – what is the tree saying to me now . . . the tree says – Ouch! My finger! The bark splintered into my finger-nail.

JERRY: Cor . . . ain't she weird. Ain't she?

JACK: Jim? What has happened?

JIM: Shut up for a minute –

JEAN: Do you know, sometimes there is a moment when you feel nobody quite knows what to do anywhere, all over the world, there is a small space of time, very rarely, but it happens. I am sure this is it now . . .

JIM: Jean.

JEAN: Say something happy, Jim? Don't joke like those two do; don't pretend to me like Cairy is doing to them. I can't act back any more. I want to prove to Marie when she comes that I'm still a good entertainer. I want to forget about Cairy altogether.

[JIM *holds her shoulder.*]

. . . Nobody can pretend for long, because somebody knows what you are doing; you can never lie about a thing that nobody else in the world knows of, you have to share a lie somehow.

JIM: What's come over you? This isn't the time to crack up.

JEAN [*stepping forward and away from Jim*]: There you are, you don't know what comes next, do you? [*Sits.*] It's difficult to imagine what will be said three sentences away. I'm the only one talking, aren't I? Yes, I'm the only one. I'm exhausted – not her.

JIM [*to Brock*]: What can you do for her too?

JERRY: Well, we do look some proper Charlies, standing around asking what next to do . . . I must say, like.

CAIRY: But you are the tree, and I'm always trying to share it with you.

BROCK: I'm still trying to listen to her.

JERRY: Then come and see the tree with us, Cairy? [*To Jim.*] . . . What tree?

CAIRY [*loud*]: Who is it then if you're not the tree! Mr Johnson. Who is in the garden besides you?

JACK: It's not me – straight – I can tell you.

BROCK: Ssshh.

CAIRY [*loud and clear*]: Who is out in the garden!

JACK: That was us, see – your pals from over the flats.

JERRY: Here, Cairy, what about them games we used to have?

CAIRY [*running to the window and leaning out shouting*]: Will you come out of that garden! Whoever you are!

[JACK *and* JERRY *smirk dim-wittedly, thinking she is playing with them.*]

JERRY [*nudging Jack*]: You wouldn't catch me under any tree with old Henry there! The things they say about him . . . the creep.

[JACK *giggles.*]

CAIRY: Go along! Please leave, get away from the tree. . . . Whoever said they could go out there? Nobody should be out there because nobody is coming back!

JEAN: I'm very tired of it all.

CAIRY [*throwing open a second window in the kitchen*]: They're out there by . . . they were pulling the branches. They like breaking things. They want to smash it down because it can't do anything for them. It's the only tree . . . he said, it's ours, and he said it was so much older than me, how old did he say . . .?

BROCK: Cairy, come back and talk to me. [*He leads her to the settee.*] . . . Now I must go. But before I do, I want you to go back to bed upstairs, and I'll come back in a day or two and we'll see you well and healthy. Will you do that?

[CAIRY *goes silently upstairs.*]

JEAN: We'll look after her, I promise you.

JIM: We'd like you to stay –

BROCK: No thanks.

[CAIRY *is wandering slowly up the stairs.*]

JEAN [*to open door*]: You will come soon?

BROCK: I'll be back before Tuesday.

JEAN: Thank you.

BROCK: Goodbye. [*Exit.*]

[*Pause.*]

JEAN [*folding her arms*]: . . . Well?

JACK: What about it then, Jim?

JIM: Well . . . let's sit down and jaw a bit first.

JEAN: Jim!

JIM [*to Jean*]: Let's try to have a laugh once, eh?

[JACK *and* JERRY *settle down.*]

JACK [*to Jean*] : . . . Are you worried, Mrs Mount?

JERRY : Proper turn up for the books – eh?

[JEAN *turns away*.]

JIM : Tell us a joke, Jerry.

JERRY : My Dad sends you his regards.

JIM [*uninterestedly*] : Yes . . .

JERRY : Do you know he's not forgot that day yet – when you found that stolen cashbox for him.

JIM : That's right – that was quite a day, wasn't it?

JERRY [*to Jean*] : Did Jim ever tell you about my old man's money, Mrs Mount?

JEAN : I don't know – I suppose so.

JERRY : He's a dark horse is old Jim. I bet he never told you nothing.

JEAN : Why aren't you both at work today? You ought not to be at home.

JACK : I work for Jerry's dad – same as him.

JERRY : My old man's a street bookie – a corner-tout; we're his runners.

JEAN [*to Jim*] : Did you know that?

JIM : Yes.

JERRY : That's what I meant when I said Jim did my old man a favour – that's what I was saying. You see my dad keeps all his money in an old rabbit-hutch underneath a floorboard under the cocktail cabinet –

JEAN : A rabbit-hutch !

JERRY : My old man fitted his rabbit-hutch inside the floorboards – and this is where he always had all his money.

JEAN : But why doesn't he use a bank, like everybody else !

JERRY : Ah – that's a good question. My old man's a canny nut, he don't believe in banks, if you see what I mean.

JEAN : No, I don't.

JERRY : He says to me he says – never give your money into a bank, they'll have it off you in no time – using your money for Building Armaments and Implements of War, my Dad says – he's a pacifist.

JIM: That's how he avoided the last war.

JERRY: As I say, my old man's canny –

JIM: He avoided the First World War too –

JERRY: That's right; they put him in the fields plucking potatoes; and that was like putting a silver spoon in his mouth. He soon had them all betting on his own Horse-Syndicate, a guaranteed foolproof system it was. He made a pile, I reckon.

JEAN: I'm sorry, I really can't follow you – if you don't mind, I don't see what –

JERRY: I'm coming to it now: because he wouldn't trust banks –

JIM: He wouldn't trust banks because he made no mistake about hiding his takings, that's the truth.

JACK: I bet your old man hasn't paid income tax for forty years.

JEAN [to Jim]: And you've been fraternizing with him all these years –

JIM: I've been playing billiards with him all these years, if that's what you mean.

JEAN: It doesn't sound right to me.

JERRY: I've passed a fair tip to you and all now and then, haven't I? Buckshee and all.

JIM: To cut a long story short, when their flat was burgled I happened to know of two coloured brothers who had just come out from lock and key for a similar offence – me and Jerry called on them in Arlington Fields – and we caught them barefaced with the loot.

JACK: Fifteen thousand quid there was.

JERRY: How about that for fancy work – and you never told your missus neither!

JEAN: So we're all good pals together, are we?

JERRY: Summat like that.

JEAN: Well – now if you'll excuse me, I've got –

JERRY [standing]: I understand – still, we called on the off-chance, see, that we might be able to help. I'm not on call for 'placings' until lunch-time.

JACK: Don't forget – tell us if there's something. We was always pally with old Cairy.

JIM: I won't.

JERRY: Well then – ta ta.

JIM: Ta ta.

JACK: Ta ta.

JIM: Ta ta.

[JERRY *and* JACK *exeunt.*]

[JIM *returns from the door.*]

JEAN: Did you know that boy was illegally 'running' bets for his father – all this time!

JIM: He's often handed a good tip to one of the boys on the beat beside their flats.

JEAN: Why do you encourage them here?

JIM: That boy Jerry's a bright one.

JEAN: But he's a hooligan.

JIM: He was.

JEAN: It wasn't that long ago when he was up in the juvenile courts.

JIM: That's right. I straightened him out – introduced him to a probation-fellow I knew. He's turned out quite bright.

JEAN: When I first laid eyes on him, I thought he's certainly not the type for my Cairy. Too damn' rough. I sent him packing last year when they tried to persuade her to join them in their pranks.

JIM: I know – you preferred nice quiet Mr Johnson, didn't you?

CAIRY [*shouting out through her window at the boys outside in the garden*]: . . . Go away . . . go away.

[JACK'S *voice replies* 'It's only us: Don't you remember us?']

. . . Go along! Please leave . . . [*She gets up and runs across the landing, pulling her dressing-gown with her. She enters again down on the stage making for the back door.*] . . . Whoever said they could go out there. [*Running and talking all in the same breath.*] . . . Nobody should be out there. Because nobody is coming. Suppose they break pieces off it. They've done that before.

JEAN: Jim?

CAIRY [*on stage*]: . . . They're out there by the – [*Opens the door and stands there stiffly.*] – they've gone. . . . He shouted to me they were pulling the branches off and I had to do something. He said – I know it was the same last week – they like breaking things. He warned you before to put up a wall instead of that fence. They jump over and seem to want to . . . Because it can't do anything for them, so they must do something back instead . . . at least, not that one, and he said – it's ours.

JEAN: Bring her back. If she should catch a cold, that would cap everything.

JIM [*to Cairy*]: You hear? . . . If you expect your Aunt to see you then you've got to act natural.

CAIRY: . . . Where is he? [*Looking round.*] He promised to be back. As soon as anything. Goodness . . . they wanted to know about the tree, just then. I told them they'd have to buy a life-interest in it before I told them. If they do, what he said was . . .

JIM: Leave her alone for a while. She'll be more natural if we act as if we are –

JEAN: Can't we imagine something prettier in the middle of it all, like she does. She can create something out of nothing –

JIM: A flower tree!

JEAN: Yes. Anything.

JIM: Where did you learn this from? Mr Johnson?

JEAN: Maybe I did, what of it?

JIM: The same to you with knobs on, silver bells, and forget-me-nots, and Christmas boxes on every branch! I think I'm the only sane one in the house –

JEAN: We are all out of step, you aren't! . . . Jim. There's nothing more real than pain. This is it. Reality. She believes in that tree because it's quite natural –

JIM: Aren't we? Skin and bone is enough, isn't it?

JEAN: That tree and the green and things – they're what we aren't. Somehow.

JIM: Baloney!

[*Doorbell rings.*]

JEAN: I suppose so. But doesn't it make you wonder just which is the reality?

JIM: Cairy – Take her upstairs to wash herself . . . they're about outside now.

JEAN: She's old enough to take herself up . . . I think I will though. I'll change these shoes . . . [*To Cairy.*] Coming? . . . Come on . . . it's like talking to a deaf mute. For all she notices. Cairy [*catching her arm*], we'd better hurry – or Auntie Marie will find me in carpet slippers.

JIM [*crossing and opening the door*]: Well – if it isn't my beautiful sister-in-law . . . [*Hugging her like a bear.*] You look all right. How is everything?

MARIE [*who is quite slim and wears a small-grey-pinhead suiting, and flat ugly shoes*]: Jimmy . . . Oh I'm fine. You're getting a little fat down there, aren't you?

JIM: Where's the rest of them –?

MARIE: Oh, they're out there . . . [*Calling outside.*] Terry – come on in . . . [*To Jim.*] I don't know what he's doing out there. [*Forward.*] . . . Isn't it quiet. Where are the others?

[TERRY *enters. He is about fourteen.*]

JIM: By Christ! When does he stop growing! Look at him now!

MARIE: He'll end up taller than Bob. Bob wasn't – how tall are you now?

TERRY: About five foot seven. Or so –

MARIE: He's much bigger than I am.

JIM: You're no giant!

MARIE: Yes. I know but –

JIM: What's Bob doing out there? I guessed he was coming as you had the car.

MARIE: He's doing something to the handle. We left the car keys behind us.

JIM: Take your things off then. Here, Terry, I'll take yours.

BOB [*in doorway*]: Sergeant Robert O'Neil reporting! ... Hallo lad!
[*To Jim.*]

JIM: Hallo.... Is that old car of yours losing its wheels or something –

BOB: No. We were all at sea this morning. She got into a flap as
usual. Cairy and all that – so we charged out half naked. Where is
she – young Cairy?

JIM: They'll be down. She's with Jean.... I'll take your coat, Bob.
... [*To Jean.*] Come on. Come on. We've got guests!

MARIE: Terry – you sit over there ...

[JEAN *crosses to go off downstairs.*]

Sit down, Bob....

JIM: Make yourselves at home. I haven't seen you for months.

BOB: You sound happier than I expected.

JIM: I'm not kidding. You're like a breath of summer in here. It was
like a graveyard yesterday. I didn't expect you to come. You
usually play sports on Sunday –

BOB: We could have played tennis. But Marie wasn't going. They
rang up the last minute – they couldn't open the groundsman's hut.
So, no game – it suited me.

MARIE: Thank God someone else has lost keys today.

JEAN [*coming on stage*]: Well now ... what a large family.

MARIE: Hallo, darling. [*They clasp hands.*]

JEAN: Sit down. Sit down ... Bob. I thought you couldn't come.
We didn't drag you from your –

BOB: More than glad to come, lovey.

JEAN [*looking at Terry*]: I can't say – young Terry any more. He
might clout me. He looks like a young bull! ... It's good to see
you. This place is like a graveyard!

[MARIE *and* BOB *laugh.*]

... What's funny?

MARIE: Darling. That's just what Jimmy said – it's a graveyard! You
are a perfect pair of glums.

JEAN: I'm not surprised. It's a nightmare in here. I wish we could get
out of it.

44

MARIE: Is it that bad?

JEAN: It's all over now. But it was like watching the world explode before your eyes last night.

BOB: Sounds as if you need the doctor. As well as Cairy.

MARIE: Oh, Bob. Where's that suit-case? We didn't forget that as well? I hope not. [*To Jean.*] That's his clothes.

BOB: I don't know.

MARIE: I reminded you about it before –

BOB: You never said a word.

MARIE: It was in the boot – I think.

BOB: I'll look. I can't remember putting it there . . .

MARIE: Scatterbrain you are.

BOB [*off front door*]: Excuse me.

MARIE: Bob. Bob!

BOB [*back*]: Yes?

MARIE: In the boot – remember?

BOB: . . . Where do you think I'm going to look – in the oil-tank!

MARIE: No – I know. Have you – have you got the keys to the boot?

BOB [*off*]: Ain't it real! . . .

MARIE: Nobody knows with that man what he has got and hasn't. He'd lose an elephant if he had one.

JIM: What's the case for?

JEAN: Terry?

MARIE: Yes.

JEAN: We've got plenty of things here. He could borrow some of Jim's things. He only wants pyjamas and things.

JIM: Can you imagine him walking round in my trousers?

JEAN: I said pyjamas.

MARIE: He'd still look like a mouse in a sheepskin!

BOB [*back*]: . . . One suitcase . . . [*Carrying it.*] *Well!* You going to enjoy yourself here, Terry.

TERRY: Mmm.

JEAN: Oh, leave him alone. You embarrass him.

BOB: Not him. Nothing can. Eh? [*To Terry.*]

JIM [*to Jean*]: . . . A bit different from Cairy?

JEAN: Nobody asked you to say that.

JIM: Oh, cut your long hair off. I was only cracking –

JEAN: Well I didn't hear it crack! Sorry and all that!

JIM: Never mind. . . .

MARIE: Aren't you two edgy!

JEAN [*tired*]: I don't know what we sound like. I couldn't care.

JIM [*to Bob*]: You haven't got any beer in that boot as well, have you?

MARIE: Where is Cairy? I thought she was with you –

JEAN: She's upstairs. She wouldn't come down.

JIM: If she keeps looking at that flower tree – she'll wear it away!

JEAN: She's crazy for that tree.

MARIE: Perhaps it's because of what's-his-name –

JEAN: It must be – they – that's our handicap, they did so many things together, and we can't know half of them. I think she wants to bring them all back –

BOB: Take her to see a specialist.

JIM: That's no damn good. Dr Brock said it would take a couple of days to clear up. If it doesn't – then – I tell you – I'll willingly beat it out of her myself. What I think is, she's worrying about him. Being caught or not. She doesn't want to tell us.

MARIE: Jean, did he examine her physically?

JEAN: Nothing – at least he hasn't harmed her. It was so spontaneous – well – there was nothing –

BOB: Only mental shock.

JEAN: Yes.

JIM: Say that as much as you like. Believe me, that wasn't spontaneous. From the minute he came here, he'd worked it all out. I said to Jean he was an old hand at it.

JEAN: She looked so lovely, like a spray of flowers . . . there was blood on her lips . . . she could have been a jewel box – suddenly broken open and they all fell out . . .

MARIE: Jean –

JIM: Poetry! There's always blinking poetry when someone is ill!

JEAN [*coming forward to Marie*]: ... Have you ever felt that there's a voice inside your head screaming itself hoarse at you – and the pain; I feel dreadful – all I want –

MARIE [*holding Jean tightly as if she might fall down*]: Now, you shouldn't have asked us round – there was no need. You're not fit –

JEAN: Hold me like that ... you're a fine sister you know – you don't grow old, do you, like me? You are very clear-skinned – how do you do it? [*Her voice is a whisper.*]

MARIE: We never get a chance to see each other –

JEAN: That's all wrong, isn't it? We should be next to each other – Oh God, I wish something would happen terribly quick.

MARIE: Never mind, darling.

BOB [*stretching*]: What a sickly sounding bunch we are ...

MARIE: You do come out with some sane remarks, don't you!

BOB: Oh, I've got millions of them! ... You know what I mean? ... There's an air about the house –

JEAN: Don't worry, Bob. We are dead.

JIM: What's up with you?

MARIE: Leave her alone –

[CAIRY *walks on slowly*.]

BOB [*seeing Cairy*]: There she is!

MARIE [*up*]: Hallo, dear.

JEAN [*moving to Cairy*]: ... Darling, come and sit down –

JIM: Leave her alone. Let her find her own way here – she's not blind –

JEAN: I was only getting up –

JIM: She doesn't have to have you –

MARIE: Come over here, Cairy. By me. You look a little – isn't she pale? She's quite white compared to Terry.

BOB: Terry. [*Looking at him.*] You haven't said a word since we got in.

TERRY: I'm all right –

BOB: I wish you'd say something. Your old man's sitting here holding the fort – talking his head off – and you don't back him up!

TERRY: What shall I say?

BOB: You think of something.

JIM [to Terry]: He's kidding you!

JEAN [to Cairy]: . . . You know Aunt Marie and Uncle Bob? . . . And Terry?

MARIE [holding Cairy's shoulders]: You haven't seen Terry for a long time.

JEAN: Say you know them, Cairy – you're not dumb . . .

MARIE: Well? . . . Are you pleased to see us?

JEAN [waiting]: Ssshh.

JIM: Oopsie-boopsie-boo! You whine like school kids! Can't you talk properly to the girl? She's not two years old! You'd think this was her christening!

MARIE: . . . Never mind. Look, this is Terry – [Exhibiting him to Cairy.] He's staying with you for a few days . . . you don't mind that?

BOB: How would you like a bit of company, Cairy? Terry's a good playmate! Go on, Terry – you're not shy!

MARIE [laughing]: They're both a little tongue-tied! Don't you want to say anything, Terry?

JEAN: She's staring . . .

CAIRY [turning round to the kitchen door]: . . . Quiet . . . [Looking round.]

JIM [following her eyes]: Eh?

CAIRY [to herself]: Isn't it? . . . [As if listening.] You see you were right after all . . . I can see them . . .

JEAN [tentatively]: . . . There's no one out there now, they went – please don't go out there – we've got friends, Cairy.

CAIRY: . . . I said if they were quiet, I could hear them . . .

MARIE: What is it?

JIM: That blinking tree!

MARIE: Sssh! She's listening to something . . .

JIM: She'll listen to me in a minute!

CAIRY: Every time they talk, he says something, and I miss it.

He wanted to say it then. Even if your skirt rustles, or – and it's lost.

MARIE: Let her take Terry outside then. They can't come to much harm, can they?

JEAN: If I could get some peace and quiet –

MARIE: Well then.

JEAN: Jim. Send them out.

JIM: She's spent the whole morning trying to get out there. I might as well.

BOB: Go on, Terry, then – with Cairy.

JIM [to Cairy]: And you – [Taking her hand.]

MARIE: All right, Terry?

JIM [moving to door]: He's fine.

TERRY: Where to?

JIM: Blimey! That's the first word he's said to her! [Opening door.]

BOB: Out in the garden. Cairy will look after you. Now you do whatever she says. And – well you've got to help her to get better; you know that?

TERRY: Yes.

BOB: You don't know, do you? Never mind.

JEAN: And don't move away from each other. You stay together.

JIM: How far do you think they're going – Brighton?

JEAN: I don't want those children from the flats – interfering –

JIM: They won't touch her. [Holding door wide.]

TERRY [beside Cairy]: . . . What's out there? . . .

[The stage blacks out.]

SCENE TWO

This time it is the evening of the same day, Sunday. Upstairs there are no lights except on Cairy's face and Terry's. They are in bed. Downstairs the hall and kitchen and to the left are shaded in half light.

The two single lights pick up Cairy's face more strongly. Terry is turned the other way, you can see the back of his head. Downstairs the large clock's ticking is magnified. The rhythmic beating comes quite clear and loud all the time during this scene.

CAIRY: Terry . . . Terry . . . Terry. . . . Now you remember the fair at Tooting? There was the Whip. And the cars swung round in a huge circle. It was loose, on one of its wheels. In that one next to us. Didn't he swing round – that fast, that much. Then snap and the whole carriage shot right through the barrier. He, there was – how many were in it? Two? An old man and a boy. He was about – he was younger than me, Terry. Are you awake –? He was the same age as you. Did you hear? Terry . . . Like you. It was just as if you – he shouted as loud as he could. And it hit the barrier. And – and you were dead. One minute you are looking at – it comes charging towards you, hits you, and you don't see any more. You haven't got any eyes. Or heart. That clock downstairs – it's beating like a heart. I can hear it quite plain. That's what tells our time – our hearts – ticking away. [*Joking.*] My heart's on my wrist! . . . You were dead. The car had twisted over, and rammed your head against the wall. . . .

[TERRY *turns over and gapes at her dully.*]

The old man cried. I had never seen a man cry. It seems unnecessary – because he's too old. . . . His face was wet, he wanted to die instead of you – they wouldn't let him. It wasn't his mistake – and – it was – all – over. He shouted out, 'I can't live, and him die! I can't live –' Why don't you ask him? . . . Ask him . . . [*No answer.*]

Are you frightened to? It's only old Mr Johnson! [*Giggling.*] . . .
He's listening . . . [*Gets out of bed.*] Look – come over here –
  [TERRY *folds the blankets over his head in amazement.*]
It's all right. It's safe, Terry! Terry! I'll bring him to you – now
stay there – everything will be correct and in orderly fashion. [*She
moves along landing, with the light on her face.*] Now, now where are
we –? . . . We are not alone. . . . You know – there's Terry to think
about! . . . He is awfully talkative! . . . He might tell anybody – I
can't see in the dark. Don't move . . . and I'll touch you.

TERRY: You are sleepwalking, Cairy – there'll be trouble! You –

CAIRY: Ssssh, I've got him. He's terribly shy with new – you are his
  friend? Yes? You are – aren't you? Here he – say – say you are his
  friend . . . say . . . No. He won't! You remember the Whip at the
  fair? When the car swung round and lost a wheel, the carriage shot
  through the barrier at an old man and a boy – your age. The old
  man started to run but it caught you and rammed your head against
  the wall. You saw it. I needn't tell you! And that clanging the
  ambulance made! You did see it. Yes. I was with you. And the
  most beautiful moment. You said it. That it was the loveliest
  second in your life. We were up there, right on the top of the
  switchback! You couldn't be any higher. In the back of the car.
  As it dipped, and we stood up for a moment. There was everything beneath us. Nothing was missed out. The lights, and far out
  to the end of London. You could see it stop. There were cows, and
  streets, and tall buildings and things, then a park and gas-works.
  Quiet sort of colour, and the roads were less sharp. Didn't we stand
  up and shout out! What did you say after that? . . . You only learn
  to love something by seeing enough of it. We saw enough! We
  saw so much then, there were millions of people, you were in love
  with the whole world. Go on – listen Terry – I saw it then more
  than ever before. I'd never been up in a plane. When I looked at all
  that ground. People I had never spoken to, millions, they'd never
  heard of me. I couldn't shout loud enough, up there, to tell even
  one of them who I was. And that I loved them! I'm so small. . . .

If they could hear my name, once. I did once; I wrote to the personal column in an evening paper; I was willing to pay double – I told them. All I wanted was a simple line – like 'I'm Henry Johnson'. But they refused! They said it didn't mean anything! It wasn't a trick-advertisement, or a message home, it didn't do anybody any good. That was the worst thing to say. It would have helped me. Wouldn't it? . . . Does everything in this world have to be of use to somebody, can't the smallest thing just stand there, and people take notice of it, just because it is being there? Terry doesn't. [*To Terry.*] Do you? You don't?

TERRY: You're crazy! It's – it's – I'll shout for somebody!

CAIRY: I do. Out of everybody. Even the tree. I know some people are like electric bulb-sockets. You fit them – and the lights go on.

TERRY: Aren't you cold? Go back in to bed.

CAIRY: No.

TERRY: Why?

CAIRY: Come on. [*She pulls the blankets partly off him.*]

TERRY: Don't do that; it's too late to mess about –

CAIRY [*softly but urgently*]: You must. Because he's going soon, he's going out.

TERRY [*scrambling out from under the coverlet; Cairy nearly pushes him out*]: Who is?

CAIRY: He is –

TERRY: I don't care –

CAIRY: You can stop him – you can try –

TERRY [*bewildered*]: Look at me – you can't look at me straight; your eyes are blank. Aren't you mad? You must be mad.

CAIRY: I've got no time –

TERRY [*making for the door*]: Nor have I –

CAIRY: You can't go without me –

TERRY: I can. Because I'm going; to tell them.

CAIRY: You mustn't go out! I didn't say –

TERRY: Please don't stop me. I'm going. [*He pushes her aside.*]

    [TERRY *runs out of the door, but* CAIRY *slams herself down on his heels, grappling at his legs; she can't quite hold him. She screams at the top of her voice.*]

CAIRY: ! . . . Oh no! Not to them – they wouldn't believe you. Nobody would. It's a complete pack of lies. He never even existed! . . . But it doesn't matter, because I was there. Because, in the fair, when it happened, and the wall hit you – I screamed!

[TERRY *runs away from her, leaving her on the floor yelling.*]

. . . No one can scream louder! I screamed right out loud because I thought you were dead!

TERRY: I wasn't there – it was a mistake . . . Hey! [*He hammers on Jim's door at the end of the landing.*]

JIM [*appearing*]: For Christ's sake, Terry! [CAIRY *lies still on the floor, breathing heavily.*] . . . Ssssh, your Aunt's asleep.

CAIRY: Each time they say anything they are not the same person; whenever I look – the face isn't the same . . . I'm dizzy with it.

JIM [*hissing*]: Will you shut up!

TERRY: What shall I do?

JIM: What has she been doing?

TERRY: What?

JIM: Look; you go in my room. You can sit on the bed for the moment. Cover yourself up. [*To Cairy.*] Now you; I wish you could see yourself, right now – you wouldn't like what you saw.

JEAN [*off*]: Jim? . . . What is it?

JIM: I don't know; you stay there.

[CAIRY *is coughing.*]

JEAN: What are you doing? Is that Cairy?

JIM: Yes.

JEAN: Put a light on.

JIM: I will.

JEAN: Where is she?

JIM: She's here.

JEAN: I'm getting up.

JIM [*beside Cairy*]: You can stay there.

JEAN [*on landing*]: Put the light on – I can hardly see.

JIM [*kneeling beside Cairy*]: Come over here and look.

JEAN [*to Terry*]: Now stay there. [*Over to Cairy.*] Is she out?

JIM: No. She's awake. Put your hand there, by her mouth.

JEAN: It's blood!

JIM: It's spit. She's salivering all over the place.

JEAN [*away to left to switch light on*]: Ugh! I don't want to be sick. [*Lights on.*] Is that better.

JIM: I'll take her back to her room.

JEAN: I'll call Brock.

JIM: You'll do no such thing! [*Lifting Cairy.*]

JEAN: I won't have her left on her own. Jim!

JIM: I'll stay with her then. Now go back to bed. You can look after Terry. He was shivering out there.

JEAN: Where are you going to sleep?

JIM: We'll be all right. Turn the light off. [*He carries Cairy back to her bed.*] Go on. Hop it. And close your door. [*He shuts his.*]

JEAN [*turns the light off. And stands by her door looking at Terry*]: ... We shouldn't have brought you here, Terry, so soon, I'm sorry we did that – [*Her voice fades as she shuts her door.*]

[*The stage blacks out.*]

CURTAIN

[*Only when the curtain has fallen does the loud ticking of the clock stop.*]

ACT TWO

SCENE ONE

The next morning.

[JEAN *shouts upstairs.*]

JEAN: Terry . . . Cooooeeee . . .?

TERRY [*poking his head out from the bathroom*] : . . . Yes?

JEAN: You're not still in bed –?

TERRY: I'm up.

JEAN: Are you ready then? The food is down here ready –

TERRY: Mm.

JEAN: Two minutes then – and come down. [*She hums to herself.*]

TERRY [*whining from off in the bathroom*] : . . . Where are they –?

JEAN: Yes?

TERRY: They're not here!

JEAN: What's missing?

TERRY: Auntie, have you got them?

JEAN: Oh yes! I keep everything in this house in my pocket!

TERRY [*standing on landing in a long white shirt, but no trousers*] : Where
   – where have they gone –?

JEAN: Bring yourself down here and tell me.

TERRY [*off a moment, descending, on again*] : . . . Look at me!

JEAN: What's this!

TERRY: I've lost my trousers!

JEAN: That I can see! Well now – there are ladies in this house, you
   know! You can't toddle about like that.

TERRY: I came in a pair, didn't I?

JEAN: I hope you did!

TERRY: I think they are in – her room –

JEAN: I thought you changed in the bathroom last night?

TERRY: No.

JEAN: Go up and see if Cairy's got them. On your bed.

TERRY: No. I don't think – they . . .

JEAN: Now, you're not frightened?

TERRY: I can't go.

JEAN: I'll go with you.

TERRY: You go up.

JEAN: We'll both go together.

TERRY: Let's not go up there at all. She doesn't want us, does she?

JEAN: You'll catch cold otherwise. I suppose I must. There's no – really I asked you over, Terry, to stay with her; you're not filling that job very well, are you? . . . [*Going off.*] You're fourteen now . . . isn't that – Oh, Terry – [*Off.*] How much pocket-money did Marie give you?

TERRY: I never had any – she never –

JEAN [*on landing*]: She? Who is She?

TERRY: Mother –

JEAN: So you want a bit of money too – I'll be broke by tonight.

TERRY [*playing about with the furniture; to himself*]: . . . She doesn't want anybody . . . and that – what does she imagine? . . . That tree – [*Balancing himself on the chair arm.*] If I had that tree – I'd cut it down – You can't see the kids out there playing – it blocks up the view! . . . Auntie? . . .

JEAN [*in Cairy's room*]: . . . Cairy? Awake? You'd best get up. It's late enough. Cairy? I'll take that blanket off you today. You don't need it now. Isn't it stuffy in here! [*Opening window.*] That's better. How's that?

TERRY: I'm standing here naked! Auntie – [*He is playing about with the breakfast food.*]

JEAN [*bustling*]: Yes. They're here, Terry.

TERRY: I'm waiting.

JEAN: Come up then.

TERRY: Bring them down.

JEAN: Oh, you children! Do parents ever stop doing things for you!

Even after you are married and gone – you still come back. And ask for something! . . . Now, you be up. Cairy, there's some food left on the table – if you feel you want it. I suppose you're hungry too, are you, Terry? [*Off, descending. Then, on stage again, to Terry.*] Now jump in them.

[TERRY *sits and puts them on; upstairs* CAIRY *goes into the bathroom, carrying her morning clothes.*]

You look quite odd putting long trousers on – do all boys your age wear long pants? . . . Now what shall we do? [*Looking round.*]

TERRY: Can I eat?

JEAN: You've been scratching about at the table already –

TERRY: I was hungry.

JEAN: You should ask if you want anything. Find a seat – then you can dive in. You want milk, don't you? Or, now you wear long trousers, is it coffee?

TERRY: Please –

JEAN [*with it*]: There is milk in it . . . [*Puts the cup in front of him.*] Oh my gosh! What a wonderful weekend! Everything that could happen, has happened! Do you agree? *You're* too young, aren't you? You don't understand what's been happening.

TERRY [*eating*]: Yes.

JEAN: Do you know whether there's anything worth living for – more than your own child? . . . When you're grown up I hope you don't have the same trouble – with yours!

TERRY: With what?

JEAN: Your children, dear! You're going to have plenty of them. I can see that – by the way you look.

TERRY: Yes.

JEAN: Are you brainy?

TERRY: No – well yes – and no.

JEAN: Make up your mind whether – what's it like to be fourteen or fifteen? I've completely forgotten. It was a long time ago. What is it like?

TERRY [*timidly*]: Oh, I'd like to be older.

JEAN: You would?

TERRY: As old as you.

JEAN: Thank you very much – am I a good age to be?

TERRY: How old are you?

JEAN: Ah now! That's an improper question. Don't ask me that. You are punching below the belt there.

TERRY: If I was your age I could go on my own – anywhere.

JEAN: Do you believe that I can? If I leave this house for half an hour – my daughter is – well – anything, in fact everything happens that shouldn't when I'm gone. But I know. It's all so safe and clean, at your age. Is that daft?

TERRY [vaguely]: Yes . . .

JEAN: Aren't you useless to talk to. You're merely discouraging. Well? Have you finished grubbing yourself? I can't see that there's much left on the table. Now suppose Cairy is hungry?

TERRY [up]: I don't mind what she does – but I'm not doing it with her.

JEAN: You know best. I won't force you to play with her. What will his lordship do? Have a rest?

TERRY [lightly]: I've just got up.

JEAN [playing up]: Oh yes, of course! Well, there's – or take a walk. You haven't seen the local surroundings for a long time. Scan your notes for the day!

TERRY: Can I go out?

JEAN: In the garden only. With respects to your royal person, you must be watched over. But only the garden. Until Cairy has come down. I hope she doesn't want to eat as well. The doctor gave her a bit of food,

[CAIRY crosses back to her room, fully dressed.]

when he was here. This morning. Oh blimey these meals are as irregular as a dog to a lamp-post! Aren't they? . . . Go outside for a while.

TERRY: Yes. But – will she be down, Auntie?

JEAN: That certainly won't bother you.

TERRY: Don't send her out.

JEAN: Nothing to worry about. Now off . . . [*She opens the back door for him. He exits.*] Cairy – do you want breakfast? . . . You've had something already. . . . [*To herself.*] I'm at sixes and sevens here – hardly anything to eat . . . [*Calling.*] Cairy?

CAIRY [*calling out of her window, off*]: . . . What are you doing out there? Come away!

TERRY [*off, loud*]: No! I'm not touching . . .

CAIRY [*agitated*]: Yes! Yes! Yes!

TERRY [*more timid*]: Not because of you –

CAIRY: You're not to be . . . you're not allowed!

TERRY: Hen –

CAIRY: What?

TERRY: Hen. Hen. You are a hen!

CAIRY [*taking off her slipper and banging it violently against the window frame*]: No right! No right!

TERRY: Hen-Henney! Hen-Henney!

CAIRY: He said no one must go near it – without him! And you have! It will change colour. Or break. It can snap in two if you touch it. It can vanish, and they'll all go if it –

TERRY: If it what? Cairy?

CAIRY: When it does. It's so wrong. Because because nobody nobody said you – stop that! You are lousy! You – [*Her voice rises.*]

JEAN [*shouting*]: Cairy! You can stop that noise now! Making that row! Do you hear?

TERRY [*off*]: Henney . . . Henney. Henney . . . Henney. Henry Johnson! . . . Henney – Henry – Johnson! [*His voice fades. He is retreating up the garden.*]

CAIRY [*quieter, more pleading*]: . . . . . Oh please! [*As if it really hurt.*] . . . Don't do that! It hurts – like – [*very softly*] a knife into –

TERRY [*still distantly*]: Henry Johnson . . . Henry Johnson . . .

JEAN [*hurrying off and up, then across landing to Cairy*]: . . . . I'll have no more . . . and shut the window . . . [*Off.*] Get yourself dressed properly . . . there are flats opposite. What do you think they are saying? . . . [*On landing.*] Cairy, this isn't right to anybody here. [*By her door.*] Making up – that's all you are doing. You're playing a game. Now finish – please.

[CAIRY *slowly shuts the window, and turns round; she chucks herself down disconsolately on the bed. And* JEAN *stands at the far end of her bed, speaking softly.*]

JEAN: . . . Darling, you are getting better, every hour. Don't slow things down. Until you practically go back to where you started. You are doing – I mean gradually, improving, the whole time. And with Terry – isn't it more right to play the same game as he does?

CAIRY [*burying her head in the pillow*]: Oh, I've heard it all before!

JEAN: Perhaps not enough.

CAIRY [*slowly*]: If I believe in what I think – I can do without you –

JEAN: But nothing you say is right. Now is it? Ask yourself.

CAIRY [*up from her bed*]: I'll go.

JEAN: Ask yourself, is it right? What do you do to me, and the others –

CAIRY: I'm quite as old as anyone else is.

JEAN: And – and we're all children – if that's the case I'm as old as you and vice-versa!

CAIRY [*nearly off*]: Am I talking too much? . . . Yes . . . Am I? Yes?

JEAN: I wish I could show you – it's quite an honour to become a woman when you grow up! But I haven't reached that stage yet. I'm still in the kindergarten. I'm not very good am I? I can't give you that – I'm not old enough! It is – it – what is it? You can tell me! It's terribly funny – I want to cry my eyes out, and nothing will come out. I must be dried up somewhere. You can, you're young. Why don't you cry for me, Cairy? This time it would be a good exchange. You must have all my tears by now. I'm much too old.

CAIRY: I know more than you, and he gave it to me, when it was lost, nobody can find it, you couldn't . . . that's for certain.

JEAN: Life begins at eighty!

TERRY [*off*]: Jean, Jean.

JEAN [*off*]: The name's Auntie!

TERRY [*opening the door, he stands there*]: ... There's two men out there.

JEAN [*on stage*]: There are two men.

TERRY: Yes.

JEAN: Not there's! Who are they?

TERRY: Just two fellows. Spivs, I think.

JEAN: I know. They come from the flats.

TERRY: Are they spivs?

JEAN: Street touts.

TERRY: What?

JEAN: They're bookie's runners.

TERRY [*uninterested*]: Oh.

JEAN: They're friends of your uncle.

TERRY: He's got some funny friends, hasn't he?

JEAN: They're nice boys though – not as tough as I thought they'd be.

JERRY [*off*]: Hey! Missus!

JACK: Wanna buy a good horse! [*Both laugh.*]

JEAN: Perhaps you'd like to play with them.

TERRY: No thanks.

JEAN: I'll have to let them in.

JERRY [*opening kitchen door*]: Hallo there!

JEAN: Hallo – goodbye!

JACK [*both inside*]: Seriously though – how is she?

JEAN: All right.

JACK: Really, I mean?

JEAN: She's all right!

JACK: Is she?

TERRY: That's what the lady said.

JACK: Who are you?

JERRY: Joker, ain't you?

JEAN: This is my nephew Terry. This is Jack and –?

JERRY: Jerry's the name – Jerry Maloney.

JEAN: Terry's come to lend a hand with Cairy.

61

JACK: Been old friends, like?

JEAN: That's right.

JERRY: Older friends than us?

JEAN: Just about.

JACK: See – we was going to offer some assistance like, this afternoon –

JEAN: That's very nice of you, but –

JACK: We thought you and Jim would need a hand-out like.

JEAN [calling]: Cairy! Come down will you?

JERRY: Ain't that right?

JACK: Yeah.

JEAN [to them]: Are you hungry?

JACK: We just ate.

[CAIRY walks across above stage.]

JEAN: Do you want to play with Terry then?

JACK: Nah . . . we're too old for games.

JERRY: We're not kids.

TERRY [challenging]: How old are you?

JERRY: How old are you?

TERRY: How old are you?

JACK: How old are you?

[CAIRY on stage.]

JEAN: Cairy . . .

CAIRY: I only want a cup of coffee.

JEAN: Yes dear – it's over there.

TERRY: Good morning.

[CAIRY ignores him.]

JEAN: Say good –

CAIRY: No!

TERRY: Don't you know me?

CAIRY: No.

TERRY: You knew me all right last night.

CAIRY: No! No! No!

JEAN: Leave her be then – let her be.

JACK: What a carry on then! in't it?

JERRY: It's a chuckle.

JEAN: Shush – let her eat.

JACK: Are you going out?

JEAN: No. Why?

JACK: We could stay and look after things – if you was.

JERRY: We ain't back on the beat until the last race.

JEAN: And what time is that?

JERRY: 4.30. Newcastle.

JEAN: I wasn't going to go –

JERRY: Here's your chance.

TERRY [*slumping down, watching Cairy whispering provocatively*]: ... I know who the Hen is ... Henney ...

[CAIRY *jumps nervously.*]

JEAN: Well, I can't ask you two to shop for me.

TERRY: Henney.

JEAN: Can't trust boys to fetch the right things.

CAIRY [*to Terry*]: When I speak to him about you, he'll do something dreadful to you!

TERRY: He's a hen, a rotten mangy hen.

JEAN: Stop that! I heard what you said – clever dick. You can stop that or you'll be outside the door.

JERRY: We do want to stay. When we met Jim on the corner he said it was O.K.

JEAN: Could you handle these two?

JERRY: Jim said we might change old Cairy round to the good. Seeing as how we're a bit different like from her usual friend.

JEAN: Friends, not friend.

JERRY: That's what I meant.

JEAN: All right – I'll go and do my errands. I won't be long.

JERRY: That's right – go on then.

[JEAN *picks up her bag and coat.*]

JEAN: Put that boy in the garden if he's any trouble.

JERRY: Yes.

JEAN: Ta ta, Cairy.

[TERRY *clucks like a hen.*]

TERRY: Curout cut cut! Curout cut cut!

[CAIRY *jumps up and throws a plate at him. He runs playfully out of the kitchen door.*]

CAIRY: Now will you stop that! Oh! he does that – don't you listen to him! What time does the bus come? Just in time for him to hurt you – why won't you leave him alone? – because he is jealous of our companionship . . .

JEAN: Cairy . . . please try not to do that, please – Terry may be playing you up, but please don't scream like that.

CAIRY: He's not hurting me – he's doing it on purpose to him –

JACK: Who is he?

JEAN [*to Cairy*]: You mean Johnson?

CAIRY: I mean what I say. No, don't touch me – I mean what I say.

JEAN: You must let Terry play with you, darling.

JACK: Run along then, lovie . . .

JEAN: Open the door for her . . .

JACK [*does so*]: There you are.

CAIRY [*hesitating, crosses to the door, and looks out*]: Why doesn't he come back? and the flower tree would be different. It's begun to wilt . . . as if it is going away too . . . usually it brightens the whole garden this time of year. He takes his time as if it doesn't matter to him.

JEAN: You see – you terrify Terry, that's why he acts up.

CAIRY [TERRY *whistles off key*]: I'll play a game with him. Shall I play that if I come out and wish something touching the tree – and he has to guess what I'm wishing – but he doesn't know, I'm wishing him dead all the time.

TERRY [*off; stops whistling*]: Hey Cairy – don't just stand there – I'm pulling at the branches – see!

CAIRY: I'm coming. [*She exits.*]

JEAN: I'm all in a terrible dither. [*She changes into a pair of high heels.*] . . . I wish I could mark everything fragile; that's how I feel, tucked in here. Listening to her; I feel like a bull in a china-shop . . . these shoes of mine are tight somewhere – I'll leave the rest of the dishes. I want to get some money. [*She opens a side drawer and takes out her purse.*] . . . Bag? gloves? and handkerchief? . . . Now I won't say anything else: only keep them out of trouble. I suppose you know what you are doing?

[*She exits.*]

JACK [*looking around*]: . . . ain't it silent?

JERRY: Ain't it.

JACK: Yeah.

JERRY: I'm bloody hungry.

JACK: Open up shop then.

JERRY: Shall I? [*Opens a cupboard.*] . . . cheese, mouldy cheese!

JACK: Cook yourself something if it's that bad then.

JERRY: Here – you wouldn't believe it wouldja –?

JACK: What?

JERRY: Cairy and that . . .

JACK: Queer, in't it?

JERRY: I spoke to that fellow once – Johnson. Right customer! I said 'Here, you lives around these parts, don't you?' He says 'Do I?' – like that! Some nut he was. He says 'Do I?' to me, he does on my life!

JACK: Weird.

JERRY: And I said 'Do you like a bit of a gamble?' and he looks up at the sky goofy as golf balls – then he looks at me –

JACK: Stuff it will you!

JERRY: What?

JACK: Pack it in.

JERRY: What for?

JACK: You get me down you do – always reminiscing and that –

JERRY: Me?

JACK: Can't you take it serious?

JERRY: For Christ's sake!

JACK: Don't it ever strike you something serious has happened?

JERRY: Aw – don't be so stupid.

JACK: Aw – don't be so stupid.

JERRY: Don't be then.

JACK: Drop!

[*Suddenly* CAIRY *scrambles through the door from the garden – breathless. She pulls Terry after her. They are chuckling together.*]

CAIRY: I've got a dog at my heels! . . . I've got a dog at my heels.

[CAIRY *drags him too quickly. She seems to panic at Terry's laughter.*]

TERRY: Hey!

CAIRY: Leave go! will you? [*She pulls too hard, releases herself, but Terry slips and falls.*]

TERRY [*scrambling up*]: . . . You're mad! she's mad!

CAIRY: As much as you are.

TERRY: Oh, but you see things – that aren't.

CAIRY [*heatedly*]: And you're stupider; you see things that are!

TERRY: Perhaps if you knew more about the truth – you might understand.

CAIRY [*to herself*]: You'd say to him something sharp – and he'd regret it. Tell him you know more about the truth than he does.

TERRY: You need watching you do – you're a proper case!

JACK: Shut up, will you! We're in charge – no mucking about like.

JERRY: We're in charge! Who are you?

CAIRY: Who am I? I'm Henry Johnson.

TERRY: Nuts.

CAIRY: You play a game like that – that's right, aren't you hiding from me? No, you are forever hiding from people.

JACK: You see – she's talking to him. Ain't she?

TERRY: Nuts.

JACK: See – she is.

CAIRY: Listen! that tune – he wanted that played at the Reunion Dance. You remember that they hadn't got the music sheets to it. The man tried to play it on the piano. . . . The strangest moment when you're so close to somebody. Your breath mixes, you've eaten fruit – smells sweet.

JERRY: In't she queer, in't she, eh?

TERRY: Ssh. She's mad.

JACK: You see – he's in here. He's in the room.

JERRY: Get out of it!

CAIRY: Now I remember what you were talking about. You said you are the thief. Now why do I say that? Oh, I don't know, that's what you said. I say a word you said and my face answers back. That's when I steal. You said, I'm stealing your eyes from other people. When I look at you they belong to you. Please don't ever stop giving me something. I want to be a great thief of you. . . . Why? Where did you come from? Lancashire. From a village? Yes? But you never talk of parents: I hated them. They embarrassed me. They were so stupid, they died before they knew they were dead. And you never ever married? No. But you won't talk about it? No. Have you ever loved somebody? Oh, I had an aunt who had a pony and trap who hid me under her shawl when she caught me out walking in the rain. That was years ago. Yes. [*She carries the chair to the front stage, and sets it down ceremoniously in front of her and she addresses it.*] . . . I mean really love? Yes, I love someone. Now? Yes. Who? That's my secret. Oh, I'm sorry. Won't you tell me? No.

TERRY [*bored*]: What a lot of stuff, Hen. . . . Hen – don't you talk like a hen? [*He squats on the floor studying her closely.*]

JERRY: What is she doing?

JACK: Like I said – she's bringing all them things back. . . .

JERRY: Like hell.

JACK: She's talking to him, see –

JERRY: I reckon winning at Doncaster on Saturday went to your head.

JACK: Get out of it.

JERRY: How much did you make for my old man – and how much did you keep for yourself?

JACK: Good night.

TERRY: Do you back horses?

JACK: Do we? Do we!

JERRY: They're our bread and butter, kid. . . .

TERRY: I'm not 'kid'.

JACK: What are you then?

TERRY: I'm about a year younger than you. . . .

JACK: So?

TERRY: So.

JACK: So?

TERRY: You're all right, you've only got to stay here a couple of minutes, I'm booked in for the week. Some school holiday this is. . . .

CAIRY [*moving away from them*]: Now – the big experiment; can you do it? Everything or nothing this time. . . . Are the doors shut? And the windows? Oh, no . . . I left the window, oh, golly . . .

JERRY: Come on ducks – here what about us, eh?

CAIRY: There . . . everything is shut tight. Yes – what is still happening? I don't know. . . . Yes I do. We are moving, aren't we? So stop us. Now – you are moving! Be still –

JACK [*to Jerry*]: Stand up straight then – do as she says.

JERRY: What?

CAIRY: Don't breathe . . . hold your breath. . . . And you too? Yes. It's hard. Stand still!

JERRY [*doing so*]: If the lads could see me now!

JACK: Be humorous like – join in her game.

[CAIRY *holds her breath. She lets herself fall down slowly. She lies down – then jumps up giggling.*]

CAIRY: I'm going giddy. . . . I'm going . . . I'm gone. . . . I've stopped everything. I've stopped the sun. I've stopped myself. What do you think about that? Oh – so so. Nothing more? Well – so so so. Huh! You don't know how to enjoy yourself.

JERRY: Oh – is it over now?

JACK: You're a bit dim, aren't you?

TERRY [*to Cairy*]: Why can't you act normally [*gripping her arm, swinging her round*] – do the things everybody else does? Stupid I call it.

CAIRY [*away*]: . . . But I forgot my own heart; I didn't stop that, did I? Oh, you silly little girl – how do you make me laugh so much? Me? Kind sir? You . . . you . . .

JACK: I couldn't act like that – I couldn't do all that; shows what a state he must have left her in –

JERRY: Shows – hell! You soppy old thing. What a custard pie you are and no mistake.

JACK: Bloody higorant type you are – I'm helping her.

TERRY [*chasing after her*]: Hey – do something else instead! Perform, be different!

CAIRY: . . . What is it you most wish? I've thought of that. I suppose you want me to say – be terribly generous or good-natured. Not at all. But to break something – oh, yes. That's what I'd do. That's more my style. I could walk into the highest domed cathedral, and inside it would be cool, and the silence could be a fragile glass ball. I'd kick it, my feet would shatter it, and the cool stone would burn up before my eyes.

TERRY: Don't you ever put the radio on in this house? Why can't she go for a long walk – and forget all about it?

CAIRY: . . . Could I put my hands on the jewelled cloth and drag it down, candlesticks, alterpieces, and saucers crashing about – the noise! I'd walk back – leaving it behind me . . . or I'd stand up on top of it, and looking at the grey slab of stone beneath me – now look about, the lectern is broken, and let me shout at the top of my voice above them all. Gallery seats and pews and tall windows – the echo hums away. Tremendously far, like an audience of leaves, swinging like tiny cradles, whispering down, green fingers prattling and tinkling behind choir boxes. It would be a music of silences. . . .

TERRY [*from the kitchen, clashing pan tops together*]: . . . Music! Music! Music! . . . Crazy old Cairy!

JACK: Shut up!

TERRY: Oh hell!

JACK: You're hurting her . . .

TERRY: Oh hell!

CAIRY: He says shut up, shut up, shut up! He says shut up!

JACK: Go on, Terry – go and play in the garden.

TERRY: Why should I play?

JACK: Go on.

TERRY: Who are you, anyway?

JACK [*chasing him half-heartedly*]: I'll give you what for in a second!..

[TERRY *runs out slamming the door behind him.*]

JERRY: ... Nervous, aren't you?

JACK: What time is it?

JERRY: Races don't start until three.

JACK: I don't know what to do now.

JERRY: Play with her – Genius!

JACK [*to Cairy*]: Come and sit down over here. Cairy – you've about said your lot.

[CAIRY *sits beside him.*]

JERRY: That's right, you sit beside this dirty old man here!

JACK: Got any more of them funny games of yours? Course not – they're all going now, aren't they?

JERRY: Isn't it agony!

JACK: Try for yourself then, if you can do better.

JERRY: Not me matey – I'll, eh – make some tea . . .

JACK: No, no, think of something – think of anything.

JERRY: You're the psychiatrist, cock.

JACK: But what for example?

JERRY: Pretend you're this fellow then – that's what the quack was doing.

JACK: Will you talk to me then, love? Perhaps it ain't so easy like to have it out with your old man, he's a bit rough like, isn't he? Tell old Jack here what else there is to tell?

[CAIRY *remains silent.*]

... now imagine I was Henry Johnson, see, now what would you say?

[*No reply.*]

... Would I say, why haven't you been out with me lately? Would I?

[*No reply.*]

JERRY: Don't ask her, just say it.

JACK: Why haven't you been out with me, playing our old games and that, Cairy?

CAIRY: Is it a game then ...

JACK: Games can be serious.

JERRY: You see – what did I say!

JACK: I'm on your side Cairy – I'm not laughing.

JERRY: See – what did I tell you?

CAIRY: I suppose you really do these things for my sake. You don't? Oh, I think you do. You don't take me very seriously.

JACK: Course I take you seriously – see, course I do. Hey! Wakey! wakey!

CAIRY [*suddenly understanding*]: You do?

JACK: Yes.

CAIRY: Really?

JACK: That's right, see – I'm your mate.

CAIRY: But you must admit you're a bit too old to play games?

JACK: Oh I don't know – you're never too old and something something.

CAIRY: I'm exactly a third your age. You've had three times my life – are there three of me inside you?

[JACK *looks blank.*]

JERRY: Answer her then. ...

JACK: Look – let's change the subject; what did we do on Saturday? Did we do something special like?

CAIRY: You were going to take me in the evening to see – oh, I forget if you did or not. And you said in the afternoon – but I don't quite remember ...

JACK: Think hard then.

CAIRY: Why didn't we go then? Isn't it so? You often make promises but when the time comes –

JACK: Well, I suppose I did promise you, but something came up sudden see, I must have changed my mind.

CAIRY: Yes?

[JEAN *opens the back door and listens.*]

JACK: But you were getting dressed, weren't you? And your Mother was out, wasn't she?

CAIRY [*vaguely*]: What time was that?

JACK: About half past three.

CAIRY: It all goes black somehow –

JACK: But try . . .

CAIRY: I can't, I really can't . . .

JACK: Did we talk?

CAIRY: You are always getting up to things. It doesn't really matter what – as long as it is you. You must always be ten feet tall imagining yourself doing this or doing that. You're rather frightened of everybody, aren't you? Admit it to me?

JACK [*lost*]: What?

CAIRY: That you aren't quite as big as you think sometimes?

JACK: Oh, I don't know . . .

JERRY: Big head!

CAIRY [*fervently*]: Are you? Tell me – are you? Tell me – are you? What? What? What?

[*While* JACK *looks surprised and bewildered the boiling kettle Jerry put on begins to whistle.*]

JACK [*to Jerry*]: Turn it up!

[JEAN *enters from the back door with* TERRY.]

JEAN: I found him in the garden. Is anything wrong?

JERRY [*pointing to Cairy*]: Sssh . . .

TERRY [*mimicking*]: Sssh!

JEAN: I'm back, has anybody noticed! Oh I'm sorry – I didn't quite remember my place properly – [*sarcastic*] Cairy is it?

[*She takes off her coat and hangs it up. She is very worried and tense.*]

JERRY: Old Jack here has been doing wonders with her. . . .

JEAN: But what were you doing out there on the lawn, Terry?

JACK: I put him out there, see – I thought –

JEAN: But he's meant to be in here helping her, isn't he?

JACK: I thought –

JEAN: Please don't!

[*Embarrassed silence.*]

JERRY: What is it?

JEAN: . . . I'm sorry – I'm a bag of nerves, I'm sorry.

JACK: That's all right.

JEAN: How is she?

JACK [*putting his arm round Cairy's shoulders*]: She's fine.

JEAN: How can she be? Fine?

JACK: I've been talking to her. . . .

JEAN: You know the people in the shops look at me – they look at me . . .

JERRY: Doesn't she look all right?

JEAN: How should I know!

JACK: Ask her then . . .

JEAN: Why? Why? I'm terrified of her!

JACK: Try.

JEAN: I get nothing from her. I've already tried. I heard what she was saying to you. I get no more than that out of her.

JACK: This was all about Saturday?

JEAN: I was getting ready to go out. She knows – oh, she knows. She's like a tape-recorder bringing it all back.

JERRY: Tell the quack then . . .

JEAN: He knows.

JERRY: He doesn't know it's Saturday and Friday she's talking about.

JEAN [*exhausted voice*]: He knows.

JACK: Well, we ain't done badly, have we? Eh?

JEAN: You've done very well.

JERRY: See – my idea.

JACK: Who asked you!

JERRY: It *was* my idea.

JEAN: . . . Cairy? . . .

73

[CAIRY *wanders off slowly. She reappears on the upper landing.*]

JACK: She's all right.

JEAN: What do you mean 'she's all right'! She's not all right.

JACK: She's all right.

JEAN: She's not! She's my daughter, and she's not all right.

JACK: Just as you say, just as you say.

JEAN: I know my daughter. I know what those faces out in the street mean when they study me. They watch my face and I know my daughter isn't all right. Don't worry about them – but I know.

JACK: . . . I wonder why she's gone upstairs?

JERRY: Would you like some tea? I've boiled the kettle.

JEAN: No – yes.

JERRY: Do you like it weak or strong?

JEAN: Anything, anything.

JACK: I wonder why – eh?

JEAN: What? Oh – do you mind if she goes upstairs for one minute?

JACK: No, I don't mind –

JEAN: Then that's fine, isn't it?

JACK: Yes, yes, I suppose it is.

JEAN: Good.

[*They stand staring at each other limply.*]

JERRY: Sugar?

JEAN: Yes, please.

JERRY: And milk?

JEAN: Oh God!

JACK: Pack it in, will you – can't you see she's not well!

JERRY: Have I said something wrong?

JACK: Here, Terry – why don't you pop upstairs and offer Cairy a drop of tea – see if she's all right.

TERRY: She is all right . . .

JACK: How do you know?

TERRY: I know.

JACK: Go on, be a pal.

TERRY: Knock it off will you, I'm not your servant, am I?

JEAN [*exhausted*]: He doesn't need to go.

JACK [*to Terry*]: I thought you were her friend ...

TERRY: I play with her – sometimes.

JACK: Do her a favour then?

TERRY: I don't want to. She's dead odd ...

JEAN [*to Terry*]: Darling, you're upset too ... because of last night. But you mustn't be afraid of her.

TERRY: I can't help myself.

JERRY: Is he kidding!

JEAN: What did you all do, Terry – while I was out?

TERRY: We mucked about ...

JEAN: Is that all?

TERRY: Oh, I don't know – ask them.

JEAN: Look, I'll ring up your Mother tonight, and ask for her to take you back. I think that will be better for all of us. You don't want to hear any more of this shouting and things. ...

[CAIRY *is walking about on the landing above.*]

JACK: Sssh – do you hear?

JERRY: What?

CAIRY: ... And who did you say? Crikey, and Mrs ...

JACK: She's off again.

JEAN: Is she? Do you hear that, Terry? Can you hear your cousin? Cairy's talking to herself, what do you make of that now?

JERRY: Don't it all seem weird, don't it?

CAIRY [*moving about*]: ... I've never seen you angry. Do you ever lose your temper? There's nothing to lose it on. Children must make you mad at times. Nothing does. They don't really enter into my world. I do though. ... Yes. Every time? Wherever I go, whatever I look at. I always include you. Cairy ... Cairy ... Cairy. ... Children never bothered to talk to me when I was a child – called me the odd one out.

JEAN: Did you hear that?

JACK: Yes.

JEAN: Did you hear that? That was on Saturday – after lunch. The exact words. I was just going out and I heard her say 'I've never seen you angry. Do you ever lose your temper?'

CAIRY: ... We do that. I know. But it's too much like starting a treasure hunt. But I've been given a lead. I'll catch you up then.

JEAN: Isn't that queer ...

CAIRY: ... I could miss all this house. But not you. I want you nearby, you can make me look for things. To see them in an entirely different light. Then again, say I went away from you, what would you do? I'd become my own age again. But you're always you're own age. No – not when I'm with you. With you, when your Mother goes out and leaves us alone, I'm as old as you are.

[*They wait downstairs for more, but Cairy is silent.*]

JACK: She's not saying any more.

JEAN: No?

JACK: She's stopped.

JEAN: Oh ...

JACK: Here – has Jim heard any more about catching the fellow?

JEAN: I don't think so.

JERRY: He told my old man this morning that there was a big search on.

JEAN: All I know is they'll phone when they've got him.

JACK: There's not much else we can do now, is there?

JERRY: No, that's right.

JACK: Don't you think we ought to toddle along?

JERRY: I got these slips to place for the 4.30 –

JEAN: Never mind your slips, they can wait. You've been very kind staying with me.

JACK: It was nothing.

JEAN: I mean you're not the sort of fellows one thinks one ought to rely on. You're a couple of spivs really – aren't you?

JACK: Oh, I wouldn't say that.

TERRY: I would!

JEAN: You're not exactly a pair of church wardens are you?

JERRY: No . . . no . . . I'd admit you're right there.

JACK: I don't look like a spiv, do I?

JERRY: Course you look like a spiv, in fact you look right common, if you got down to thinking about it.

JACK: And what about you?

JERRY: But I admit it, see – quite right, I'm a bit of a spiv. If you look at it that way – like.

JEAN: What I mean is – you look like the types who throw bottles through windows and fetch out razors. . . .

JACK: Really? I really look like that?

JEAN: You've got narrow trousers and long hair – what else is any self-respecting person expected to think?

JACK: Proper carry on, isn't it?

JEAN: But don't go –

JACK: Eh?

JEAN: But please don't think I want you to go. I need you.

JACK: Well, it don't exactly sound like it, does it. . . .

JEAN: Go over there, anywhere. . . . I want to talk about Henry Johnson. I want to describe him. He wasn't very tall. But big and heavy. He used to creep around on brown boots all day. Dirty old brown boots. Never cleaned them. Or pressed his trousers. And the same old tie each day. He had sandy, thinning hair. The type that goes bald quickly. He was ugly and he had a lisp.

JERRY: He sounds like Heaven, doesn't he!

JEAN: He never spoke about women. But he never spoke about his job either, the boys at school. He could only mention Cairy. I don't think he knew anybody else's christian name but hers. Then if I asked him how many people he knew before he came here, he wouldn't answer me. He'd say he never knew people long enough to become friends. So much mathematics and stuff, you could never really talk to him. He'd calculate his answers. Every time, weigh them up to see if they balanced. And try to talk to him! He acted timid. He told me once, people are like houses. As they grow older they shut some windows, those that they particularly dislike.

But the others they leave open, and if they are not wide enough, they break down the bricks around them so as they can have more light just there. But he said children were merely exploring the houses, trying to find out what all the windows looked upon. What I think is – he did everything purposefully. From the moment he set eyes upon her, he worked it out carefully. Games and telling stories. They had little secrets. He must have watched her like an eagle above a sheep; I'd swear even before Saturday morning, he had all his clothes packed. He knew we'd all be out at some time or another, like any Saturday. I suppose he had his ticket and money ready. Reserved. I must have been the fly in the ointment. And the old tricks came out. The stories and paraphernalia. He told me he was restless. That he had to keep on the move. Terry, you're not like that, are you? You don't hold a secret inside you until it's ready to burst out . . . children get like that. I suppose he was a child. You won't forget Cairy and Mr Johnson, I can see that. What do you think of them, Terry? They've done something bad, haven't they? What do you think?

TERRY: . . . I don't know.

JEAN: Oh, but everybody's told you – but really you are too young – everyone's told you to steer clear of that sort of person?

TERRY [*wildly*]: I said I don't know!

JEAN: But they do tell you, don't they?

TERRY: Yes – anything! Yes!

JEAN: You see, I'm right!

TERRY: Can't I go now –?

JERRY: Jean, let me talk –

JEAN: I'm talking –

JERRY: You're making a big mistake. These aren't children any more. Cairy is thirteen. You treat her as if she were ten! And Terry – how old is he? Fourteen or so – and you make him out to be half that age! Let them grow up.

JEAN: My house is all tumbling down. Oh God, when you've got four walls surrounding you – you wish to high Heaven, you only wish to Heaven you – that there could be five, to turn round to – and see something new and clean, that wasn't there before. Why can't I hear more and see more than there is now in front of me?

[*They all pause.* JIM *off whistling loudly.*]

JIM [*entering*]: . . . Whatcha, girl! Ay! Who do you think I am? The postman?

JEAN: Where did you spring from?

JIM: Don't you want to hear some news?

JEAN: Yes. Of course.

JERRY: About who?

JIM: Aha!

JEAN: Cairy? Is it?

JIM: Not telling.

JEAN: Yes you are. What is it?

JACK: Somebody has found him?

JIM: Where is that girl? Shouldn't she be down here? Hi, tosher! You haven't seen your cousin, have you?

TERRY [*pulling away*]: . . . Tish!

JIM [*calling*]: Cairy! . . .

JEAN: She's upstairs. If you want her. I want to know –

JIM: Yes. Well. It's not very much – they've – ah – seen him.

JACK: Johnson?

JERRY: Wonderful!

JIM: It's not important.

JERRY: I should say it is!

JIM: The night watchman spotted him at the Edward the Seventh Dock. London dry docks. The alarm went off – but there was no one on duty round there – and we weren't told until mid-day.

JERRY: He could be anywhere now.

JIM: No matter, we know he's in London – or thereabouts. Does that make you feel better about it?

JEAN: I'm not worrying in the least. Am I?

JIM: Well, you look edgy –

JEAN: I won't be satisfied though – until he's under locks and bolts.

JIM: They are going to ring me tonight. If they hear anything more. Or that they've got him. But it doesn't matter, believe me – if he has to crawl around in a London dock – last night – he can't have much money.

JACK: Well, I suppose we must go.

JIM: Yes. Well. Thank you very much! Everybody's grateful.

JERRY [*still standing*]: O.K.

JACK: Bye-bye, Terry – Jean. Give our love to Cairy, won't you?

JIM: I wouldn't entertain it!

JERRY: Bye! [*Goes off.*]

JACK: Bye! [*Goes off.*]

JIM: . . . That's that.

JEAN: That's a relief!

JIM: It's strange to find ourselves on our own – nowadays.

JEAN: At least I know nobody dreams nightmares like this –

JIM: Don't worry. There'll be more tonight. If that phone call doesn't come through.

JEAN: Why don't you sit down –

JIM: I ran into young Brock, over here. I told him a few things! . . . He says not to worry. But he might be in here tonight, sometime. She might be violent again – so he's coming over.

JEAN: God! I've been sweating – as if it's a hot summer's day. I'm wet right through me. He said not to worry?

JIM: He did –

JEAN: He should try taking my place then. He'd soon change his mind.

JIM: I'm not worrying about anything.

JEAN: I know that.

JIM: Yes – well?

JEAN: I say everybody should at this time!

JIM: This would be a fine old world then. Everybody shouting at everyone else! Eh?

JEAN: Don't argue with me, Jim. You're right every time. I don't know why you bother to. I don't know a thing, do I?

JIM: You'll do.

JEAN: Oh yes.

JIM: I could cry for you.

JEAN: And tonight and after tonight, and then later on – isn't it our tragedy? Isn't it?

    [*No answer.*]

    . . . Isn't it? . . . Jim? . . . Jim?

    [*The stage blacks out completely.*]

SCENE TWO

The evening of the same day.

JEAN: There was a young boy walking in the middle of the road today. He was absolutely cocksure of himself. And all the cars were streaming past him. He had on those sandals with no backs in them. He stubbed his toe somehow – and the sandal came off his foot. He stopped and turned round to pick it up. Then he saw the cars behind him – like that, without his shoe on, on one foot. His whole face changed. He was terrified. Just at that moment when he realized he shouldn't be there. And what might really happen to him. . . . Where all the cars . . . that's what I mean – it's terribly bad when people don't see what's happening to them – until it hits them and it's too late. . . . What's the time?

JIM [*reading*]: There's a clock up there.

JEAN: It's slow.

JIM: Blimey! You only put it right a minute ago!

JEAN: You don't have to snap!

JIM: I was not.

JEAN: Well then . . .

JIM: Let's not both upset each other again – tonight. Eh?

JEAN: I'm not going out of my way to try exactly. Am I? You do act as if you're quite uesless at times – and I get agitated.

81

JIM: I get the blame every time, don't I?

JEAN: . . . They won't ring later than twelve, will they?

JIM: What?

JEAN: I said they won't ring later –

JIM: I'll be in bed by then.

JEAN: I'm staying up. In case –

JIM: You can –

JEAN: I might as well. Because that phone won't wake you – upstairs – will it?

JIM: I can hear it all right.

JEAN: It might be urgent –

JIM: Someone might blow up Scotland Yard! What does it matter?

JEAN: Now that's what I mean! This don't-care attitude of everybody!

JIM: Never mind. Forget I said it.

JEAN: . . . There's nothing much to do in the evenings, is there? . . . Now if we had a television set – it would be different . . . isn't it boring? . . . I don't believe the town is made for anything else but to work in . . .

JIM: Ssshhh –

JEAN: Why should I?

JIM: I'm concentrating –

JEAN: I'm going outside. The atmosphere seems sticky in here . . . it looks clean and fresh out there . . . [*Opening door, and standing staring out.*] Jim? Come out and look at the tree. . . . The lights from those flats is all caught in the branches. It's quite pretty. It does look different at night-time. . . . Jim? . . .

JIM: No, I'll stay in –

JEAN [*off*]: There's a cat out here – Jim?

JIM [*more to himself*]: You're as restless as I don't know what.

JEAN: . . . I can't imagine . . . it must be a stray . . . nobody's got a cat anywhere near us . . . Jim? . . .

JIM [*over to door*]: . . . Don't bother. I won't come out –

JEAN [*further away now*]: It's cool out here.

JIM: Yes ... I know.

[CAIRY *has got up out of bed, hearing Jean outside, and she is watching her out of the window.*]

CAIRY: ... That's not for you to touch ... leave it ...

JEAN: Cairy – go back to bed.

CAIRY: I said that's not for you to ... you didn't hear me –

JEAN: Keep quiet! Terry's asleep!

JIM: That reminds me – wasn't he going home tonight?

CAIRY [*soft*]: I don't care ...

JEAN: Does it bother you, Cairy? I'll go in ...

CAIRY [*runs back to her bed, and sits on it. She is taut again*]: You were shaking the tree ... because of a cat! ...

JEAN [*calling softly*]: ... Cairy? ... Go to sleep. You'll wake Terry up! ...

JIM: I'll go up to look at her.

CAIRY: ... Can you hear her? ... No. I think she's gone. She does that at times – uses the back way. You were saying about a game. Has she gone? And I said yes. Well, let's start. What? The game then. You tell me? ... It's got a long – story ... Yes? When you are asked to remember someone's face, what do you do? I think. Yes? Right down deep inside. That's if it is difficult to – somebody's inside. That's if it is difficult to – somebody's face, or go right back as far as you can remember. That sort. I can think like that – it gets ...

[JIM *on stage above watches Cairy by her door.*]

Don't look at me like that, I'm not an ogre, am I? You don't want to put them there, put your hands there – like that. [*She topples slowly to her knees as if pushed there. She holds her hands up limply.*] ... No, this is wrong. It's perfectly correct. It's what everybody has to face at one time or another – and this is our moment. It never was this way. Oh yes. But like this? Oh yes. But never with as much care and attention, never with so much love you see – please, please, please. Not throwing it away, I want to try to understand so much more. But please ... please ...

please . . . Don't. Don't hurt. But please . . . [*Her knees give way and she lies gently on the ground. Downstairs the telephone has started to ring.* CAIRY *sits up silently. After a pause,* JEAN *swiftly runs down to the phone.*]

JEAN: Jim? Jim! Do you hear it?

JIM: What do you think?

JEAN [*dazed*]: I'll answer it. . . .

CAIRY [*looking up at Jim*]: Hallo . . . Hallo, stranger. [*Smiling at him.*]

JEAN [*lifting the receiver*]: Hallo. Yes, that's right.

JIM: Now you stay quiet. Don't say another word. It's all over now. Don't say another word.

JEAN: Yes . . . yes. This is she speaking.

CURTAIN

JOHN ARDEN

in collaboration with Margaretta D'Arcy

The Happy Haven

THE HAPPY HAVEN

First produced at the Royal Court Theatre, London, on 14 September 1960, with the following cast:

DR COPPERTHWAITE	Peter Bowles
MRS PHINEUS	Susan Engel
MRS LETOUZEL	Rachel Roberts
MR GOLIGHTLY	Barrie Ingham
MR HARDRADER	Nicholas Selby
MR CRAPE	Frank Finlay
ROBINSON / LORD MAYOR	James Bolam
SMITH / SIR FREDERICK HAPGOOD	Edward Fox
NURSE JONES / LADY MAYORESS	Mary Watson
NURSE BROWN / LADY FROM THE MINISTRY	Rosalind Knight

Directed by William Gaskill

THE play is intended to be given a formalized presentation. This involves the use of masks, which are worn as follows – the Five Old People wear character masks of the *commedia dell' arte* type, covering the upper part of their faces only. The Doctor does not wear a mask, except at the very end, when he is shown in one that covers his whole face, and represents himself as a child. The Nurses and Orderlies have their masks and noses covered by hospital antiseptic masks. The Distinguished Visitors wear masks similar to those of the Old People, but less individualized.

The Setting should suggest a Hospital atmosphere, clinical and rectilinear, but the scenes are not localized to any particular rooms.

The Dog is to be imagined by the audience, but must be understood to be seen by all the characters on the stage – it is not a 'delusion'.

The stage directions are those used for the original production at Bristol University, when the play was presented on an open stage, following roughly the Elizabethan model. There were two doors opening from the back wall of the stage, with between them a recess closed by sliding doors, which accommodated the Doctor's laboratory equipment. Above this recess was a small upper stage. At the Royal Court, the play had of necessity to be played within the proscenium arch. This is a necessity that will doubtless be imposed upon most productions of *The Happy Haven* in this country, but it is none the less a regrettable one. The unsatisfactory organization of the English theatre in general and the archaic design of its buildings continually hamstring any attempts on the part of dramatists and directors to open out the conventions of the drama; and I must record my gratitude to Bristol University and its Department of Drama for making it possible to prove to myself that the leanings I have long had towards the open stage and its disciplines were justifiable in practice as well as in theory. I would urge anyone who wishes to produce this play to do so, if at all possible, on an Open Stage. Structural limitations may prevent the use of the upper stage: but it is not an essential part of the setting, and the scenes set on it may be brought down to the main acting level without undue difficulty.

ACT ONE

SCENE ONE

[DOCTOR COPPERTHWAITE *enters on upper stage and addresses the audience directly.*]

DOCTOR: Ah-hum. Good evening, ladies and gentlemen. First, let me say how glad I am to see you here and to extend a cordial welcome to the Happy Haven. We are, as you know, as yet only a small institution and our grant from the revenues of the National Health Service is alas not as generous as it might be – but, well, I dare say you'll know the old proverb – Time mends all. I'd like you to meet some of the old people who are in our care. As the phrase is, the evening of their lives – well, I've more to say about that later – but at present sufficient to indicate that this hospital for the amelioration of the lot of the aged is situated in pleasant rural surroundings, almost self-supporting – own produce, eggs, butter, and so on – within easy reach of London, and, I am happy to say, the most up-to-date facilities for both medical treatment and – most important of all from my point of view – research. I'm the Superintendent, my name's Copperthwaite, I've been here five years, and – er, yes, well, you want to meet the patients, don't you Nurse Brown, Nurse Jones.

[*The* NURSES *enter on main stage.*]
We're ready to meet the patients.

[*Exeunt* NURSES.]
We call them patients, but you'll understand they're not really ill, they're just old, you know, the passage of time, the gradual declension – it's a physical fact, you look at it scientifically, it all fits the picture – above all things in an establishment of this nature, *must* preserve the clinical approach: can't be too often stressed.

[NURSES *enter with the five* OLD PEOPLE. MRS PHINEUS *is brought in in her wheel-chair, the rest walk. They sit down in a formal row on the two benches, with* MRS PHINEUS's *wheel-chair placed in the centre. The* NURSES *stand at either end.*]

And here we are. We might say today is really an auspicious occasion for meeting these five old people. You see, the old lady in the middle is enjoying her ninetieth birthday, and, of course, there's a bit of a celebration. Shouldn't there be a cake, Nurse?

[NURSE BROWN *exits.*]

Right. Well, she's going to cut the cake and they'll congratulate her. She's our oldest, Mrs Phineus her name is, and she's been a widow for twenty years.

[*Enter* NURSE BROWN *with cake. She carries it to* MRS PHINEUS, *and puts the knife into her hand.*]

Now here's the cake, and here's the knife to cut it: and Mrs Phineus is just about to cut it; and she's *cut it*!

[*As* MRS PHINEUS *cuts the cake, the* NURSES *and* OLD PEOPLE *all clap.*]

Now they're all about to congratulate Mrs Phineus in the traditional fashion.

OLD PEOPLE [*sing*]:

> Happy birthday to you
> Happy birthday to you
> Happy birthday, Mrs Phineus,
> Happy birthday to you.

[*The cake is cut up by* NURSE BROWN *and a piece handed to each patient.*]

DOCTOR: And the party is in full swing. While they're all enjoying themselves, it would perhaps be appropriate if I were to give a brief resume of their names, ages, and case histories.

[*He refers to a sheaf of notes. As each old person is mentioned, he or she stands up, formally, and bows or curtsies to the audience. The others sit quite still and are eating their cake in a completely formal fashion.*]

We'll start with Mrs Phineus – not much to be said about her, general condition remarkably promising considering her years. Some obstruction recorded in the condensers, sandbox apertures require occasional overhaul, but by and large answers very well to her regulator. Now then: number two. On Mrs Phineus's right we have Mr Golightly, seventy-five years old, bachelor, very good state of preservation. Fitted six years ago with improved Walschaerts valve-gear replacing original Stephenson's link motion, and injectors also recently renewed. Latent procreative impulses require damping down on the firebox, but less so than formerly. Next one, number three, on Mrs Phineus' left, you will observe the only other female member, Mrs Letouzel. Aged seventy, all moving parts in good condition, cross-head pins perhaps slightly deteriorated, and occasional trouble from over-heated bearings when financial gain is in question. General report, extremely favourable. Now next to her we have Mr Hardrader, number four, our best running specimen. Very firm original design in smokebox and blast pipe has resulted in continual first-class steaming conditions. Age eighty-eight on the thirteenth of next month. Finally, on the extreme left, you will see Mr Crape. There has been here an unfortunate case history of overall deterioration, but last year was given a complete refit, including elongated smokebox, revised cylinder-head design, and replacement of obsolete perforated splashers. Age is now seventy-nine. There is still a tendency to over-exceed the power-potential beyond nominal capacity, but provided this can be overcome – well, I think we can say, further outlook quite hopeful. This is about all I can usefully tell you at the moment. Their little party is well under way, though they mustn't be allowed to get too excited –

OLD PEOPLE [sing]:

> Knees up, mother Brown
> Knees up, mother Brown
> Knees up, knees up, don't get the breeze up,
> Knees up, mother Brown.

DOCTOR: I think we'd better tactfully put an end to the evening now, a little kicking over the traces goes a long way at this age.

[OLD PEOPLE's *song repeated.*]

Ye-es, I think so. Nurse. I think that had better be all, Nurse. Off to bed, boys and girls, you're half an hour late as it is, burning the candle at both ends, y'know, have to go easy, don't we, that's the way, off to bed now, Nurse. Good night, good night, boys and girls. If you've not ate your cake yet, you can take it to bed and finish it there. That's right.

OLD PEOPLE: Good night, Doctor.

DOCTOR: Good night.

[*Exeunt* NURSES, *taking in* OLD PEOPLE – *each one holding half-eaten slice of cake.*]

And for the time being, that's that. Now the next thing, ladies and gentlemen, is my laboratory. I dare say it would be of interest if I were to give you some short exposition of the type of research I'm at present engaged in? Smith, Robinson.

[ORDERLIES *enter on main stage.*]

Get the lab ready, will you? Thank you very much.

[*Exeunt* ORDERLIES, *into recess.*]

If you'll just wait one moment, ladies and gentlemen – I'll be with you directly.

[*Exit* DOCTOR. ORDERLIES *re-enter on main stage, wheeling out from the recess the lab bench with its equipment. As they place it in position, the* DOCTOR *enters on the main stage.*]

We can call it the next morning now, and this is my morning routine – every morning, very early, before the patients have their breakfast, just about the time they're beginning to be washed. This is also, I suppose, how shall I call it, well, you will no doubt best understand me if I say, that this is the one true 'Ratio Operandi', the 'Reductio ad Quem', the – oh I don't know – the over-riding purpose and ambition of my work in this hospital. My research. My project. My daily work for the full five years I've been Superintendent here. To quote, somewhat tentatively, a literary example as being perhaps most appropriate for this audience, you can call me if you like, a Doctor Faustus of the present generation. It's not an exact parallel – Faustus sold his soul to the devil, I believe. I'm selling mine to nobody. But what I have here or what I shall have here, ladies and gentlemen, is nothing less, or will be nothing less, than the Elixir of life – of Life, and of Youth. I haven't got it yet. Now I'm near, I'm extremely near, oh I can tell you that, in certainty. Perhaps this very morning will prove the last of all the mornings I've had to stand in this lab, and calculate, and attempt, and slowly progress, experiment by experiment, formula by formula. Those five old people you saw go to bed last night are to be the raw material upon which I shall work. They don't know it yet, but they are. If I am successful, and the Elixir is found – *Copperthwaite's Elixir* – or might I call it the Happy Haven Elixir – the institution is greater than the man – *if* I am successful; then those five old people will not be at the end of their established term of years, but at the beginning! They will be able, they will be able, to be completely reborn! To any age we may see fit to lead them. Think of that. Think of that! . . . But let us preserve our professional detachment. The experiment, ladies and gentlemen, is by no means over yet. [*He turns to his bench.*] We'll have a look at it now. Notebooks please.

[ORDERLY SMITH *hands him books as he names them.*]
Number thirty-two, thirty-three, thirty-five-A, and the current one. Thank you. Experiment Number One; two-eight-six, Stage Four. Are you all paying attention, I want you to take particular note of the equipment mounted here, and containing, in the vessel, the solution derived from yesterday's work, reading nine-by-three by four-and-a-half scantlings, ledged braced battened and primed. This solution is now cool, yes, it's cool, and it has been allowed to stand for twenty-two hours. I term this the secondary or tensile state of leading. To it I am about to add nought point three-double-six degrees of *this* [*He holds up a second retort, also with liquid in it.*]

– which is a five-eighth screed, three parts three-sixteenth aggregate, one-and-a-half parts plastic terrazzo. The resulting precipitate will then be heated for three hundred and twelve seconds, all headers, stretchers, and squints removed by oxidization: and then I – and *then*, why perhaps *then* – ah, well, we'd better take it as it comes, hadn't we? [*He pours the second liquid into the first.*] Bunsen burner, please.

[ORDERLY ROBINSON *lights the burner.*]

I want absolute quiet. This is very tense, very delicate. Thank you. Before heating I add the necessary trimmers and binding members. Number four.

[ORDERLY ROBINSON *hands him a test-tube of liquid which he pours into retort.*]

DOCTOR: Number eight.

[*Similar business.*]

Twelve-B.

[*Similar business.*]

Eighteen. Eighteen . . . where's number eighteen? Come on, come on! God's sake, Robinson, have these things ready –

[*Similar business, rather flurried.*]

Now then, timing dial. Thank you.

[ORDERLY SMITH *hands him large stop-watch.*]

DOCTOR [*reads the seconds off stop-watch*]: Three-twelve. Three-ten. Three-eight. Six. Four. Two, one, three *hundred*.

[ORDERLY ROBINSON *has taken the retort and is holding it over bunsen while* DOCTOR *calls the time. Every twelve seconds – indicated by* DOCTOR *jerking up his arm – he whips retort away from flame and agitates rapidly in the air, then holds it back again above bunsen.*]

This is done every twelve seconds exactly, to prevent coagulation of sediment. After the first hundred seconds, we do it every five. Two-nine-four. Two-nine-two. Two-ninety. Two-eighty-*eight*.

[*Mixture agitated again.*]

All right so far. Seems to be all right. This is the most dangerous part though. . . . Two eighty-four. Two-eight-two. Two hundred and eighty –

[CRAPE *enters*.]

CRAPE: Er, excuse me, Dr Copperthwaite –

DOCTOR [*whirling round, startled*]: Eh, *what*! What is it, what are you doing here –

CRAPE: Excuse me if I interrupted. Doctor –

DOCTOR: *Interrupted!* You bloody dog, get out! [*He looks at the retort.*] Oh my God: coagulated. The whole damn thing's coagulated. It's no damn good at all. Clear it out, clear away, it's three weeks' consolidated work, oh no, it's nothing, no – it's all the luck of the game, *isn't it*, you interfering old – [*He pulls himself together.*] Eh, what's the use. I'm sorry, ladies and gentlemen. I'm afraid you're disappointed. We didn't reach it after all. But we will. Very shortly. It's a long road that has no turning, as they say. We all find these little setbacks. Don't we?

[*The* ORDERLIES *have wheeled away the bench etc. into the recess.*] Cleared away, Smith? Good. I'm not doing any more this morning. Tomorrow we'll start again at Number One-two-eight-one, Stage two. All right? And tell Sister that I want all male patients to be given an enema before this evening. I'm a little alarmed about the state of their bloodstreams. There seem to be symptoms of mortification. . . . Thank you.

[*Exeunt* ORDERLIES.]

You know very well I am never available to patients when I am working in the laboratory, Mr Crape. So what do you want?

CRAPE: I do beg your pardon, Doctor, if I in any way intruded – of course we're all of us aware how important your work is –

DOCTOR: Are you? There are rules in this hospital, you know, and they're meant to be obeyed –

CRAPE: Oh naturally, naturally, Doctor, I do indeed apologize, yes – but this is as you might say special, as a matter of fact, a delicate question, you see –

DOCTOR: And why can't it wait till a more normal time? There are stated hours for making complaints about the other patients, as you know perfectly well, Mr Crape – you take advantage of them often enough.

CRAPE: But Doctor, in these cases, one is often impelled to, well, like, to break with decorum, on account of the importance of imperceptibility – I mean, I don't want to be seen here, do I? I mean, bad for the value of our little talks, Doctor – after all it *is* only out of loyalty to the hospitality, eh?

DOCTOR: All right, all right ... So what has Mrs Letouzel been up to this time? I hope it isn't more pilfering. I told them to see that the collecting box for the spastic children had a padlock put on to it. Hasn't it been done?

CRAPE: Oh yes, yes, I think so, Doctor, yes – it's not about Mrs Letouzel really this morning. Mr Hardrader.

DOCTOR: Well?

CRAPE: He's still got it, you know. He takes it for walks.

DOCTOR: In the hospital?

CRAPE: Not exactly, no ... but –

DOCTOR: In the grounds then?

CRAPE: Well to be quite frank, Doctor, I am not entirely sure –

DOCTOR: Mr Crape, I see nothing whatever to prevent Mr Hardrader possessing a bull-terrier or any other sort of dog, provided he does not infringe my regulations by keeping it on the premises. If you can't bring evidence to show that that *is* what he's doing, then you can please stop wasting my valuable time! Is there nothing else? Are they satisfied with their diet? There's far too much of a tendency for grumblings and grumblings and nobody ever tells me – one has to know these things – Well?

CRAPE: I think Mrs Phineus sometimes gets into the larders when there's no one about – Mrs Letouzel said she keeps a pot of strawberry jam under her bedclothes, but I don't think it can be very likely –

DOCTOR: I suppose a pot of jam won't do her any harm: but it could be a dangerous precedent ... all right, Mr Crape. That'll do for now. Off you go to breakfast.

CRAPE: Oh, but Doctor, I've just thought –

DOCTOR: Off to breakfast, Mr Crape, I've a great deal to attend to this morning –

CRAPE: You asked about Mrs Letouzel. There *is* something, you know. It's about what she is, Doctor. That old woman – she's a Spy.

DOCTOR: Spy?

CRAPE: That's right.

> Ooh, Doctor, she's a greedy Spy
> Ooh, Doctor, she's so sharp and sly!

And what she wants to find out, Doctor, find out, here . . .

[*He makes a series of gestures around him and towards where the bench etc. have been taken out.*]

DOCTOR: Now please, let's have it in English.

CRAPE: Sh-ssh . . . I'll whisper it. She wants, to find out, what it is, you're at!

DOCTOR: I dare say she does. Anything else?

CRAPE: Isn't that enough? Of course we all know the importance of your work –

DOCTOR: How?

CRAPE: How?

DOCTOR: Yes, Mr Crape. *How* do you know my work is so important?

CRAPE: Why . . . it stands to reason, Doctor. I was saying to Mr Golightly only the other day – 'Dr Copperthwaite, Mr Golightly, is what they term an Intellectual – he's a real scientist,' I said. 'And what he does in his Laboratory, I'll wager you nor I couldn't come near comprehending it, not if we tried for twenty years.' Could we, Doctor? It stands to reason.

DOCTOR: H'm.

CRAPE: Now you and me, Doctor –

DOCTOR: Mr Crape, you have been talking for nearly ten minutes, you have told me absolutely nothing: and you *ruined* my experiment! I don't want to see you again for a very long time.

[*Exit* DOCTOR.]

CRAPE: Ah, disappointing. What we might term a disappointing
devolution? But they aren't all, you know – oho no. There's times
when I've been able to learn that Doctor some most remarkable
things, yes: *he* knows my value. [*He sings.*]

> The darkening age of James J. Crape
> Yet burns with one surviving fire:
> To see the old fools all a-shiver and a-quiver
> At the secret probings of my power!

Oi-oi, what's this? [*His eye falls on a loose leaf which has fallen from
the Doctor's notebook at the time of the interruption, and has lain un-
noticed on the floor. He picks it up.*] The Doctor's dropped his – hey,
Doctor! Doctor! Doctor, you've dropped your – he doesn't hear
me, I'm too late. Good. [*He has called in a careful diminuendo, ending
in a whisper.*] Not but what there's much advantage to be gained
out o' *this*, I don't imagine. Signs, calculations, arithmetics, alge-
bras, squared paper, crossing out – real Doctor's handwriting, too –
I can't hardly read it. . . . 'Optimum ages and reduced minimum
of estimated reductions – thirty years, forty years, fifty –' A list of
names – oho . . . 'Letouzel, Phineus, Hardrader, Golightly – *Crape*.'
Well: I don't know what it is, and I don't like it. But it's got *their*
names on, as well as mine. Forewarned is forearmed. I'd call it
worth preserving.

[ORDERLY ROBINSON *enters.* CRAPE *whips the paper into his coat.*]
Oh, Mr Robinson, er, looking for something? Left something
behind? No . . . no, nothing here . . . but I'll keep a sharp eye –
ha ha, good morning . . .

[*Exit* ORDERLY.]

This place isn't safe. I'd better make meself scarce. I'll go and find
Letouzel – see what the old nutmeg-grater's plotting today.
Maybe something there to advantage? Ha ha . . . maybe . . . [*He
goes out singing.*]

> All a-quiver and a-shiver
> At the secret probings of my power . . .

SCENE TWO

[*A* VOICE *over the loudspeaker.*]

VOICE: Mr Golightly, please. Mr Golightly to report to Sister's office. Mr Golightly, if you please.

[*Enter* MRS LETOUZEL *pushing* MRS PHINEUS *in her wheel-chair.*]

PHINEUS: Yes ... I think I do, yes.

LETOUZEL: No, dear, no.

PHINEUS: Yes.

LETOUZEL: It comes more expensive.

PHINEUS: No.

LETOUZEL: Oh yes it does, dear, much more expensive. Besides, it's better to drink Indian. Not so much tannin.

PHINEUS: I beg your pardon, Mrs Letouzel?

LETOUZEL: I said Indian tea, dear, does not contain so much tannin. The China tea is very corrosive, you see.

PHINEUS: Corrosive?

LETOUZEL: To the intestines, dear. It corrodes them.

PHINEUS: Yes ... I spoke to Dr Copperthwaite. He said I could have China tea if I asked for it. He said so. I want it.

LETOUZEL: It's much more expensive.

PHINEUS: Yes.

LETOUZEL: I'll see about it. Next week. .... Oh, by the way, dear, I wonder if you wouldn't mind putting your name on this. [*She produces a document and a fountain-pen.*]

PHINEUS: Oh dear ... what?

LETOUZEL: Your usual signature, you just write it *here*. We have to make sure that your Anglo-Ethiopian Copper Shares remain well consolidated, don't we?

PHINEUS: I don't quite understand ...

LETOUZEL: Consolidated, dear. If we are to spend so much more on having China tea, we must preserve for our investments a degree of consolidation, you know. Sign here, dear.

PHINEUS [*signing*]: Yes ... yes ...

LETOUZEL [*sings to the audience*]:

> One thousand pounds she thought that she could save.
> For no true need, you see:
> Indeed for naked greed.
> The State will pay to dig her narrow grave.

[*She takes the document back.*] That's right, dear . . . thank you. I shall send it to the Solicitor's by the afternoon post. Here is the letter to go with it. [*She produces a letter.*] Would you like to read it over? It refers to your quarterly payments to Dr Copperthwaite, you know he has put his fees up this summer, don't you?

PHINEUS: Has he? Oh dear. I expect it will be because of the extra cost of the tea. . . . No, no, I don't want to read it, Mrs Letouzel, I'm afraid it might perturb me . . . must I put my name?

LETOUZEL: If you don't mind, dear. Here.

PHINEUS [*signing*]: Yes . . . yes . . .

LETOUZEL [*sings as before*]:

> One thousand pounds she thought that she could save.
> For no true need, you see:
> Indeed for China tea.
> A marble teapot should adorn her grave.

[*She takes the letter back and puts it together with the other document into an envelope, closes it, but does not seal.*]

PHINEUS: Is Mr Golightly coming to see me this afternoon, do you imagine?

LETOUZEL: I've no idea, I'm sure. He usually contrives to. So I expect he will today. . . . Oh by the way, dear, you've forgotten your contribution for the Spastic Children Fund, haven't you? Dr Copperthwaite wants all of us to be regular contributors, you know. [*She produces from the recesses of her clothing a small oblong collection box which she presents.*] Half-a-crown, dear.

[MRS PHINEUS *finds a coin after much fumbling in her huge knitting bag.*]

LETOUZEL [*sings to the audience during the fumbling*]:

> One thousand pounds she thought that she could save.

The children's need, you see,
To me is dear indeed.
This narrow box more fruitful than the grave.
Thank you, dear. Tired? Yes. Why don't we have a nice rest,
that's right, close your eyes, dear, a nice rest ... yes ... [*She wheels
her away.*]

SCENE THREE

[*Enter* GOLIGHTLY.]

GOLIGHTLY: Ah, well, thank goodness that's over for today. Undignified, yes, but alas, you will tell me, necessary. Dr Copperthwaite
says necessary, a good working bowel is the foundation of a good
working life. Even in the evening of our days the heart may – may
it not? – beat its wings a little, unencumbered by the more brutish
obstructions. It will shortly be time for my cup of tea with Mrs
Phineus. You understand that most days she condescends to receive
me, and – a cup of tea, a Bath-bun, or Eccles-cake, a few mild words
of tender and respectful intercourse, and if she is so minded – a
little sport or game, a gay twenty minutes. Sometimes dominoes,
sometimes spillikins, sometimes halma – *today* – ha ha – [*he produces a small dartboard from under his coat*] I have obtained permission,
with some difficulty, for this. Darts, in a hospital, may be said to be
hazardous. But I pressed the point. I emphasized to the Doctor
that my skill was considerable and there would be no damage. Mrs
Phineus can't play darts. But if I can teach her, shall I not in some
manner be putting her in my debt, and is not that an enviable state
for a yearning heart? Hey? Let's hang it up. [*He hangs the board on
the rear wall of the stage.*] Now then: three darts – let's see what we
can score. [*He throws the darts. They all miss the board.*] Oh. Never
mind. Practice makes perfect. Try, try again. [*He throws them again.
They all hit the board but with a very low score. He quickly takes the two*

worst and improves their position.] Ye-es. Well, we'll call that one bull, one twenty – oh, we'll allow this one, a five – not so good, but it *got* there. [*He now pretends to talk to his opponent.*] Your turn, Mrs Phineus – no, no, dear lady, hold it so, the helping hand, the tentative touch on the shoulder – ah dear, dear dear, balance, above all, *balance*! Splendid! Splendid! Next time they'll *all* be on the board. Remarkable progress for such a beginner. ... Perhaps we're a little tired? Tea? Oh, *tea*, Mrs Phineus – how very kind, certainly, dear lady, or may I use a more familiar name? This tender moment, Margaret, this – oh Margaret, all my life, all my life I have waited for such a – Margaret, I melt, I weep, forgive me, my presumption, so sweet, so tender, oh so very vulnerable and in need of my protection, dearest love, my heart, my chick, my chuck, princess of pulchritude – oh love, dear love –

[*In his emotion he is now kneeling at an imaginary pair of feet.* MRS LETOUZEL *enters wheeling* MRS PHINEUS *in her chair.* MRS PHINEUS *is asleep.*]

GOLIGHTLY: Oh, good gracious, how do you do, dear lady – Mrs Letouzel – I seemed to have broken a shoelace. Careless, but undaunted, I should wear elastic-sided boots, should I not?

LETOUZEL: Ssh, she's asleep.

GOLIGHTLY: Oh.

LETOUZEL: Do you think I could have a word with you, Mr Golightly? Now, quickly, before she wakes up? She'll be asking for her tea.

GOLIGHTLY: Ah, yes, her tea –

LETOUZEL: How does it go?

GOLIGHTLY: I beg your pardon?

LETOUZEL: You: her: how does it go? Let's play the Truth game – we're old enough, aren't we?

> Truth or Lie, till the day I die
> Strike you dead if you tell me a lie.

Come on, Mr Golightly, oho come on, rogue, *I* know the tickling heart. Who's the discreet one – **you** or me? Who sends her tea in

every day and always asks the nurse for two cups? Who contrives
the Eccles-cakes or Bath-buns on her plate and sees that always
there's an *even* number? Who's your fairy-godmother, Mr Golightly? Dr Copperthwaite – or me? Oh come on – come on, you
rogue –

GOLIGHTLY: You put me to a confusion, Mrs Letouzel, I had not
realized that I was so apparent. . . .

LETOUZEL: The tender heart calls to the tender heart, you know.
Yes: but: ah no: no, no: yet, but: I *do* wonder . . .

GOLIGHTLY: You wonder?

LETOUZEL: If perhaps I haven't been a half-inch stupid, a quarter-
inch too easily swung, by sentiment maybe – she will eat you up.

GOLIGHTLY: Eat me?

LETOUZEL: What happened to *Mister* Phineus?

GOLIGHTLY: Mister? Why, post-operative complications following
an appendicectomy, I understood.

LETOUZEL: Yes. But complications; not always organic, are they?

GOLIGHTLY: What? but –

LETOUZEL: I am saying not a thing. Only reflecting. I see you: and I
see her, and ah, it's not always so good to be too warm and trusting.
The trusting heart, the fallen fledgling.

GOLIGHTLY: Mrs Letouzel, really, I must protest. These are insinua-
tions, yes, that is what they are, dear lady, I'm sorry, but there is no
other word. And in fairness to Mrs Phineus I must ask you either to
keep them to yourself, or at least not behind her back, or in the long
run to establish evidence, madam, but not just to *toss* – this broad-
casting, this subversive, this cruel undermining – I must insist,
madam: *no!*

[MRS PHINEUS *wakes.*]

LETOUZEL: Ssh, she's awake.

PHINEUS: It is now half past four.

LETOUZEL: Not quite yet, my dear. Twenty past.

PHINEUS: Eh.

LETOUZEL: Twenty past. Twenty past four, dear.

PHINEUS: No. Half past. I never make a mistake about the time. When I wake up I know to the moment the exact hour of the day. Your watch must be fast, dear Mrs Letouzel. Ten minutes. Yes.

GOLIGHTLY: You are quite right, Mrs Phineus. It *is* half past four.

PHINEUS: I beg your pardon – I am a little hard of hearing – ah, Mr Golightly, how very agreeable to see you this afternoon and what a pleasant surprise. Yes. You're quite right, it is half past. Dear Mrs Letouzel, as you go out, perhaps you would be so kind as to ask nurse to bring in my tea. Mr Golightly, will you join me? I do hope so. Two cups, my dear. You just ask the nurse. Yes.

[*Exit* MRS LETOUZEL.]

PHINEUS: Sit beside me, Mr Golightly.

GOLIGHTLY: Shall we have our little game, before tea, my dear lady.

PHINEUS: I beg your pardon? I'm a little hard of –

GOLIGHTLY: I said would you like to play our –

PHINEUS: Oh no, I don't think so today, I am very tired of dominoes. Dr Copperthwaite says that the black and white, so often repeated, must eventually affect my eyes. Yes.

GOLIGHTLY: Not dominoes today.

PHINEUS: No, no, not dominoes. Dear Mrs Letouzel will send in the nurse and she shall bring us tea.

GOLIGHTLY: I thought you might prefer to play –

PHINEUS: I have asked this week for neither Bath-buns nor Eccles-cake, but a small tomato sandwich. One has to consider the intake of protein. Dr Copperthwaite does not seem very aware of the danger of starch in my diet. I have spoken to him about it. Yes. Twice.

GOLIGHTLY: To play *darts*?

PHINEUS: I beg your pardon?

GOLIGHTLY: Darts? You see, there is the board all ready for us. Three darts and they're very light and easy to throw. Perhaps if I could demonstrate –

PHINEUS: No no. Not dominoes today. Hopscotch.

GOLIGHTLY: Hopscotch?

PHINEUS: Yes. You see, you must mark out the floor – and then – oh we're neither of us too old to jump here – and then there. Are we? No. Dr Copperthwaite says I must leave my chair for a good half hour every day. Give me a piece of chalk.

GOLIGHTLY: Oh, chalk? Well I should have a piece –

PHINEUS: I have a piece. [*She takes a huge piece of chalk out of her enormous reticule.*] Mark out the squares.

GOLIGHTLY: I don't think I quite remember how –

PHINEUS: I do. [*She jumps out of her wheel-chair and points out the position of the squares on the stage for him, moving with surprising agility, and always being a couple of moves in front of him.*] One there.

GOLIGHTLY [*drawing hastily*]: Here?

PHINEUS: Then two. Here.

GOLIGHTLY: Here?

PHINEUS: There.

GOLIGHTLY: Oh. Here.

PHINEUS: Then three. Three there.

GOLIGHTLY: Here.

PHINEUS: Three more. More.

GOLIGHTLY: Yes.

PHINEUS: Two.

GOLIGHTLY [*puffed*]: Oh ha hoo – Two.

PHINEUS: And one. And one. And one, here. Here. Here. One there. There.

GOLIGHTLY: And one and one and one . . . would you like first turn?

PHINEUS: No, you.

GOLIGHTLY: Are you quite sure you wouldn't –

PHINEUS: Go on. Go on. Hop!

GOLIGHTLY: But shouldn't there be a stone, or a tin, to – to kick?

PHINEUS: What have you got?

GOLIGHTLY [*produces a matchbox*]: This?

PHINEUS: No.

GOLIGHTLY [*produces spectacle-case*]: This?

PHINEUS: No. No.

GOLIGHTLY [*produces gold cigarette-case*]: Well, all I have left is –

PHINEUS: That one. Yes.

GOLIGHTLY: But, dear lady, it's real gold –

PHINEUS: Very pretty. That one. Yes. Now hop.

GOLIGHTLY [*hopping with difficulty*]: One: and two: and – [*He rests on both feet.*]

PHINEUS: No no no! Not to rest yet. One foot, only. *This* square, you can rest.

GOLIGHTLY: Oh dear. Yes. Ah . . . Ah . . . Oh dear. [*He falls down.*] I don't think I can quite –

PHINEUS: My turn. The rules are strict, you see. Not to rest except in the outside square. *My* turn now. [*She hops.*] One. Two. Oh . . . Oh . . . Three! I'm allowed a rest. [*She rests.*]

GOLIGHTLY: No.

PHINEUS: Yes. The second time, you see. This is the *second* hop. So we have extra rests. Yours was the *first* hop, wasn't it?

GOLIGHTLY: But this is the first hop *you've* had.

PHINEUS: No. In the whole game: the *second* hop. Now then: [*She hops further.*] One two three. Ah . . . Ah . . . A little rest, here. Yes. Now then: one two three. I'm allowed another rest. Here. Yes. This is the second hop. Now then: one two three – [*She accidentally kicks the cigarette-case out of play: but picks it up and puts it in the final square.*] Home! I won. I won. I won. I won. Yes. I won. I won. I won. Yes. I won. I won. I won. Yes. I won. I won. I won.

GOLIGHTLY: No!

PHINEUS: I *won*.

GOLIGHTLY: But you used your fingers. Picked it up with your fingers. It has to be *kicked*.

PHINEUS: No. No. The second hop: you see. Those are the rules.

GOLIGHTLY: Oh? Are they? Oh. I didn't quite remember them like that, I must say, but –

PHINEUS: Shall we have tea? Yes.

[*Enter* NURSE JONES *with tea-things.*]

Here it is. I thought it would come now. Thank you so much, Nurse. So very kind.

[NURSE JONES *helps her back into her chair, and then leaves.*]

I'm mother, am I not? Yes. So while I pour the tea, dear Mr Golightly, perhaps you would sing to me? It would be so kind. Yes. The melancholy song, perhaps.

GOLIGHTLY: Oh, please, not that one – I had really rather not . . .

PHINEUS: The melancholy one. It begins, you know how it begins – about the Sea Captain who steers his ship in vain, and then about the whales. You remember, don't you? Sing it. Yes.

[*She attends to the tea-things.*]

GOLIGHTLY: As you wish, dear lady – [*He sings.*]

> It is in vain the bold sea-captain
> Steers his ship toward a star
> The world turns round, the star is turning,
> His voyage wanders wide and far.
>
> He cannot mark the course he's taking
> His eyes are blind with salty scale.
> The storm destroys his very heart root
> As tears the harpoon through the whale.
>
> The whalefish dies in a bloodred whirlpool
> The sailor dies on the frozen strand.
> Washed up by waves for years that drove him
> Brought him at last to an unknown land.
>
> The life of man is lost and lonely,
> Whereas the porpoise and the whale
> They both have meaning and conclusion –

[*The song loses coherence.*]

> But he finds no meaning nor conclusion
> He finds no meaning nor –
> Whereas the porpoise and the whale –

I don't believe it! have always said love, Mrs Phineus, I have always believed it, I must still believe it, you cannot but credit that I have always certainly held to it, and even if without true experience, look, I have never really been able to put it to the proof – oh my dear, dear Mrs Phineus, I have never killed a whale, I have never *seen* a whale, nor yet travelled on a ship, except to the Isle of Wight when my sister lived in Shanklin – but, Love, it must surely be Love, *there* is a star that will not turn, I have had faith in this, for years, years, please, it must be true, *Love* is the meaning, say it is the conclusion – say it say it – *please!* .... Why, you've finished up all the tea, Mrs Phineus.

PHINEUS: Oh no, not all of it. Surely not.

GOLIGHTLY: But then, I suppose, I suppose, why not? Is it not your prerogative? Indeed, dear lady, are you not fully entitled – perhaps there is just a little bit left at the bottom of the pot? Oh dear, oh dear. Well then ... And after all she brought very few sandwiches, and small ones, small ... Perhaps I may have eaten one without actually noticing? I *do* feel quite full, as though I *had* had tea. I am quite absent-minded. Yes.

PHINEUS: Yes.

GOLIGHTLY: Yes?

PHINEUS: I am particularly partial to tomato sandwiches. I am so glad that you are as well.

[*Enter* NURSES *and* MRS LETOUZEL.]

LETOUZEL: Time for your bath, dear. Isn't it, Nurse? Half past five, dear.

PHINEUS: No. Five and twenty to six. I always know the time. I always know the time. I don't think I wish to have my bath tonight. No bath tonight, no bath tonight. No –

LETOUZEL: Oh but you must, dear, you must have your bath –

PHINEUS: No, no, no, no, no bath tonight –

[*Protesting in panic, she is wheeled out by the* NURSES.]

GOLIGHTLY: Give her a bath. Give her a bath. Hot, seething, pitch and brimstone. That's what she deserves. Cruel. Oh: here, here, there's a fish hook, here – [*He touches his throat.*] She's jerking it, tugs at it! Cruel!

LETOUZEL: It's true what I said then?

GOLIGHTLY: I would ask you not to concern yourself, madam, with what is not your concern. Permit me, if you please, to confine my misery to my own private bosom.

[*Exit.* MRS LETOUZEL *then sits down and takes out her collection box and documents. She starts looking over these, making ticks with a pen etc.*]

LETOUZEL [*as Golightly leaves*]: Ye-es, well, now that the interference seems to be at least temporarily eliminated, perhaps we'd better check our current totals, h'm? . . . 'One thousand pounds she thought that she could save . . .'

[*Enter* CRAPE *creeping up behind her. He starts singing, and she jumps to her feet, whipping the documents etc. out of sight.*]

CRAPE [*sings*]:

> There was an old woman in our town
> In our town did dwell
> And she grafted in a thousand pounds
> But she wanted more as well.

LETOUZEL: Highly diverting, Mr Crape, but it would be more to your credit if –

CRAPE [*laughing fit to split*]:

> Whip she larey tidifoo larey
> Whip she larey oh
> She grafted in a thousand pounds
> But she –

LETOUZEL: I said I had no doubt it is highly diverting, but you don't astonish me, Mr Crape: and particularly I am not astonished to find you creeping about, behind a lady's back, in carpet slippers. It's all of a piece. Go to the devil.

CRAPE: That's a very disagreeable sentiment, Mrs Letouzel. I prefer to ignore it. . . . Heh, ha ha, I see you sent off our little Golightly with a good sharp nip to his backend. Crabs' claws or lobsters', eh? [*He picks up her hand and examines her fingers.*] They look a bit blue, dear. I'd call it lobsters. . . . Let's play the Truth Game. Old Mrs Phineus's thousand pounds isn't as easy to get at as you thought it ought to be? A snippet here, a snippet there, but no real achievement – true?

> Truth or Lie: till the day you die
> Strike you dead if you tell me a lie.

Go on . . . true? All right. *Your* turn. You ask me.

LETOUZEL: I have no intention of being so childish.

CRAPE: As you like then. I'm only playing fair.

LETOUZEL: Wait a minute. Wait: I *will* take a turn.

> Truth or Lie: till the day you die
> Strike you dead if you tell me a lie.

CRAPE: Granted.

LETOUZEL: You have little talks with the Doctor, don't you, two or three times a week?

CRAPE: Eh? Now, now look here, old woman –

LETOUZEL: Truth or lie?

CRAPE: Uh . . . true. But don't you go thinking –

LETOUZEL: I know the sort of thing you trot along to tell him, Mr Crape, make no mistake about *that*! But I'm really far more interested in what *he* tells to you.

CRAPE: He doesn't tell me anything – or anyway if he does, it is under the seal of confidence. I wouldn't dream of infringing it.

LETOUZEL: What about this Bounty?

CRAPE: Bounty? What Bounty?

LETOUZEL: I know because he said so. I went to see him on Friday to make a very justified complaint. I said to him: 'Dr Copperthwaite, the present-day cost of living is very very hard upon we older people who have lived through two world wars.' And he said to me –

CRAPE: 'Bah wah wah wah-wah, Robinson, Smith, clear it up, sweep it away, that's all for this morning!'

LETOUZEL: And I said to him –

CRAPE: 'But for we *older* people, Dr Copperthwaite, who have lived through two world wars, the Old Age Pension is scandalous, the National Assistance gives us nothing –'

LETOUZEL: 'The Socialist Party in 1947 quite deliberately stole my savings.'

CRAPE: 'There are those of us, Dr Copperthwaite, who have lived through two world wars!'

LETOUZEL: And he said to me –

CRAPE: 'Bah wah wah wah-wah, Nurse Brown, Nurse Jones, swabs, basins, towels, liniment, ointment –'

[*They both dissolve into excessive laughter.* CRAPE *emerges from it first.*]

'Mrs Letouzel, you cantankerous old bag, what d'you mean, by complaining about your money! Your board and lodging and medical treatment in this benighted Bridewell is free! It's paid for by the voluntary contributions of our worshipful Patrons, and also, in part, by the Government. All *you* are asked to provide, God damn your eyes, are those few small comforts which –'

LETOUZEL: Which –?

CRAPE: '*Which* in the fullness of time will be rendered unnecessary by –'

LETOUZEL: 'By the Bounty paid out by the Ministry of Health.'

CRAPE: That's not what I was going to say.

LETOUZEL: No. But it *is* what *he* said. I'm afraid he had lost control. He was most ill-tempered and abusive. But that was what he said.

CRAPE: I've never heard of no Ministerial Bounty.

LETOUZEL: No more had I, Mr Crape. And the Doctor made it perfectly clear that I was not supposed to have done, either. He turned red in the face and went stamping and bumbling away. A slip of the tongue, you see: but what did it signify?

CRAPE: Steady, steady – here comes the Heavy Brigade – 'The Colonel said, die hard my boys. And by God they died hard. . . .'

[HARDRADER *enters. He looks around for his dog, sees it is not with him, then goes back to the door, opens it, calls* 'Hector, Hector'. *The dog (imaginary of course) comes apparently running in and leaps up at Crape. He and* MRS LETOUZEL *react in a panic. The dog barks.*]

HARDRADER: No no, down boy, down – go to heel, Hector, heel, boy, *heel*!

LETOUZEL: Must you bring that dog in here, Mr Hardrader!

CRAPE: Hey, hey, down you devil, down!

HARDRADER: Down, boy, down, leave him alone, he's all right, Crape, don't be frightened, he's as gentle as a goldfish. If you show him you're afraid of him, of course he comes round on you. Now Hector, sit down. Behave yourself. I shan't tell you twice. That's better. There, you see: perfectly disciplined – the word of command. He was only having his fun. Do you know, we've made a splendid walk this afternoon, Hector and me – eight miles out, eight and a half miles in again, over the hill past the housing estate, along the arterial road, railway line, gasworks – out into the fresh air, beautiful. I composed two verses in praise of nature – then sharp about turn at the bridge over the motorway, back we came, eight miles, half a mile detour at the cemetery corner to visit Mrs Hardrader's grave, flowers on the grave, a few words, composed a verse in praise of the departed, Hector gives her a howl too in commemoration – oh he remembers, don't you, boy? Then home again for tea, fit, tired, splendid.

LETOUZEL: You ought to see he stays in his kennel. It's not fair on other people. Good boy, then, good boy . . . er Hector, there you are now, Hector – keep him away, man, keep him away for heaven's sake!

HARDRADER: Hector, I said *sit*!

LETOUZEL: It is quite wrong to bring a dog that size into the hospital, Mr Hardrader. I'm surprised Dr Copperthwaite –

HARDRADER: Nonsense, Mrs Letouzel. Best friend a man ever had. Why, he used to live in my own room when I first came here, but some busybody made a complaint. Do you know this, Mrs Letouzel: I'm not an unsociable man, but I can only claim to have had two real friends in the whole of my life. That's Mrs Hardrader, and Hector. And Hector is the better of the two. Aha, boy, aha, nearly time for your biscuits. . . . What *you* need, y'know, Crape, is a bit more physical exercise. Nothing else necessary. A few strong walks, ride a tricycle, up and down with the dumbells! I tell you what, when the equipment arrives for the Doctor's new Gymnasium, I'll give you two afternoons a week on the parallel bars and the climbing ropes. I'll put something like a framework back inside *you*, man: completely rejuvenate you in less than a month!

CRAPE: *Parallel bars!* What are you talking about! He's not going to waste his money getting us parallel bars at *our* age! Why, I couldn't *possibly* –

HARDRADER: Maybe not now, but I think you'll find you will. Astonishing what a man can do with a bit of training. The equipment certainly has been ordered, y'know. The storekeeper told me himself. *He* was a bit surprised, as well . . . H'm, yes . . . Oh, it'll do us a power of good! You can give me ten years, I suppose, Crape: but you take a look at me. There's good fresh air in here – [*Thumping his chest.*] What have you got? What have you got there? Smog.

VOICE [*over the loudspeaker*]: Mr Golightly, please. Mr Golightly to report to Sister's Office. Mr Golightly, if you please.

HARDRADER: Ha! Sounds like the silly old pansy's got to have another enema! Hope he enjoys it. Ha ha.

VOICE: Correction to the last announcement. Correction. Mr *Hardrader* to report to Sister's Office, *not* Mr Golightly. Mr Hardrader, if you please.

HARDRADER: Indeed I shall do nothing of the sort! I have no use at all for that sort of treatment. It's merely pandering to one's natural sluggishness. No good. No good. [*He sings, with gestures that alarm Crape and Mrs Letouzel.*]

    I will not stoop, I will not bend,
    I live my life to the uttermost end.
    And when they come to drag me in –

Ho! Left, right, straight to the chin!
Bang, crash, ho, ooh, wallop, out –
Take him away!
Hardrader, Hardrader,
Hardrader wins the day.'

What do *you* say, Hector?

Ho! Grab him, get him, sick him, go for his throat –
Take him away!
Bold Hector, Bold Hector,
Bold Hector wins the day –

[*Enter* NURSE BROWN. HARDRADER *nervously tries to escape the other way.*]

Yes, Nurse, right away. Yes . . .

[*He tries to drive the dog out the far side.*]

Go away boy, go on, go – you're not wanted now. Get rid of him, Crape. Go on, be off! . . . [*The dog is pushed out by* CRAPE *and* LETOUZEL.]

Oh, yes, Nurse. Yes. Indeed, yes: Sister's Office, I was just on my way – yes.

[HARDRADER *goes out with the nurse.*]

LETOUZEL: I shall speak to Dr Copperthwaite. That abominable dog. It's entirely ridiculous.

CRAPE: He says to me rejuvenated? *That* old man – rejuvenated!

LETOUZEL: Rowdiness and rhodomontade, dogs and smells and great muddy boots –

CRAPE: What possible good can any of us get from wanting to be young again? It's only when you're old that you can see how it all sets up – you need experience, you need wisdom – you're not kidding me I'm sorry for my age!

LETOUZEL: Oh? Now you don't believe that, do you, Mr Crape?

CRAPE: Eh?

LETOUZEL: Do you mean to say that there's any sort of value in knowing how to get, when you've no time left you to *spend*? Here we are, look at us, dried up in this Institution, the only things we know how to do are the worst things we ever learned – plotting and planning, avarice and spite. Well, why not? We have no opportunity for anything different. . . . *We* should stop quarrelling : we ought to be friends.

CRAPE: Ah yes, we ought. . . . Oh that stupid Copperbottom, he's wasting his time. What he needs to be working on, if he wants to be worthwhile, is a *real* rejuvenation ! If he could discover a drug that'd make us all young again, yet not destroy our memories – eh? *There* there'd be some value.

LETOUZEL: Who knows? Perhaps he is.

CRAPE: Wait a minute –

LETOUZEL: What d'you mean, wait a minute –

CRAPE: Oh wait a minute . . . we're talking flat rubbish. It's too much to hope for . . . *He* said : Gymnasium. Why build a Gymnasium? Right?

LETOUZEL: I suppose so –

CRAPE: Wait a minute. *You* said : Ministerial Bounty. Why give us a Bounty? It's not been provided for in any Act of Parliament so far as *I* know. Right?

LETOUZEL: No, you're right, it hasn't . . .

CRAPE: But supposing –

LETOUZEL: Supposing –

CRAPE: Supposing *you* was a mermaid, you'd have a lovely silver tail – right? And you'd need water to swim in !

LETOUZEL: Right !

CRAPE: But supposing, supposing, instead of a mermaid, you was a young woman ! You'd need some sort of dowry to start you out in life ! And if *I* was a young man – parallel bars ! I could *swing* on the parallel bars ! Oh my good Lord, I'd be jumping like a monkey !

LETOUZEL: It isn't very likely.

CRAPE: Not? Is it not? [*He pulls out the paper he found in* SCENE ONE.] Now take a look at this. Disregard the mathematics. Look at these names. Optimum ages, estimated reductions, here we are, months, years, you see ! He's *doing* it !

LETOUZEL: He must be!

CRAPE: That's what he's doing!

BOTH TOGETHER: He's going to *rejuvenate* us!

[*Startled by a sudden noise, they go rigid, saying:* 'Ssh!']

CRAPE: It's all right: it's nothing. Someone slammed a door....

LETOUZEL: When will it happen?

CRAPE: I was in with him this morning. There was a sort of an accident. Bound to hold things up a little. We've got time to reflect.

LETOUZEL: Ye-es.... *How* dare he! *How* dare he! Without one word to us!

CRAPE: Quite right – how dare he.... But it stands to reason, after all, he's got to keep it secret till he's worked out his formulas. What *you* want to fix your mind on, y'know, is this question of the Bounty.

LETOUZEL: H'm, yes, of course. There is that point of view ... ah, it's bound to be inadequate. Public funds, bureaucratic parsimony – and just when I was really reaching my nose into the true fat meat of *her* savings.... I have it! I shall go into partnership with her.

CRAPE: Partnership in what?

LETOUZEL: In a little Agency, Mr Crape. She'll still have what I've left her out of her thousand, we'll invest it intelligently according to my system. All my life, I have been waiting for this. Scheme after scheme, absolutely foolproof, has been baulked from the beginning by my never having quite enough capital to carry it through. In 1945 everything was set for such a speculation in transport shares that – oh, that shameful General Election! The black ingratitude of the British public.... Enough of this. I shall set up my Agency.

CRAPE: What sort of Agency?

LETOUZEL: A general Agency. No staff. Just myself (and of course, the sleeping partner, dear Mrs P – oh yes, and she will sleep!). Our clients will write in and I shall conduct their business for them entirely through correspondence. The letters come, the transaction is performed, the letters go out again, and the percentages accrue.

Each profit invested, and each investment profitable! Life, Mr Crape: *life*, to be re-lived once more. I can't wait for the day!

CRAPE: *I'm* going into business, and all. I'm going to open a warehouse. Export-Import. Y'know, packing-cases, oil-drums, boxes of porridge-oats – there are going to be *men* working for *me* – fifteen of 'em, in green aprons and a cap with a leather peak. 'Three more lorries to be unloaded, hurry it up, ah, Parkinson, how's the kiddies? And the missus? Good ... Hardrader! Get them iron girders to the other end of the shed before lunch-time and when you've done that you can carry them big bales right up into the loft.'

LETOUZEL: You're not going to employ *him*!

CRAPE: Ho ho, I am so – you see him young again and out into the world – he'll be as helpless as a babe! He was put in here in the first place by some of his own family. Too hearty about their house by far, he was. They lived in a semi, y'know, only about a mile away, and he brought all the half-timbering down one night sleep-walking – he strides into a bow window and he carries it straight out into the garden with him! But when he's thirty-five and I'm twenty-six, I'll have that physical phenomenon working for me till the floor-joists rock beneath him! Bow wow, bow wow, down, ye devil, *down*! What about Golightly?

LETOUZEL: What about him?

CRAPE: If he marries Ma Phineus, and he might very well – you won't find much partnership left, will you? A bit of rejuvenation could make a great deal of difference.

LETOUZEL: Then I'd better go and court him myself, I suppose, and you'd better court Hardrader, if you want to make sure of him before he gets his own ideas. But for God's sake keep it secret!

CRAPE: Strike me dead if I utter a word! *We* know, don't we, and nobody else! We're on a stance of power, *we* are – like, hand in hand, aren't we? ... We ought to get wed! Why, who knows *what* we're going to turn out like? We might be like *Gods*!

LETOUZEL: Ah no, Mr Crape. It's Business is our business, that's all.

CRAPE: Oh, but I used to be handsome – you know, they called me Dandy Jimmy! You wait and see! [*He sings.*]

> To be born into this world again
> As a little child to grow
> Where the young need the old
> For to show them the road –

LETOUZEL [*sings*]: And the old need the young to go.

[*They sing the song through, once more together, and dance out.*]

VOICE [*over the loudspeaker*]: Mr Crape, please. Mr Crape to report to Sister's Office. Mr Crape, if you please.

SCENE FOUR

DOCTOR [*offstage*]: Robinson! Mr Robinson! Mr Smith! Mr Smith! [*Enter* DOCTOR, *followed by* ORDERLY ROBINSON *who carries a retort full of liquid.* ORDERLY SMITH *enters by other door and meets them. He carries notebooks.*]

DOCTOR: Notebooks? Have you got the retort? Let's have a look at it … Ah, aha, ha. You see, you see – dark blue, dark blue, look at it, and it shades into black down at the bottom. Black sediment: blue: just as I thought. It came in a flash. I never even dreamt – I'll tell you by God I think this is it! What a devil of a good chance that damfool patient interrupted us when he did! He doesn't know it, no, but he's speeded up his own chances by a third, by a half, I should think by *threequarters* – you see what he's done? The very fact it coagulated, may be the one clue we need! I must have been blind. This is one of those discoveries in the history of science that –

[*He leafs through his notebooks.*]

Yes, yes – here we are – ha: six point eight-six-nine, seventy-two, four by three by two, *divide,* cross the coordinates, bending-moment, bending-moment – quick –

[ORDERLY SMITH *finds a place for him in a log-table and does a quick calculation in the margin with a biro.*]

Good boy, good: right, right – and by the power of three – and there we are! So. Twenty-four hours more: there should be one more change in the colour. I'm certain there will be. Then we'll try it again over the bunsen, add in your accotile and heraclith solution – half-quantities, make a note – and if it turns green, we've got it! A short cut at last. It's more than a short cut – it's much more than that – I hardly dare say it but it's opening out a whole new field of development. This means, this means that I'm going to be able to put this Elixir straight into full production, straight on the world market! Robinson, I want you to get a draft report made out, as soon as you have time. We must tell the Ministry. It alters our whole timetable. An agonizing – a *wonderfully* agonizing reappraisal of the entire Copperthwaite Project! You know, I'm going to have those five young again by the end of next week. I tell you they're going to skip like mountain bloody goats! All right, Robinson. Take it away. Put it back in the rack. And make sure you check that temperature. Twenty-four hours more. How on earth am I going to live through it? Go on, boy, go on . . .

[*Exit* ORDERLY SMITH *with retort.*]

Get me the telephone. I want to talk to Charlie Sanderson. You know his number, don't you?

[ORDERLY SMITH *fetches from the recess a telephone on a long lead. He rapidly dials a number, then hands receiver to Doctor.*]

Hello – Charlie? . . . Jack. How are you, sport? Ha ha, go on, go on, you don't tell me, he he, watch it, Charlie, watch it, she'll have you at the altar before you've buttoned your breeches. . . . Now seriously, Charlie, look, I'm going to have to scratch from the match on Saturday. . . . No no, of course it isn't because of last week, of course I don't bear a grudge, boy. I was off form and I knew it, you were quite right what you said to me, I'd have told you the same. . . . All right, sport, all right. Forgiven and forgotten.

But the fact of the matter is, there's something big coming up at the hospital. . . . Oh the usual line, you know, nothing earthshaking, bedpans and thermometers – but it may be important and I just daren't commit myself, I'm sorry. . . . Well what about Jimmy Ricketts, then, can't you play him in the second row, make that new type with the big 'tache your hooker – what's his name – Hawkins? – and then swop your scrum-half with – take it easy, Charlie, I know you're the Captain, I know it's short notice. And I may be damn good, boy, but I'm not indispensable – in any case, we're only playing a Teachers' Training College, they'll be outclassed, sport, no question – you'll never even notice I'm not there. . . . Oh, good. Well that's damned accommodating of you, Charlie, I'm bloody grateful, really . . . what? . . . Ho, ho, no! Oh, you look out for *her*, chum – and make sure you know where you've hidden your bedroom key. . . . All right Charlie, I'll remember. I'll put 'em in the post for you. Medical goods, a plain envelope – *I* know the drill. We'll keep you a bachelor yet. . . . Yes, on the Health Service. Taxpayers for ever! So long, sport, so long. And best of luck on Saturday. I'll be round for the beer in the evening. . . . So long. [*He rings off.*] Thank you Mr Smith. Put it away, please.

[ORDERLY SMITH *removes telephone.*]

Oh, while I've got it in my mind – I want you to take a letter – I heard a dog bark in the corridor this afternoon. Before we know where we are, we'll have old Crape along with more of his eternal complaints: so I'm damn well putting a stop to it, *now*.

[ORDERLY SMITH *prepares to take dictation in one of the notebooks.*]

To Mr Hardrader. Dear Mr Hardrader, it has been brought to my notice that in defiance of the permanent regulations of this hospital, you persist in retaining your pet animal on the premises. I would be glad if you would arrange to have the dog removed within thirty-six hours or else I shall have no option but to give instructions to have it destroyed. Yours, etcetera etcetera, J. Copperthwaite, Superintendent. Sign it pp me and see he gets it at once. . . . That ought to make the place a little more hygienic. I don't like dogs anyway. . . . Dogs . . . I may need that dog. Cancel the letter. Write it like this: 'The dog must be delivered to my Office within thirty-six hours or else.' Then get someone who knows about these things to put a value on the beast. I think it's only a mongrel: but I wouldn't want to take it from the old fellow without paying him something. . . . That'll do for this afternoon. Will you attend to it directly? Thank you.

[*Exeunt severally.*]

SCENE FIVE

[MRS LETOUZEL *enters cautiously. She creeps across the stage to the opposite door, peeps through it, and then flattens herself against the doorpost as* GOLIGHTLY *enters, slowly. He does not see her, nor the mitten which she has taken off and dropped in his path.*]

LETOUZEL: Ha h'm. [*He turns round, sees her, inclines his head, coldly but politely, and continues on his way.*]

LETOUZEL: Mr Golightly! I'm afraid I've dropped my mitten.

GOLIGHTLY: I beg your pardon, Mrs Letouzel. I was in a brown study. Pray forgive me. [*He hands her the mitten and leaves her.*] Good evening . . .

[*She gives an exasperated exclamation, and dodges out of the door by which he has entered. He sits down dejectedly. She re-enters by the door of her original entry: or rather, peeps round it to see what he is doing. He gets up and starts toward her, but without realizing she is there. She retreats behind the door, and when he reaches it, pops out at him with a startled little squeak.*]

LETOUZEL: Oh! Mr Golightly, really! . . . We seem to be running into each other everywhere! I was just on my way to – well, I didn't expect to meet any gentlemen in *this* corridor, Mr Golightly!

GOLIGHTLY: Good gracious, madam, I really *do* beg your pardon! Excuse me! I will return to my quarters at once.

LETOUZEL [*detaining him*]: Mr Golightly.

GOLIGHTLY: Madam?

LETOUZEL: I am truly sorry for you, Mr Golightly. Please believe me when I tell you that. I know what you came here for, you see.

GOLIGHTLY: You do? Oh . . .

LETOUZEL: You hoped to catch some fleeting glimpse, did you not? One last appeal to her implacable divinity, as she is swept from room to room – But it wouldn't be any use. She will never change, never. . . . Dear friend, I beg you: put her out of your mind!

GOLIGHTLY: No. . . . No. . . . I cannot. . . . And you are as bad, you know! Oh yes you are! You gloat and look on. I know what they think – Namby-pamby little Golightly, tripping about, ogling, smirking, ha ha, yes, the lady-killer: but all that he's fit for is the queen-bee's dirty work! But I can tell you: when I was a young man I was most certainly admired! It was not considered disgraceful, in those days, to appear spruce and to behave with chivalry. If I could be young – for just one evening, Mrs Letouzel, *I'd* show up the crudities, the brutalities of this age! There are young women who would be *astonished*! And that is no fable!

LETOUZEL: Suppose – why not suppose – suppose that you *were* young. Suppose *she* was too. You'd still allow it to go on, just as it goes on now.

GOLIGHTLY: Oh no I would not.

LETOUZEL: Ah, you would not? You'd tear her right out of you, leap away like a rattlesnake, and ravage alone through the hips and the hearts of innumerable others! Oh you promiscuous, you un-controlled, you terrible danger!

GOLIGHTLY: I don't mean that either. All I intended to say was, that I should be able for once to pay my court where my inclinations have dictated, without prejudice from my old age and my con-comitant ridiculous appearance.

LETOUZEL: But I told you: she will eat you up.

GOLIGHTLY: Only because of my age.

LETOUZEL: No! If you were no more than eighteen years old tomorrow, and she no more than – you stupid little man, do you not understand that that's all you are going to be! And she, she, she, will already be more than *thirty*! Mr Golightly, what you need is a *friend*: a loving, loyal, and vigilant friend. [*To the audience.*] I have said too much. [*To Golightly.*] I should not have told you. [*To audience.*] I should not have told him. Business is business. Business isn't passion. Passion and rage: to me, that *must* be business. I have let myself go. I think I am an idiot. But let's look for advantage. [*To Golightly.*] I'll accept it: I've told you. I'd better tell you more. Tell you the lot. Come on.

[*Exeunt.*]

SCENE SIX

[*Enter* HARDRADER *with a piece of paper, pursuing two nurses.* CRAPE *follows him.*]

HARDRADER [*trapping the Nurses in a corner*]: Excuse me, excuse me, Nurses, I won't keep you a moment. Don't be in a such hurry to get away – I may be an old man, but I'm not an old ghost, y'know. I can assure you, if you listen, you'll find yourself edified. There now, sit down, sit down, Nurse Brown –

[*The* NURSES *reluctantly do so.*]

Ha ha, Brown, down, what do we make out of that?

> I watch Nurse Brown
> As she sits down
> On the seat beside Nurse Jones.
> Two diamond stones
> Upon one golden ring.
> To view them both,
> Sets my old heart to sing.
> Hey ding-a-ding, ding.

Only an improvisation, of course. Rough, rough, I know. But what about this? This one's *considered*, this is what I want you to hear: [*He reads.*] To Hector – that's my dog.

> Old fellow. You and I through life
> Have wandered without hurt or strife
> Between us, man and dog. How few
> Of humankind can say so too!
> How few can say, that with a wife
> The years have passed so freely, as with you!
> Alas, how few!

Well, there you are? There's the Sentiment: is it the Truth? Oh, come on, young ladies, don't be bashful. A poem must be true or else it's no good – so tell me, be honest. . . .

LOUDSPEAKER: Nurse Jones, Nurse Brown, to report at once to Sterilization Room. Nurse Jones, Nurse Brown, please. Sterilization.

[*Exeunt* NURSES.]

HARDRADER: Oh. Thoroughly disheartening. Every time I try to teach these young women something, there's something else calls them away. Always the same. They never seem to allow them any free time.

CRAPE: They're supposed to be on duty. Stands to reason they're going to be called for.

HARDRADER: But if they were *off* duty, d'you imagine they'd stay and listen to me for more than two minutes? All they want to do is to jig around with yellow-faced young doctors at these, at these I think they call them 'boogie-woogie' parties, far too late at night. It's not as if they even took any sensible interest in a few out-of-door activities. Look at Dr Copperthwaite, certainly he plays a very respectable game of Rugger every Saturday: but who bothers to support him? No one from this hospital. Except me. No one at all.

[*Enter* ORDERLY SMITH *with letter.*]

Ah Mr Smith? A letter? For me? For me! What's the matter? Er, wait a moment – Mr Smith, I say, I say, please –

[*Exit* ORDERLY SMITH.]
What d'you imagine this is?

CRAPE: I should expect it's from the Superintendent.

HARDRADER: I hope nothing's wrong.

CRAPE: It's just the usual routine bureaucracy – you've been here long enough to know about *that*.

HARDRADER: Dr Copperthwaite only sends notes if there's something wrong. D'you imagine there could be a – a serious discovery, I mean, for instance, my last X-ray? Cancer? TB?

CRAPE: At your age?

HARDRADER: Why not?

CRAPE: Well at your age, why worry? We're all waiting for it, aren't we?

HARDRADER: I have always prided myself on my continued robust condition. I have always been happy to think that when I go, I shall go – straight: suddenly: upright to the end. I have never a cold, never a cough – which is more than can be said for you –

CRAPE [*with a snuffle*]: Colds and coughs are nothing –

HARDRADER: Yes they are, they're symptoms. If there is one thing I have dreaded, it is that something might come – say, cancer, without warning, without *any* symptoms. Every time the Doctor examines us, I say to myself – 'Not this time, oh my God, not this time.'

CRAPE: Why don't you open it?

HARDRADER: Open it. . . . Goddamit, who's afraid? Who cares a brassknuckle for any blasted young sawbones! Ha – [*He tears the letter open and reads it to himself.*] Good heavens. . . . Oh good heavens. . . . Oh . . . Crape: are you a man?

CRAPE: What sort of a man?

HARDRADER: Breathing. Feeling. Living. That sort. Well, are you?

CRAPE: What's the matter?

HARDRADER: Read it. The man who wrote this letter was not a man. Even if this letter is a joke, if it is mistimed pleasantry in a juvenile bad taste, it was written by no man. Because it is an inhuman letter: and I can tell you Crape, it has made me wish to die.

CRAPE [*having read the letter*]: Oh dear dear dear, Mr Hardrader, summon our spirits, man, come on, old chap, cheer up cheer up, rally round the flag, boys. You've still got the dog, I take it?

HARDRADER: I suppose so. I keep him in a potting-shed to the north of the tennis courts. I feed him every day under cover of going to examine the hardcore and the greensward. They all know I like to inspect the sports grounds regularly, and I thought I had been taken for granted down there. Some of the nurses are in the secret of course. But I said to them: please turn a blind eye. And they are good girls, loyal. They did so. But now – Crape, Crape, what on earth am I going to do?

CRAPE: Give me the dog.

HARDRADER: Give you the –

CRAPE: Get him out of that shed. Let me take him. And don't ask me where. When they come to tell you to hand him over: why, you deny all knowledge. Tell 'em he's run away. What could be easier?

HARDRADER: But what will happen then? Hector can't live without me, why, he –

CRAPE: Of course you'll get him back, old chap, old chap. When the hunt's died down. But don't put him in the potting-shed again. No. Now see: what about the old greenhouse among the rhododendrons west of the cricket pavilion? You go up there to inspect the state of the wicket, don't you? get it . . . eh?

HARDRADER: I would never have trusted Hector to anyone, before, ever. And then, there's another thing. How can I repay you? I am not a man to stand in debt, to anyone, ever. You see, I don't even know that I can manage to survive this business. I have not admitted this very often, but I *am* old, Crape, an old man, older than you. And the shock of the separation may –

CRAPE: Temporary separation.

HARDRADER: It is still a separation, and an unendurable one.

CRAPE: It's true you haven't very long to live –

HARDRADER: No. I haven't, now. Under no circumstances, now. Today I know this: I am altogether too old for all those things that I have lived for. Energy. Vigour. Strength of the body. Comradeship. Hector. What does it matter if Hector is destroyed. I am a dead man too. I was a big, strong man. Yes, Crape, I was. But it is finished, you see. This letter –

CRAPE: Oh no, old chap. No.

HARDRADER: What do you mean?

CRAPE: I wasn't going to tell you – [*To audience.*] I wasn't going to tell him. [*To Hardrader.*] But you're so down in the dumps, it looks as if I'll have to. [*To audience.*] I don't give a damn for *her*: do I? And do you? No, you don't because I'm the quicker of the two of us: you know it – and whatever she plans, I'll be the paymaster at the end of it all. [*To Hardrader*] Old chap, we're going to save Hector. And you're going to understand how very very much it is going to be worth it. You talk of repayment? Aha, you'll have your chance. Come on, and I'll tell you. And then we'll find the dog. Come on, come on. Old chap. Old chap.

[*Exeunt.*]

SCENE SEVEN

[*The telephone rings in the recess.* ORDERLY SMITH *hurries in, brings out the apparatus, at the same time answering it. Before he has time to speak, the* DOCTOR *enters and takes it from him.*]

DOCTOR: All right, Mr Smith, all right – I hear him, I'll take it. Hello, Superintendent here ... Eh? What? I didn't catch it. Hello! ... Damn nuisance, they've disappeared. You pick up the phone, there's some silly chicken on the other end, she says 'burble burble' will you hang on for one moment please, I'll put you right through! – and I'm damned if I know who she's putting me through to. Buckingham Palace for all I'm informed. Hello, yes, your Majesty, how simply super of you to call! Yes, of course,

Your Majesty, five o'clock would be splendid – shall we wea
court dress or is it going to be formal? Eh, hello, yes? . . . Yes, ye
of *course* I'm Copperthwaite. . . . What? (Oh my God, it *is* th
Queen – or next best anyway.) Good morning, Sir Frederick
I'm really sorry, I didn't quite recognize . . . Eh, dear dear dea
no no no no, Sir Frederick, *any* time of the day is a convenient tim
except when I'm . . . Oh. Sunday. I see. . . . Of course, I can'
very well say no. But it *would* be a bit happier for me if you coul
see your way, sir, to deferring it a week. You see, I have to . .
why, if you put it like that, Sir Frederick, of course. Yes. . .
Sunday. Very well sir. . . . No question, no. No no no. *Quite* a
right, Sir Frederick. Very happy. Very proud to see you here
Yes. . . . And good-bye to *you*, sir. [*He rings off.*] And good-bye t
you, sir. And, sir to you, sir. And good-bye, good-bye, good-by
I'm talking to my peace of mind, that's all. To my careless exist
ence. Good-bye ! . . . There, Smith, it's gone ! Look at it disappear
ing. Flight of a swallow. D'you want to know the reason? S
Frederick, no less. The Lord Mayor and the Bishop. The Mayore
and Mrs Bishop. The Town Clerk and Mrs Clerk, I dare say. Ha
the bloody Ministry straight down from Whitehall. They'r
coming, on Sunday. A ceremonial visit. We'd better buy a flag
Get a carpet. Scarlet. Buns, tea, cream in the buns. But I'm no
giving 'em drinks. This is a hospital, not a country club. No drink
no cinema shows, no dancing, no billiards. . . . This is Robinson'
report, y'know – too damn keen by far, that chap – I *told* him not t
make it so melodramatic. They want to see the Elixir, and the
want to see it at work. I'm not ready for an audience ! Who do the
think I am ! They'll be asking for a sputnik or a descent in a bathy
scaphe before we know where we are. . . . Well: let's have
organized. Shoulder to the wheel boy, your back to the wal
They're coming on Sunday. Dial me 36786 will you. And then g
away. I want this one private.

[ORDERLY SMITH *dials the number, hands back the phone to doct
and exits.*]

Hello, is that you, mother? Jack here. . . . Yes I'm very well indeed, mother – now, look – . . . Just a minute mother, I'm trying to tell you – . . . I'm *telling* you mother, I can't come on Sunday. Well of course I hadn't let you know: I'm letting you know now. Look, I can't come on Sunday because there's a man from the Ministry of Health and a whole lot more of the nobs and they're coming down to look at the hospital and I have to be here. . . . No, mother, you *can't* meet them. It's not social, it's official, and . . . now, look, love, I'm sorry: I like to come home as much as you like me to come . . . oh, *was* she? Did I ask her . . .? For God's sake let me invite my own girls to tea. . . . I *know* Joyce is a nice girl, I'm sure she's a lovely girl, she'll make a positively splendid wife for some stupid . . . All right, mother. I'm sorry. The tongue is sharper than the sword, or the thought is slower than the knife, or whatever they say. I didn't mean to be rude. Make my excuses, tell Joyce I'm sorry. If you must have her to tea, she can come the the weekend after –

[*Barking heard.* DOCTOR *becomes aware of dog on stage.*]

What's that! Get out of it! Get down there! Down! Smith – I say Smith.

[*Enter* ORDERLY SMITH.]

Get this damned dog out! Who let it in? There's a dog in the room, I shall have to ring off. . . . No mother, no, there's a bloody great dog. . . . I'm sorry, mother . . . NO! You can ring me next week! [*He rings off and thrusts telephone at* ORDERLY SMITH.] Where's it gone? Here! No, no, stop it! Here!

[*They pursue the dog round the stage in a flurry.*]

Lord help us, use your sense man, get it to the door – go on, now, go on, don't be afraid of it, it isn't going to bite you –

[*The* ORDERLY SMITH *bitten, screams.*]

Get it out of the door!

[*The dog is got out of the door and they slam the door behind it, and take breath in relief. The barking starts again at the other side of the stage.* CRAPE *enters, struggling with the dog at that side.*]

CRAPE: Down, boy, down – go to heel, good boy, good dog, Hector, Hector – no . . . Doctor, I'm sorry, it's nothing to do with me – he seemed to run away, I was trying to catch him –

DOCTOR: Robinson – Where's Robinson?

[*Enter* ORDERLY ROBINSON *above.*]

Who let this dog in!

[ORDERLY ROBINSON *shrugs and shakes his head helplessly.*]

Well we've got to get it out. Entice it, entice it. Get some food for it – *quickly* – How should I know what food – meat, eggs, fish, hurry!

[*Exit* ORDERLY ROBINSON *right.*]

hurry!

CRAPE: Watch him, Doctor, he's beginning to snarl. I think you've got him vexed.

DOCTOR: Keep still. Just keep still. Smith, I said *still*! Robinson, where are you?

[ORDERLY ROBINSON *enters on main stage with a plate of food.*]

What have you got there? Stew? All right, I dare say it eats stew, now attract him, attract him; lead him along with it – gently, gently – look dog, there's a plate of stew, look at the bloody stew, will you – good dog, good dog – rattle the eating irons, Robinson, make some effort to attract him, man – dinner, dinner, dinner – what do they call him?

CRAPE: Hector.

DOCTOR: Hector, boy, Hector, dinner for Hector, that's right, boy, that's right, come to the Doctor – give me the dinner – [*He takes the plate of stew.*] Doctor's got dinner, dinner for Hector, Doctor for Hector, Hector for Doctor, Doctor, Doctor, Hector, Doctor, dinner, dinner, dinner – [*He has worked his way backwards to the recess and quickly lays the plate down inside, clapping the screen closed behind him as he comes out. The barking is heard muffled.*] Three brass balls and be damned for his dinner. Where did he come from? Hardrader? Is it?

CRAPE: Now, doctor, all I was doing was –

DOCTOR: Poking your nose in, that's all you always do – red nose, Mr Crape, thick nose, carbuncles. Too much blood, Mr Crape. Too much. A nose like that needs a good blistering poultice. I shall bear it in mind. Get out of my sight.

[*Exit* CRAPE.]

Now then, the dog: go in after him – *carefully* – put him in a basket, strap down the basket, come out again, *carefully* – lock the door behind you. Look sharp.

[*Exit* ORDERLY ROBINSON *into recess.*]

So we're all set for Sunday. There's nothing now I need worry about. The Elixir is fermenting all according to plan, Sir Frederick and his friends are all fermenting according to plan, the dog's in a box according to plan – my God, the patients. I hadn't given them a thought. They might none of them be fit – snap check-up, all five. lay it on. X-rays, all the rest of the business. Robinson!

[*Enter* ORDERLY ROBINSON *from recess, carrying empty plate.* MRS LETOUZEL *enters.*]

All fixed? Then get ready. Snap check-up. All five X-rays, all the rest of the business. Smith, do you hear me . . .

LETOUZEL: Dr Copperthwaite, if you please, I maintain that it will not do. This sort of rudeness, simply snatched from my hands, I shall report it to the governors –

DOCTOR: Nurse, Nurse, Nurse Brown, Nurse Jones – All five, snap check-up, get ready, lay it on –

[DOCTOR *and* ORDERLIES *exeunt severally.* NURSES *cross the stage busily.*]

LETOUZEL: They may have given me the wrong diet, I wouldn't know, I wasn't told, but to serve me a dinner, and then to come immediately, simply to snatch it away –

[DOCTOR *crosses the stage, meeting* ORDERLIES *who cross in opposite direction.*]

DOCTOR [*en passant*]: Report cards, temperature charts, blood pressures, quick quick quick; Nurse Brown, Nurse Jones, where have you gone to?

LETOUZEL: I didn't even have time to see what was on the plate. I thought steak and kidney. But what was there with it? Pie crust – suet crust, steamed gravy, potatoes, why, I don't know – I'm not at all fond of steamed suet pudding. . . . But I should have liked to have known . . .

[*Enter* NURSE JONES.]

I tell you, I should like to have known . . .

[*Exit* MRS LETOUZEL *with the* NURSE.]

ACT TWO

SCENE ONE

LOUDSPEAKER: Attention, please. Attention, please. This is important. This is urgent. This is extra, unusual, a breach in routine. Mr Crape, Mr Hardrader, Mr Golightly, Mrs Phineus, Mrs Letouzel, will you all report, please, at once, to the X-ray department for immediate examination. The Superintendent's instructions. Will Orderlies and Nurses please ensure, at once, that Mrs Letouzel, Mrs Phineus, Mr Golightly, Mr Hardrader, Mr Crape, all report, at once, for immediate examination. Important. Urgent. Attention. Attention. Nurses and Orderlies, please, attention, attention . . .

[OLD PEOPLE (*except* MRS PHINEUS) *run across the upper stage, accompanied by* NURSES. *Then they enter on main stage and cross it, going out at opposite side.* ORDERLIES *cross the main stage in the other direction, passing them in the middle. Then the four* OLD PEOPLE *and* NURSE BROWN *re-appear on upper stage and sit down in a row. The* ORDERLIES *re-enter on lower stage, as does the* DOCTOR.]

DOCTOR: Is everybody there? One, two, three, four –

[MRS PHINEUS *is wheeled on to main stage by* NURSE JONES.]

– *And* Mrs Phineus. Right. Nurse Brown, I want to make a complete examination of each patient with as few delays as possible – time's as short as patience, remember that, so have everybody undressed and ready to come in, in turn, the minute I give the word. Right? Mr Robinson, Mr Smith, attend to the X-ray equipment inside and let's have the negatives on the dot, in my hand, the minute I give the word. Nurse Jones, you stay down here in the consulting room, please. Right. Speed it up. I'll start with Mrs Phineus in precisely one minute.

[*The* ORDERLIES *go into the recess.* MRS PHINEUS *is taken out of her wheel chair by* NURSE JONES *and led out of one door. The* DOCTOR *goes out of the other.*]

CRAPE [*sings*]:

> There were five green bottles
> A-hanging on the wall
> Five green bottles a-hanging on the wall
> But one green bottle has obeyed the Doctor's call
> So there's four green bottles a-hanging on the wall,
>
> Why we're here a-hanging
> We haven't yet been told
> There's an extra-urgent reason that shortly will unfold
> But one green bottle has suddenly gone cold –

[*As a possible explanation on which his mind takes hold – as he sits here imagining all sorts of explanations and emergencies and urgencies and all manner of unforeseen contingencies, disorders, alarms, provoked or otherwise called into being by the dark hand or instrumentality of chance – he sneezes, coughs, and splutters.*] – Doctor Copperthwaite's examining our health – how *is* our health? Mrs Letouzel?

LETOUZEL: Good.

CRAPE: Mr Golightly?

GOLIGHTLY: Good. Except for pains about my heart.

CRAPE: Mr Hardrader? Mr Hardrader? Oh tell me an answer – you can tell *me* an answer – [*In a whisper.*] I've got him away, bow-wow, bow-wow, away, away, OK *away* –

[HARDRADER *brightens up.*]

Now, how's your health?

HARDRADER: Oh by jove, by *jove* –

LETOUZEL: Mr Crape, how's yours?

CRAPE: Do you know, I think I've caught a cold – I don't believe it's serious, but you never know, do you, and at this time of year –

LETOUZEL: Don't be alarmed. I'm not alarmed. I'm relaxed: and I'm *silent*.

HARDRADER: Crape, you don't imagine –

GOLIGHTLY: Dear lady, you don't imagine –

HARDRADER AND GOLIGHTLY: That today is the Day!

LETOUZEL: I said relaxed, and I said I was *silent*.

GOLIGHTLY: Ah, yes, the word. Ssh ssh, quite right.

[*He puts his finger to his lips, and looks significantly at her.* CRAPE *puts his finger to his lips and looks at* HARDRADER, *who puts his finger to his lips and looks at Crape. On the main stage,* MRS PHINEUS, *wearing a sort of white nightshirt, is brought in by* NURSE JONES. *The* DOCTOR *enters from opposite door.*]

DOCTOR: Ah, Mrs Phineus. And how are we today? In good shape, are we? Are the X-rays taken, Mr Robinson?

[ORDERLY ROBINSON *looks out of recess and nods.*]

Now there's no need to worry, Mrs Phineus, about all this bustling about and medical business. I just want a small routine check-up, nothing to it, nothing to it specially, my dear, as you might say, a brief once-over – say Ah.

PHINEUS: Ah.

DOCTOR: Ninety-nine.

PHINEUS: Doctor, if you please – what is the meaning of all this commotion –?

DOCTOR: Ninety-nine.

PHINEUS: But, Doctor, we are not dangerously ill. No, I am in excellent health, Doctor, why do you wish to – ninety-nine.

DOCTOR [*at her knees with his little hammer*]: One, two, three, *hup.* [*Calls to upper stage.*] Will you get Mrs Letouzel ready please.

[NURSE BROWN *leads* MRS LETOUZEL *off upper stage.*]

PHINEUS: Please what is the meaning –

DOCTOR: One, two, three, *hup.* Good. Good. Waterworks all right?

PHINEUS: I beg your pardon, Doctor? Oh yes, yes, I suppose, I think –

DOCTOR: Yes. I think they are, me dear. Thank you. That'll do. . . . Now then, generally speaking, would you say you're in good shape, Mrs Phineus? I'd say you were, I'd say you were never better, I'd say I was very pleased with you – I'd say many more years, we can give you many more years. All right, me dear, off you go. Nurse.

[NURSE JONES *takes* MRS PHINEUS *out.*]

X-rays ready, Robinson?

[ORDERLY ROBINSON *enters from recess and hands X-rays to Doctor.*]

DOCTOR: Good. Good. Nothing wrong here that the odd dab of iodine won't cure. She'll do. A positive report on Mrs Phineus. Write it down.

[ORDERLY ROBINSON *writes it down.*]

Now for the next, Mrs Letouzel. X-rays taken, Smith.

[ORDERLY SMITH *puts his head out of recess and shakes it.*]

Hurry up about it then and send her in when it is.

[ORDERLY ROBINSON *goes back into recess.* NURSE BROWN *reappears on upper stage.*]

CRAPE [*sings*]:

There was four green bottles
A-waiting in a row
The next green bottle was fetched to go below
So there's three green bottles a-sweating at every pore
Three poor soldiers conscripted for the war
For death or glory or to hear the cannons roar –

I was at Passchendael, I was, oh what a terrible mess, terrible, four years in the Service Corps issuing new socks to men with trench feet, I can tell you it was a terrible bloody mess, oh God I was fair terrified.

[*He coughs, snuffles, and sneezes.* NURSE JONES *brings* MRS LE-TOUZEL, *in her white robe, to see the doctor.*]

LETOUZEL: Dr Copperthwaite, this is not the usual routine of the hospital. Now I would like to know, Doctor, because it is only fair to us older people who have been through two world wars –

DOCTOR: Now there's no need to worry, Mrs Letouzel, just medical business, a small routine check-up, me dear – say Ah.

LETOUZEL: Ah.

DOCTOR: Ninety-nine.

LETOUZEL: But, Doctor.

DOCTOR: Ninety-nine.

LETOUZEL: Ninety-nine.

DOCTOR: That sounds all right.

LETOUZEL: It does?

DOCTOR: Oh yes . . . One, two, three, *hup*.

LETOUZEL: Hup.

DOCTOR: One, two, three – hello?

LETOUZEL: Doctor, what's the matter?

DOCTOR: Again. One, two, three, *hup*. *Hup*. I dare say it's only local. Clear up by Sunday. Now don't you be worried, me dear, no need to worry. [*Calls to upper stage.*] Mr Hardrader, get him ready, please.

[NURSE BROWN *leads* HARDRADER *off upper stage.*]

How are you generally, I mean, walking, talking, reading the papers? Waterworks?

LETOUZEL: Oh I'm sure, sure, why quite sure, not a particle of doubt –

DOCTOR: Good, good, you're sure? Waterworks?

LETOUZEL: Oh, yes, I am quite sure, Doctor, really, I am perfectly –

DOCTOR: Let's have the X-rays.

[*Enter* ORDERLY ROBINSON *with them.*]

Ye-es . . . well . . . I think so. This is only routine, me dear – but, yes, many more years for you. Splendid form, splendid. Off you go.

[NURSE JONES *takes her out.*]

She'll do. Positive. Make a note, not too heavy a dose. I don't think we'd better have her going any further back than, say, thirty-five, thirty. I doubt if she's ever been that far back ever. I doubt if she could do it now. Mr Hardrader, when he's ready – I've no worries about him, nor yet for Mr Golightly. But Crape? We'll, we'll see . . .

    [ORDERLY ROBINSON *goes back into recess.*]

CRAPE: Two green bottles a-hanging on the wall. Two green bottles. A-hanging on –

GOLIGHTLY: Don't be nervous.

CRAPE: I'm not nervous.

GOLIGHTLY: I'm never nervous. Why should we be nervous?

CRAPE: I think I've got a cold. Why should that matter?

GOLIGHTLY: Not to me, no.

CRAPE: Nor to me neither. Anyone can have colds.

GOLIGHTLY: Seasonable. Rain. Snow. Sleet. Draughts from the windows.

CRAPE: Anyone can have a cold! [*He coughs.*] Or a cough?

    [NURSE BROWN *re-enters on upper stage.* HARDRADER *in his robe is brought in to the Doctor by* NURSE JONES.]

DOCTOR: Aha, Mr Hardrader. [*Calls to upper stage.*] Mr Golightly please!

    [NURSE BROWN *leads* GOLIGHTLY *off upper stage.*]

Had your X-rays taken? Good. Now don't you bother your head about all this medical business. A routine check-up, nothing to it – say Ah . . . Ninety-nine . . . One, two, three, *hup* . . . Next one, one, two, three, *hup* . . . waterworks, waterworks, ye-es . . . walking, talking, reading the papers? Good, good.

HARDRADER: Doctor, about Hector. You wrote me a letter –

DOCTOR: Don't you be worrying about that, old boy, all the best and the best of all possible worlds.

HARDRADER: You see, I was looking for him and he seems to be lost. Lost, Doctor, yes, I was trying to find him, I was doing my best –

DOCTOR: We mustn't delay the progress of science, I'm quite sure you understand, that these little sentiments, of no avail really, when looked at in proportion, as we say, the greatest good for the greatest possible number – waterworks all right?

HARDRADER: Why, yes, they're all right . . .

DOCTOR: Mr Golightly ready yet?

[NURSE JONES *brings* GOLIGHTLY *in, in his robe.* NURSE BROWN *re-appears on upper stage.*]

Now don't you get flustered, Mr Golightly, old chap, about all this medical business, just a brief once-over, routine, routine. Had your X-rays taken? Hurry up with those – Robinson, X-rays, bring both lots in. Ah. Ninety-nine. One, two, three, *hup* – next one, one, two, three, *hup* good, good, waterworks, read the papers do you, good –

HARDRADER: Doctor, I suppose –

DOCTOR: Least said, soonest mended, that's the way, stiff upper lip – where are those X-rays?

[ORDERLY ROBINSON *enters with two sets of X-rays.*]

Let's have a look. [*Calls to upper stage.*] Mr Crape, please!

[NURSE BROWN *leads* CRAPE *off upper stage.*]

Both sets, are they? Good. Nothing wrong here we can't set up with a couple of stitches. Right you are then, positive, positive – many happy years for the pair of you, eh? Don't you worry at all. That'll do, Nurse, take 'em away.

[NURSE JONES *takes* GOLIGHTLY *and* HARDRADER *out as* NURSE BROWN *brings in* CRAPE *at the same door, in his robe.* NURSE JONES *re-enters.*]

X-rays taken, Mr Crape? Now this is just the usual medical business, no need to get flustered. Waterworks all right?

[ORDERLY ROBINSON *goes back into recess.*]

CRAPE: Oh yes, Doctor. Never any trouble. Clockwork. One green bottle a-hanging on the wall.

DOCTOR: Eh, what? Say Ah.

CRAPE: Ah.

DOCTOR: Say it again.

CRAPE: Ah.

DOCTOR: H'm . . . Go on, again.

CRAPE: Ah. Ah . . . Ah . . .

DOCTOR: Hoarse . . . a bit hoarse, aren't we? Ninety-nine.

CRAPE: Ninety-nine.

DOCTOR: Say ninety-nine.

CRAPE: I said it.

DOCTOR: I didn't hear you. Say it again.

CRAPE: Ninety-nine.

DOCTOR: Louder. Like this: ninety-nine.

CRAPE: Ninety-nine.

DOCTOR: What's the matter with you?

CRAPE: Nothing! Nothing's the matter, Doctor, I'm splendid, I'm on the top of the form –

DOCTOR: Bad throat, haven't you? Bronchial.

CRAPE: No –

DOCTOR: Oh yes you are. X-rays ready on Mr Crape yet? Come on, slap it about! I'm a bit worried about you. You're not all you ought to be.

CRAPE: Oh, Doctor, don't say that. No, Doctor, please don't. If it's anything at all it could be a little piece of a chronic condition I got, back in 1917, y'know. The wet trenches, you see, it gave the boys trench feet and they'd bring in their socks to my stores to be changed, and it was the constant humidity in there, all hanging round the walls – but it hasn't troubled me serious, not for thirty years, Doctor, no Doctor, please Doctor, really it hasn't –

[*The* ORDERLIES *come in with his X-rays.*]

DOCTOR: Ah . . . good, aha . . . H'm, h'm, ye-es . . . say ninety-nine.

CRAPE: Oh, Doctor, please – if it's because of the business with the dog, I assure you –

DOCTOR: Mr Crape: ninety-nine!

CRAPE: Ninety-nine.

DOCTOR: No. It won't do. Put him down provisionally negative and mark it with a query – maybe six months' time . . . but not now, no. We can't have you prejudice yourself with a suppurated larynx, can we?

CRAPE: Negative –

DOCTOR: But don't you worry, old fellow, it's only routine. Usual medical once-over, checkups, nothing at all to be flustered about. All right, that'll do. Come.

[*Exeunt* DOCTOR *with* NURSES *and* ORDERLIES. HARDRADER *comes in* (*throughout rest of scene, the* OLD PEOPLE *are still wearing their X-ray robes*).]

HARDRADER: I'm passed. He's passed me. He told me I was positive. He's even passed Golightly. Though goodness knows I've no particular wish to meet *him* thirty years ago . . . Hoorah! I say hoorah! – oh, what you told me, bow wow, you know? It *was* true, wasn't it – you *did* do it – got him away?

CRAPE: Eh? Oh that, the dog? Oh, yes, he's away, yes, quite away, don't worry . . .

HARDRADER: When do you think we are going to be given it? Will it be a jab, or a pill, or something in a glass? God knows, I don't know, I'd never have dreamt it possible – you know, I asked Copperthwaite, you know I asked him straight out –

CRAPE: You asked him *what*?

HARDRADER: About the dog. I told him, I said: Hector seems to be lost. I said: well, Doctor, what about it? But it didn't seem to register.

CRAPE: I don't suppose it would.

HARDRADER: What's the matter?

CRAPE: I've got a cold.

HARDRADER: Oh dear. Take my handkerchief. Clean.

CRAPE: Damn your bloody handkerchief.

HARDRADER: Steady, Crape, steady. Be a man. Stand up to your new life. It's bound to be a shock, of course, but –

[*Enter* GOLIGHTLY.]

GOLIGHTLY: He passed me, he told me I was positive, absolutely passed! Hoorah! I say Hardrader, hoorah!

HARDRADER: You're very cheerful. Why? Have you heard something?

GOLIGHTLY: Me? Heard? Oh no, no. It's just that I'm – I'm passed, I'm passed, my physical condition –

[*He sings.*]

>   O I am a man and a very healthy man
>   I'm a racehorse in my prime
>   Ten thousand fields of the brilliant green
>   For my pleasuring they all are mine.

But you are cheerful too, yes I can see that – there's somebody knows something – do they? Don't they?

HARDRADER: Oh no, no no, no significance, no. But health and strength and life, man –

[*He sings.*]

>   O I am a man and a very healthy man
>   A porpoise upon the storm
>   I leap and leap ten thousand miles
>   From Australia to Cape Horn.

[*Enter* MRS LETOUZEL.]

GOLIGHTLY: Passed? Are you passed? Yes, of course, you are passed, dear lady, oh your features without doubt declare it, bright eyes, glowing cheeks, aha, aha, I shall give you a kiss –

[*He does so, spontaneously.*]

HARDRADER: You too, you too, we all know, don't we, Mrs Letouzel, no question of secrecy now: we've all found out, some-how – we're all passed fit for life –

HARDRADER AND GOLIGHTLY [*sing*]:

>   Boys and girls come out to play
>   The moon doth shine as bright as day –

LETOUZEL [*while* HARDRADER *and* GOLIGHTLY *dance round and round*]: Who's been talking? Crape?

CRAPE: Leave me alone.

LETOUZEL [*hissing at him*]: You swore you'd keep it secret.

CRAPE: And so did you, you old scragged rabbit, but *Golightly's* been told –

LETOUZEL: Not by me –

CRAPE: Oh yes he has.

LETOUZEL: And what does it matter? The question is this: everything's moving too fast. The Doctor said to me something about Sunday. Now that can only mean –

CRAPE: It means I'm left out.

LETOUZEL: Out?

CRAPE: I have a cold. I have a cold. Hoarse in my throat. It only began this morning. He said I wasn't positive. But my waterworks are perfect. Ears, eyesight, lungs, bowels, there's nothing wrong at all. Cruelty, damnable, why me? You, you're nothing but a galvanized tin money box on two jerking legs with the slit choked up – [to Hardrader.] You're a lost dog looking for a lost dog, all you can do is howl in the gutter – [to Golightly] You, you stale doughnut oozing mouldy jam, if they put the drug into you, there's only one part of you they'll ever rejuvenate and then the police will run you in for a permanent obscenity. Who wants to be young again? What'll you find to do when you are? All the things you want to do – why, you'll bloody well have to set to and do them! So how will you like that?

HARDRADER: I shall like it very much indeed, and I'd remind you, Crape, that you are in mixed company.

GOLIGHTLY: Your own disappointment is no excuse for abusing others, Mr Crape, I think you are very rude.

LETOUZEL: Go on, get lost.

CRAPE: Why don't all of you leave me alone?

[He goes to a far corner of the stage and sits down to sulk, with his back to the others. NURSE BROWN leads in MRS PHINEUS and puts her in her wheel-chair.]

PHINEUS: Thank you, Nurse, thank you. Yes, I'll be easy. Yes.

[Exit NURSE BROWN.]

I asked the Nurse to bring me to you, because I wanted to know about what has been happening. All this excitement in the hospital, commotion, disturbances, they're all so abrupt: I don't like it! No! There's no more routine. Mr Golightly, I'm frightened, whatever is the matter? What? What?

GOLIGHTLY: I don't know quite how to express it to you, dear Mrs Phineus, but –

PHINEUS [*jumping out of her chair*]: Tell me. Tell me. Mr Hardrader: are we all going to be killed!

HARDRADER: Killed – good heavens, no –

PHINEUS: I think we are. Yes. They are tired of us, they don't want to feed us any more. Mrs Letouzel: he's decided to get rid of us, that is the truth and you are hiding it from me!

LETOUZEL: No. Oh, no –

PHINEUS: Yes it is, yes it is. Yes. Mr Crape – *he* knows, look at him! There he sits, yes, and with no doubts at all. *He* turns his back and he cries.

CRAPE [*turning round*]: What do you want to know, old lady – hey?

LETOUZEL: Oh leave her alone, she's no idea what she's talking about. She's not right in the head.

CRAPE: Be quiet. Now the lot of you, shut up!

HARDRADER: Crape, nobody is talking except yourself.

CRAPE: I'm going to play a jolly game with old Mrs Phineus: she'll excuse me – won't you, me old love – if I step for a pair of minutes into Mr Golightly's slippery shoes –

> Truth or lie till the day you die
>
> Strike you dead if you tell us a lie.

PHINEUS: No. No. I won't have you doing it, you must not make me frightened, Dr Copperthwaite says –

CRAPE: Truth or lie till the day you die

> Strike you dead if you tell us a lie.

PHINEUS: Why should I play your games! I don't like you, I don't want to play with you – Mr Golightly, tell him I don't want to –

[*She falls back into her wheel-chair.*]

GOLIGHTLY: Mr Crape, please, this old lady doesn't want to –

CRAPE: Oh yes, she does. When she plays with *me* she plays my game, don't you, you dear old thing, you sweet old sweetheart you –

HARDRADER: I say there, steady, Crape, really –

LETOUZEL: Let him be. Just for a little. See how far he goes. [*To audience.*] I may use this, you know. I couldn't conquer her, but if he can, and I can conquer *him* – more use than Golightly, wouldn't you say? Watch him, watch him, he's beating her down –

CRAPE: After we've played, I'll get you your tea, how would you like that? I'll feed you your tea, everything you want, scones, and crumpets and tarts and Eccles-cakes galore, oh delicious, delicious – come on, come on, me lovely –

> Truth or lie till the day you die
> Strike you dead if you tell us a lie –

PHINEUS: Truth or lie –

CRAPE: Yes?

PHINEUS: Truth or lie till the day I –

CRAPE: Till the day you –?

PHINEUS: No. No.

CRAPE: Come on, come on, yes! Splendid, you're doing it beautifully – come on –

PHINEUS: Truth or lie till the day I die

> Strike me dead if I tell you a lie . . .

CRAPE: That's right, you've got it! Now we're really playing. Aren't we? I shall give you a kiss. [*He does so.*] There. That's for being a jolly sporting girl! I'll start. Supposing I told you the Doctor *was* going to have us all killed –

PHINEUS: Oh . . . Oh . . .

CRAPE: Supposing he was. What would you think of it. What would you truly think?

PHINEUS: I don't want to have to die.

CRAPE: Why not?

PHINEUS: I don't want to.

CRAPE: Margaret, *why not*?

PHINEUS:

> I'm an old old lady
> And I don't have long to live.
> I am only strong enough to take

Not to give. No time left to give.
I want to drink, I want to eat,
I want my shoes taken off my feet.
I want to talk but not to walk
Because if I walk, I have to know
Where it is I want to go.
I want to sleep but not to dream
I want to play and win every game
To live with love but not to love
The world to move but me not move
I want I want for ever and ever.
The world to work, the world to be clever.
Leave me be, but don't leave me alone.
That's what I want. I'm a big round stone
Sitting in the middle of a thunderstorm.
There you are: that's true.
That's me. Now: you.

CRAPE: No, no. Not yet. My turn soon. I'm playing to different rules. I play the *second* time, you see. Yes ... Now answer me this one. Supposing you died. Today. Here. Now. Just supposing. And then you were born again. Young. Strong. Not beautiful. You never were beautiful until you were old – I've seen your wedding photograph, so I know what you were like, apple-duff and custard, that was you: and your poor little Phineus-man, the pudding-cloth you were wrapped in, he was boiled all to shreds in the water! Suppose you were born again –

PHINEUS: I don't know –

CRAPE: I do. You wouldn't dare to face it. Oh Lord, it would be far too much like hard work ... Truth or lie? Truth or lie?

PHINEUS: Truth. Truth. But I'd like to be a baby, be born again to be a little baby ...

CRAPE: Teething, wetting your nappy, teething, struggling to crawl when you've barely learned the strength to move a knee or an elbow, teething, safety-pins stuck into you, squalling, teething, scalded with your bath-water, losing your rattle over the side of the pram –

PHINEUS: No, no.

CRAPE: No! Now you've said it. No. Anyone else say 'yes'?

GOLIGHTLY: I said 'yes'.

CRAPE: Did you? For *her*? Now you've heard what she's just told you. She was your only reason. Do you still want to do it; for *her*?

GOLIGHTLY: Others – there are plenty of others.

CRAPE: There always were plenty of others. How many of them did you get?

GOLIGHTLY: Never mind, Mr Crape.

CRAPE: I'll tell you what they used to call me. They used to call me Dandy Jim! The only name anybody ever had for you was Little-Wet-willy-in-a-Half-Pint-Pot. Now isn't that the truth? [*To Hardrader.*] Old chap. Old chap Hardrader. Big strong games and sports, boxing and cricket, badminton and the high-jump, Egyptian P.T. Only two friends and one of them's in her grave – you couldn't make her love you, so you went toughing it on the greensward and bellowing at your dirty dog. If you were to start again, what would *you* find?

HARDRADER: I hope I would find a healthy humane existence.

GOLIGHTLY: No no, excuse me, no: Mr Hardrader. You would be as lonely as ever you were. I know, because *I* would be, too. Isn't it terrifying.

CRAPE: Isn't it?

HARDRADER: I do not understand you, sir. You seem to have changed your mind entirely. But why should you try to change ours?

CRAPE: I'm playing the game of Truth, old fellow. It's three points wilder than a bracing set of hockey –

HARDRADER: Set of tennis.

CRAPE: Hockey, chum, hockey. When *I* call the rules.

LETOUZEL: Crape. Play with me.

Truth or lie till the day I die
Strike me dead if I tell a lie.

CRAPE: Truth or lie, ta tum tum-tum, – ah we know the rest of it – you start first!

LETOUZEL: No. You.

PHINEUS: These are the two stout players. Mr Golightly, Mr Hardrader, sit by me and we will watch them play.

[*They do so.*]

CRAPE: You don't want rejuvenation. There's nothing different between you and him, and him, and her. All your life you've burrowed for the money: and you haven't got a red ha'penny.

LETOUZEL: Ho ho, have I not?

CRAPE: Mrs Phineus's thousand pounds – you don't have much of that, old woman, and you never really did, 'cos she hasn't got it. It's all in the air, ticker-tape, dog-bump, Dr Copperbox holds the lot, he gives you pocket money for your China tea and your hair-dyes. All right, she made it over to you, put her scratching old fist on fifty-five miles of stores affidavits – how much of that money have you actually seen? Cash? Coin of the realm? Paid on the Bristol nail?

LETOUZEL: You don't understand the principles of finance. You uneducated old man, what should you know of the poetry and dreams of organized paper? Kleenex to wipe your nose with, that's about your sum.

CRAPE: I've got a cold. I can't help that. It's my bloody curse. Every damned project gets drowned in catarrh. It's a neurotic disability, it's not my fault. Don't you dare mock me with it! But you've told me the truth. You don't want the money: all you want's the notion of it. Here, in here, at your age – that's your luxury. But outside – in the world, between the bus-stops and the supermarkets and the no-parking areas, you've got to have hands on the real jingling metal: or the only place you'll find yourself is back in the Happy Haven, in seventy years' time. What happened to Mister Letouzel?

LETOUZEL: Eh? Keep to the point. What's that to do with it?

CRAPE: We're playing the game. You have to tell me. All right, I'll tell *you*. He didn't exist. You lived all your life a spinster in a little bit of a railway share, and when those rats nationalized, you found you'd no alternative, but to give yourself to Copperthwaite.

GOLIGHTLY: Just the same as us.

CRAPE: Poor dears. Poor old dears. Your only safe investment disappeared in the night and if you had any bolder gambles –

LETOUZEL: They were not successful. That was my misfortune. It wasn't my fault. Don't you dare to mock me with it.

GOLIGHTLY: I'm sure if she wishes to call herself Mrs Letouzel she has a perfect right. If she thinks it suits her. It is what we term a courtesy title. You wouldn't be expected to understand that, Mr Crape.

CRAPE: Oh skip it, skip it . . . I think I've made my point. Is there one person here has any single motive for wanting to be young again?

LETOUZEL: Truth or lie. What about you?

CRAPE: I thought that was obvious. I've been rejected.

LETOUZEL: Why, so you have. And don't you enjoy it too, you abominable coffin-carrier. You turn us against our own selves and you disgust us to the very gorge of our throat with what we've all been for the whole of our lives. It's quite made your day, hasn't it? You've never been so happy since the time you were weaned. Ah my goodness gracious me, Mr Crape, at last you've found yourself in power!

CRAPE: Truth or lie, I have.

LETOUZEL: No. Truth or lie, you have not! Now you think, because you snarl and grin and run around between our ankles, that we've all changed our minds and that we'll all stay with you at your term of years and we'll all die together a-keeping you company? Maybe we will. But for a different reason . . . We heard everything you said – good, good, it worked. Yes, we're humiliated. You've made us afraid, you see. Here we are, worms. Old ones. We don't want to die, but we none of us dare state that we want any more life. Let's look around us! Now then, who cares?

CRAPE: I don't know what you're talking about, but I'd say nobody cares.

LETOUZEL: And you would be right. Nobody, not even the Doctor. Not even him, call him our Lord, Priest, and Superintendent, great Guardian of the Mysteries – [*She sings.*]

> Take off your hats, bow down:
> The High King wears the crown,
> He lays out his land with a long directing hand
> And the measurements all written down.
> The measure of you and of me
> In numbers so clearly told –
> Say you are a field and I am a tree
> And you are a house or a road.
>
> If he wants to root out or rebuild,
> Raise up or lay level or burn,
> He draws his new line, we obey in his good time:
> We suffer, we praise him, we learn.
>
> We learn how to love and submit,
> To lie down like a frightened new wife.
> Each day and each hour we have given to his power
> To the end and beyond of our life –

That's immortality: he grants it to us and then we hand it back. He's the undisputed custodian of everything that's good for us. Security. Reliability. Though some people have said he failed to save the score the other Saturday at football –

HARDRADER: Why – yes –

LETOUZEL: They relied on him to stop the goals; when he came back from the match he was swearing, frustrated – I know because I heard him. He'd let them all through, he had to apologize, I tell you I heard him –

HARDRADER: Quite right, so did I!

LETOUZEL: Apologized – Copperthwaite – in his humility, to the Captain of the Team . . . but despite that, you silly children, we are all his worms. And he says 'Turn, worms, turn,' and he thinks we have got no choice!

GOLIGHTLY: I am not a worm. I am not a worm. My name is Henry Golightly and I walk upon legs.

HARDRADER: Two legs. Ten toes. Two arms. Ten fingers. Ribs. Shoulders. Backbone. Backbone. If my backbone *does* bend, it still belongs to *me*.

PHINEUS: Mr Crape.

CRAPE: I read my Bible. God said, he said it to the snake, I remember, he said: 'Because thou hast done this,' he said –

PHINEUS: Mr Crape.

CRAPE: 'Thou art cursed above all cattle, and above every beast of the field. Upon thy belly shalt thou go, and dust shalt thou eat all the –'

PHINEUS: Mr Crape.

CRAPE: 'All the days of thy life. Because thou has done this.' There, that's your true fortunes. Don't talk to me about bones.

PHINEUS: Mr Crape. Please. Please. What is the Doctor going to do? You haven't told us yet.

CRAPE: 'Because thou hast done this,' he said. Done what? Grown old. That's what we've done . . . And the doctor – oh, the doctor? He's going to give us medicine, dear, to make us all young again. It's not of importance. You wouldn't like it. Don't bother . . .

PHINEUS: But he never told me.

LETOUZEL: Why should he? He's a professional man, dear, he works to the rules.

PHINEUS: I call it very unfair. Very, very unfair. Yes.

HARDRADER: I don't want his Elixir now. You've confused me so much with all of your reasons. But if my backbone bends, it's mine.

CRAPE: Old chap. Old chap. You're the Doctor's patient. You have to do what he says.

HARDRADER: I shall ask to leave the Haven.

GOLIGHTLY: But where would you go?

HARDRADER: Find another Nursing Home.

LETOUZEL: And another Copperthwaite.

HARDRADER: Not necessarily.

GOLIGHTLY: But are you willing to take the risk?

HARDRADER: I don't know ... We can refuse to accept the Elixir. Obviously we can. Free country. Citizens. Voters.

LETOUZEL: He's worked on this for years. Weighed us and dieted us and taken our temperatures.

GOLIGHTLY: Humiliating forms of treatment, with, with rubber pipes and so forth: when I haven't even been ill.

LETOUZEL: He's not likely to let us ruin the masterpiece of his life, is he?

HARDRADER: But what can he do?

LETOUZEL: Turn us out, that's what.

CRAPE [to Hardrader]: Or worse, worse. Supposing he told you you'd got cancer in your lungs. Would you believe him?

HARDRADER: Oh my God, I don't know.

CRAPE: But he could, and it might be a lie – how would you know? He'd terrify you to death. Look what he wanted to do to your dog!

HARDRADER: You mean – vivisection?

CRAPE: What else?

HARDRADER: For a man who'd do that to a poor dumb animal – no punishment could be sufficiently severe.

LETOUZEL: Then why don't we punish him?

HARDRADER: By God, I wish I could ... Oh I would do ... this, and I'd do – that, and I'd do – oh, this, this, that, that –

PHINEUS: I once said to Mr Phineus. 'Why don't we have a little baby. I would so love a little baby to hold and to enclose and to have.' Some women say, oh the trouble and the worry and the noisiness and the naughtiness and the mess – but I said, 'I don't care about that. Mr Phineus shall pay for a good sensible old-fashioned girl to be his Nanny, and later he can go to boarding-school. All I want to do is to hold him and to have him and to enclose him.' I said it to Mr Phineus. And he tried. Yes. He tried to pleasure me and he tried to give me my baby, so many times, oh so often and so many times to no purpose. He was no good. No. No courage in him at all. So he died and there was no succession. I had expected a baby. I had bought all his little clothes and his toys and everything right up to when he would go to the boarding-school, where I suppose they would want him to wear uniform, so I couldn't get that for him in advance. But I bought all the rest and I kept them and I have them all here in my room, locked in my big box. I would so like to have a little baby.

[*Pause.*]

CRAPE: Somebody said he was talking about Sunday. There's something going to happen on Sunday. He hasn't got his drug ready yet, or I'm sure we'd have heard about it. But we have to find out the moment he *does* get it. To find out before Sunday. We must spy on his Laboratory.

GOLIGHTLY: How can we do that?

LETOUZEL: Oh we'll find a way. Use your little brains, you silly little fellow, or else shut your mouth while the rest of us use ours.

[*The* DOCTOR *enters on the upper stage.*]

DOCTOR: Off to bed, now, boys and girls, you're half an hour late as it is – burning the candle at both ends, you know, have to go easy, don't we? That's the way, off to bed, now – Nurse!

[NURSE BROWN *enters on main stage.*]

Good night. Good night, boys and girls.

OLD PEOPLE: Good night, Doctor.

DOCTOR: Good night.

[*Exeunt –* NURSE *wheels Mrs Phineus in. The* DOCTOR *remains above.*]

[*The* DOCTOR *is on the upper stage.*]

DOCTOR: Ladies and gentlemen. Twenty-four hours; and now I'm going to see if it works! In my Laboratory, as you know, the retort with the solution in it – is it or is it not going to turn green? Bear with me a few moments, I'll just make the arrangements, and hey presto, open sesame, abracadabra – I'll tell you confidentially, it is going to turn green. *This* time, I'm right. Mr Smith, Mr Robinson, Lab ready if you please!

[*He leaves the upper stage.* GOLIGHTLY *enters cautiously on the main stage, in pyjamas.*]

GOLIGHTLY: Why me, why me, why should I have to do it? Why not somebody else?

[MRS LETOUZEL *enters cautiously after him in nightgown and hair net.*]

LETOUZEL: Because you're the smallest, that's why. We've told you that ten times –

GOLIGHTLY: But personally speaking, I have nothing against Dr Copperthwaite – Mr Hardrader has been the worst done by, surely *he* should –

[HARDRADER *enters cautiously at the opposite door in pyjamas.*]

HARDRADER: Golightly, pull yourself together, man. If you've any chivalry at all, remember Mrs Phineus. The man who would deny a woman the child she has craved for is an unmitigated scoundrel.

GOLIGHTLY: Quite right, Mr Hardrader. You have put me to shame, sir, I will do what I am asked. [*He goes into the recess, and we hear him blundering about in there, out of sight.*] The door is locked!

[*Enter* CRAPE *cautiously, in pyjamas, holding a burglar's jemmy.*]

CRAPE: Of course it's locked, you dithering old nightingale – I told you you'd not get in till you'd waited for me! Let me have a look at it.

DOCTOR [*off stage*]: Smith!

HARDRADER: Cave!

[ORDERLY SMITH *enters from the opposite side to the Doctor's shout, carrying a tray of test tubes etc.*]

CRAPE: Freeze where you are!

[*They all crouch down like hares.* ORDERLY SMITH *crosses the stage and goes out without seeing them.*]

That's the way to do it. You stand stark still and they think you're a bush – I learnt that in France! Now, where's this locked door?

[*He goes into the recess.* GOLIGHTLY *comes out of it.*]

Aha . . . Ha . . . clickety-clock, clock-clock!

[*He reappears.*]

> Dandy Jimmy and his jemmy
> Save us all a pretty penny!

Mr Golightly, in you go lightly! [*He pushes Golightly in again.*] Ha ha, he's in.

DOCTOR [*offstage*]: Robinson!

HARDRADER: Cave!

CRAPE: Freeze.

[ORDERLY ROBINSON *crosses the stage with tray, same business as before.*]

Safe again. I told you. Come on.

[*Exeunt.* COPPERTHWAITE *and* ORDERLIES *enter.*]

DOCTOR: Let's have it, let's have it.

[ORDERLIES *open the recess and bring out the Lab bench.* GO-LIGHTLY *is crouched underneath it, and is pulled out unobserved.*]

Bunsen Burner. Right. Now let's see the retort . . . H'm ha. H'm . . . Looks promising, ladies and gentlemen. Sediment developed *just* as I forecast, and the whole thing is approximately the consistency of – of water. Good. Boil it.

[*It is held over the flame.*]

Accotile and heraclith solution? Good. You see what I'm doing? Watch for the change of colour . . . That hot enough yet? Come on, come on, come on –

> Put another nickel in
> In the nickelodeon

> All I want is loving you
> And boil it boil it boil it –

Right! She's boiled. Give it to me. *I'll* pour. [*He pours in the contents of a second retort. It turns green.*] Beautiful. Oh my beautiful. Oh my lovely girl. Green as the leaves on the weeping willow tree, where my true love lies sleeping. I've done it. I've done it. Gentlemen, you may smoke. One of mine? One of mine?

[*They stand side by side. The* ORDERLIES *remove their masks and all three take a few formal puffs at cigarettes. Then they drop their butts grind them into the floor, and turn back to the work.* ORDERLIES *replace masks.*]

Stage Two. A Practical Test. Go and fetch the dog.

[ORDERLY ROBINSON *goes into the recess. The dog is heard barking.*]

Taking a common-sense point of view, ladies and gentlemen, scientific detachment – I know that this green liquid is the Elixir of Youth, but I can't go administering it to my patients without some further evidence, can I? Besides, how would I know how much I ought to give them, unless we'd some sort of a preliminary run-through, eh?

[ORDERLY ROBINSON *re-enters with a large basket, fastened up.*]

Is the dog all right in there?

[*Dog barks.*]

Seems to be. Put two ounces of the Elixir into a saucer.

[ORDERLY ROBINSON *does so.*]

If anybody in the audience is a little worried at my giving this admittedly unproven drug to an unfortunate dumb animal: there's a lot of silly nonsense talked by so-called humanitarians – would any one of those ladies like to step up here to me and take the place of the dog?. ... NO? I didn't think that you would. You look altogether too sensible. Open the box, please.

[ORDERLY ROBINSON *does so. Dog barks.*]

Take him out – *gently*.

[ORDERLY ROBINSON *takes the dog out in his arms – cradling quite a large-sized beast. Dog continues to bark.*]

Saucer on the floor. Dog by the saucer. Let him drink.

[*The dog is set down. More barking. The men watch closely.*]

Doesn't seem very thirsty. You haven't given him anything to drink already, have you? Robinson? Smith? H'm. Come on, come on, doggie, good boy, good boy, drinky, drinky, drinky. Lap lap lap. Oh for Godsake . . . Go on, *drink*! I'm sorry, but it looks like a long wait. We might as well sit down . . .

[*They sit.*]

       Put another nickel in, in the nickleodeon –

Where's he going? He can't leave the room, can he? You've shut all the doors? . . . Oi, oi . . . Keep still, Smith. You can clean that up later, don't distract him, he's looking for the saucer . . . steady, steady, quiet everybody, absolute quiet – he's drinking, he's drinking – he's *drunk* it! Good dog, good dog, good, good –

[*Dog barks.*]

Now then we shouldn't have to wait long, any minute now, we're going to see – yes – yes –

[*The barks become shriller.*]

Yes! It's worked! It *really* has worked! Oh my God, I'm a famous man.

[*The bark is now a high-pitched squeal.*]

Don't let the dog get out – catch him, catch him, Robinson quick! Oh, the sweet little fellow –

[ORDERLY ROBINSON *is now holding a very small bundle.*]

Oh, the dear little puppy, oh, the little chick, there, there, there, did the horrid Doctor givums nasty green water forums dinners, didums didums? Put him inside and give him something to chew – he seems to be teething. That's right.

[ORDERLY ROBINSON *takes the dog out.*]

Now we'll take in my notebooks and the Elixir, please for safety: and we'll make a proper coordinated report upon the whole business, without any flights of poetic fancy. And let's not get so excited either that we forget the formalities – oh, but this is epoch-making, this is scarcely believable unless you'd been told, this is the greatest experience of your lives and I hope you'll not forget it . . . Come on.

[*Exeunt,* ORDERLY SMITH *carrying the retort and the notebooks.* GOLIGHTLY *emerges from under the bench.*]

GOLIGHTLY: Poor Mr Hardrader. However can I break it to him? Still, a little puppy, very tender, very winsome, perhaps he won't be altogether so completely cast-down? There seems to be quite a lot left – now then, a test-tube – quickness of the hand deceives the eye, oh dear, I've spilt a bit, now then – there we are, and there's enough left in the saucer to –

[*He has poured some of the contents of the saucer into a test-tube.*]

DOCTOR [*offstage*]: You've forgotten the saucer!

GOLIGHTLY: Only just in time! My goodness, aren't I brave.

[*He nips off, as* ORDERLIES *come on again from opposite sides. They clear away the bench into recess and go out, taking the saucer with them.*]

SCENE THREE

[*The sound of church bells. Enter* COPPERTHWAITE *in a hurry.*]

DOCTOR: Excuse me, it's Sunday morning already, listen! I'm in a tearing hurry, the whole place is upside down, nothing prepared, and they'll be here in ten minutes. Who will? I can just spare sixty seconds to tell you. First of all: Sir Frederick Hapgood, makes cars, makes money, and a good deal of the money he makes, he puts into this hospital – no question, I've got to impress him. Then, second: a lady from the Ministry of Health – there's a lot of government money put into this, and all – to be quite frank, they pay my salary – so I've got to impress *her*. Then thirdly and fourthly: our own local Mayor, and his good wife the Mayoress. They sit on the committee of this hospital, carry a deal of influence in this district – socially speaking, they *are* this district – county society, very conservative, very well worth keeping in with. And to keep in with them: impress them. There was to have been a bishop, but he's not coming now, thank goodness. I think he's had to go off somewhere to kick a High-church Vicar out of some parish or other . . . But there's enough of 'em, I say, there's enough. And, by God, I can tell you, they're going to be impressed. Because what they're going to see is my Elixir at work. The World Premiere, that's what. After they've all had coffee, I shall try it on Mrs Phineus.

[*Sound of arrival of motor-cars, horns blow, doors slam, etc.*]

And here comes the Establishment. Dead on time. I'd better go and meet them. Do I look sufficiently impressive? Ah well, we're all as God made us, so to speak. The Institution is greater than the Man.

[*Exit. Enter* MRS LETOUZEL *and* GOLIGHTLY, *coffee pots, cups etc.* (*In this scene the* OLD PEOPLE *are all in their best clothes.*)]

LETOUZEL: Aren't there supposed to be biscuits?

GOLIGHTLY: Mr Hardrader is bringing the biscuits.

LETOUZEL: Good. Everything else all right? Coffee, cream-jug, sugar-bowl, cups, one, two, three, four, and one for the Doctor, spoons, one, two, three, four, and one for the Doctor.

GOLIGHTLY [*producing his test-tube*]: Shall I put it in now?

LETOUZEL: Put it in where?

GOLIGHTLY: I thought we were going to pour out the – [*He waves at the coffee-pot.*]

LETOUZEL: Not till they come in! Now take it easy, Henry, don't be in a hurry, all the time in the world.

GOLIGHTLY: I don't like having to put it in when they're all in the room – one of them might notice –

LETOUZEL: The quickness of the hand deceives the eye.

GOLIGHTLY: Yes, but I wish it didn't have to be *my* hand – Mrs Letouzel, I think I've done sufficient, cannot somebody else –

[*Enter* HARDRADER *with a plate of biscuits.*]

HARDRADER: Here are the biscuits. You have it on you?

[GOLIGHTLY *shows him the test-tube.*]

I'd be obliged if you'd give it to me.

LETOUZEL: Why?

HARDRADER: Dear lady, if you please. *I* should be the one to put it in. Hector would have wished it so. Would he not, Golightly?

GOLIGHTLY: Oh, I'm sure that he would, sir. Here you are.

[*He hands him the tube.*]

HARDRADER: Thank you.

GOLIGHTLY: But you know, Hector isn't dead.

HARDRADER: To me he is dead. My Hector is dead. Whatever is alive, it's – it's some other dog. Where the devil is Crape?

LETOUZEL: He's gone to make sure we shan't be disturbed. No nurses, no orderlies, nobody here except for ourselves, and our visitors, and our leader and teacher.

> Take of your hats, bow down.
> The High King wears the Crown.

HARDRADER: Cave: Here they come.

[*The* DOCTOR *enters with the four* VISITORS. *He leads them round the stage as though showing them round the hospital.*]

DOCTOR: The Convalescent Wing, as you see, to our left, facing the sun, big balconies, very airy, very spacious. To the right, my Operating Theatre, and ancillary departments, as you might say, perfection of function is in itself beautiful – but of course, Sir Frederick, *you* know all this already – Mr Mayor and ladies, we see over there the Sir Frederick Hapgood Ward, opened last year by Sir Frederick himself, there's a large bronze plaque in the foyer commemorating the occasion, and of course, the Annigoni portrait of the late Lady Hapgood, which we account one of the Happy Haven's most treasured possessions. And now, perhaps, if you'll come *this* way – ah, I see coffee – a cup of coffee awaits us – made and served specially by one or two of our patients – from the Special Research Ward, they are of course to be the subjects in the special experiment I have been explaining to you – I wanted you specially to meet them, before – ah, before we begin – [*Aside to Mrs Letouzel.*] Where's Mrs Phineus?

LETOUZEL: She's having a little rest, Doctor. She seemed rather tired –

DOCTOR: Would you mind fetching her, Mrs Letouzel? [*In a furious whisper.*] When I said all of you, I meant *all*. She ought to be here. Why can't people listen when I give a few instructions? Hurry up and get her.

  [*Exit* MRS LETOUZEL.]

Let me introduce – Mr Golightly, Mr Hardrader –

  [*The coffee etc. is handed to the Visitors. When the* OLD PEOPLE *make conversation with them, the* VISITORS *reply in wordless gobbling noises which sound both patronizing and genial.*]

HARDRADER: Some five or six years now. And I wouldn't exchange it for home, goodness gracious, no . . .

GOLIGHTLY: A charming place, a very charming place, dear lady, indeed to retire to . . .

HARDRADER: The countryside, the open air, contemplation, peaceful surroundings, nature . . .

DOCTOR [*who has not taken coffee*]: And of course, the beautiful scenery and fresh air in themselves as we say a continual therapy . . .

GOLIGHTLY: Oh dear me no, Sir Frederick, it is often only too stimulating here, when you reach *my* age, a peaceful and secluded existence is really the only one that charms – [*aside to Hardrader.*] Is it in?

HARDRADER [*aside*]: Not yet. How much?

GOLIGHTLY [*aside*]: About half. We don't want to overdo it.

HARDRADER [*aside*]: All right. Half. [*With his back turned to the company, he carefully empties half the contents of the tube into a cup of coffee, and then offers it to the Doctor.*] Doctor, would you like a cup of coffee?

DOCTOR: No, thank you, Mr Hardrader. I don't normally take coffee. Have some yourself. [*To the Visitors.*] And another point, of course, the freedom from continual contact and only too often conflict with relatives, in itself acts as a –

HARDRADER: Doctor, if you don't care for coffee, perhaps we could get you a cup of tea?

DOCTOR: What? No. No thank you.

HARDRADER: Oh. Very well . . .

[*Enter* CRAPE. HARDRADER *takes him anxiously apart.*]

He won't take the coffee.

CRAPE: Give him some tea.

HARDRADER: He won't take that either.

CRAPE: You've already put it in?

HARDRADER: Half of it.

GOLIGHTLY: And I often say, we were gay then, yes and very happy. Though I wouldn't really have those days again – but there *is* a nostalgia, ah Vienna, Vienna, and the Emperor's mounted band riding round the Ringstrasse, and that wonderful, wonderful Strauss music . . .

CRAPE [*aside to Hardrader*]: Give me the other half.

HARDRADER [*aside*]: Why?

CRAPE [*aside*]: I'll tell you later. Quick.

[HARDRADER *gives him the test-tube.* MRS LETOUZEL *wheels in* MRS PHINEUS.]

DOCTOR: Aha, Mrs Phineus! Sir Frederick, Mr Mayor, ladies, let me present you to our oldest, and perhaps I'd better not say it, but she is, nevertheless, our best-loved and best-privileged inhabitant – ah – Mrs Phineus –

CRAPE [*aside to Mrs Letouzel*]: He won't take any coffee.

LETOUZEL: Then offer him some tea.

HARDRADER [*aside*]: It's no good. He won't.

LETOUZEL: Leave it to me.

[*She goes and whispers to Mrs Phineus.*]

CRAPE [*aside*]: Let him just drink the coffee and we are in the clear. I've locked the communicating doors. Orderlies and nurses can't get in unless they break through the windows. We've got all the time in the world –

PHINEUS: May I have a cup of coffee?

CRAPE [to Hardrader]: Give it her. Quick.

    [HARDRADER does so.]

PHINEUS: Thank you, Mr Hardrader... It seems to be rather hot. Perhaps Doctor Copperthwaite, you wouldn't mind taking a sip to test it for me, would you? I'm so afraid of burning my mouth, you see.

DOCTOR: Of course, it's a pleasure, Mrs Phineus – [He sips.] Oh I think you'll find it quite cool enough. In fact, it's rather cold. Been poured out a long time, I expect, it –

PHINEUS: Oh dear, it is cold? I don't think, if it's cold, I ought to take it at all. No. You yourself have warned me, Doctor, of the possible danger to the kidneys, have you not? Perhaps you would drink it for me?

DOCTOR: Eh? Oh, well, I suppose I might as well, as I've got it in my hand ... It's not very sweet. Has anyone any sugar?

    [MRS LETOUZEL hands him the sugar.]

Ah, thank you, Mrs Letouzel ... Well, I put a lot of sugar in, but it's still pretty bitter –

    [To Visitors.]

Is *your* coffee all right? Sure? Do say if it's not, because –

    [He finishes the cupful, dubiously. Then, aside to Mrs Letouzel.]

Here, who made this stuff? I feel quite – [He hurries off the stage.]

    [The next three speeches are delivered simultaneously, in great excitement.]

GOLIGHTLY: And always for ever the beautiful climate, the snow on the Dolomites, the sparkle of the wine, the roses and the music, dear lady, the sun in our blood, crying love, love, love, ah the enchantment of the South –

HARDRADER: The one thing I regret here is the absence of the river, a good strong scull up against the tide on a Sunday morning as far as Hobson's Lock, refreshing pint in the Barge and Anchor, then home again with the current and the wind with you, and every artery tingling like quicksilver – wonderful, wonderful –

LETOUZEL: Mrs Phineus is rather deaf, and perhaps a little over-excited, but she wishes to say that she is very happy indeed to meet you, Sir Frederick, and how much, how very much she has always admired you and of course dear Lady Hapgood and the wonderful things you have done for us all!

[*Meanwhile,* CRAPE, *with his back to the others has taken the empty coffee-cup, poured out some more coffee, and is preparing to pour the rest of the Elixir into it.* MRS LETOUZEL *suddenly sees what he is up to. She comes sharply across to him and seizes his wrist.*]

PHINEUS: Yes, yes, Sir Frederick, ah Lady Hapgood, dear good Lady Hapgood, I was so sorry when I heard – was it not so very sudden? But we have the portrait here. That, we shall always treasure.

[MRS LETOUZEL *has been having a silent but strong struggle with* CRAPE.]

LETOUZEL [*aside to him*]: What do you think you're doing!

CRAPE [*aside*]: Please let me do it, let me, let me – just because I had a cold, *he* was trying to stop me but I thought that *you*, you wouldn't be so cruel as to –

LETOUZEL [*aside*]: *NO!* You don't want it! It's all of us or none of us! There's no more time for tricks – besides, you and me, we need one another: if we're alone, we're lost!

[*She succeeds in getting the test-tube from him. In the final effort, the coffee-cup is thrown on the floor. The* DOCTOR *re-enters.*]

DOCTOR: All well, all well, enjoying your coffee, Sir Frederick? Mr Mayor, Mrs Mayor, er Miss, er – the biscuits all right, are they? You're quite sure, Sir Frederick? Good ... [*He comes down to Mrs Letouzel. Aside to her.*] I'd have you know, Mrs Letouzel, I've just been extremely sick. What's the matter with the coffee? Who made it? ...

[*He turns back to the Visitors.*]

Ah, Sir Frederick, if you've finished your refreshment, perhaps we can get on to the next item in our little programme – Er, h'm, patients! Boys and girls, if you wouldn't mind clearing away the coffee things and, er, back to your rooms, and Mrs Letouzel, perhaps you could leave Mrs Phineus here with us, I believe Sir Frederick wishes to –

[*He breaks off uncertainly as he sees that the* OLD PEOPLE *all have their backs turned and are whispering together.*]

CRAPE: It hasn't worked.

HARDRADER: What do we do?

GOLIGHTLY: We'll have to do something.

CRAPE: The coffee, the coffee must have killed it!

LETOUZEL: We've still got the other half – no thanks to *you* –

PHINEUS [*suddenly*]: Here: all to me!

[*They all crouch round her wheel-chair in a tight huddle like a football scrum. The* DOCTOR *and* VISITORS *watch in bewilderment.*]

DOCTOR: Well, now, I'm not sure what – we must appreciate, of course that these old people have their periodic eccentricities, it's maybe that they feel their little half-hour of recreation with us has been cut short too abruptly – we always find it best to humour them, you know, Sir Frederick –

LETOUZEL: Right. Now. Begin. Mr Crape. Mr Golightly. The bench. Quickly.

[CRAPE *and* GOLIGHTLY *pick up a bench by its end and run against the Visitors with it, pinning them across their bellies against the edge of the stage.*]

DOCTOR: Hey, wait a minute –

LETOUZEL: Mr Hardrader. Neck. Arms. Quickly.

[HARDRADER *grabs the Doctor's arm and twists it behind his back, at the same time bearing down with his other hand on the back of his neck. The* DOCTOR *is forced to bow right over.*]

Right. Now then. Needle.

MRS PHINEUS *takes from her reticule an enormous hypodermic needle which she opens.* MRS LETOUZEL *swiftly pours in the contents of the test-tube.*]

DOCTOR: Oh, oh, stoppit, leggo, ow, ouch, yarroo –

[*The* VISITORS *gobble.*]

PHINEUS: For a long time I have kept this locked up in my big box. It was lucky I thought to bring it along today. Yes. I said to myself: 'One day, it will be needed.'

LETOUZEL: Needle filled. Screwed up. Ready? [*She hauls up the Doctor's coat and hauls down his trousers.*] NOW!

[MRS PHINEUS *sticks the needle into the Doctor, who gives an appalling yell. The needle is withdrawn.*]

LETOUZEL: Come on. Take him in.

[*She and* HARDRADER *rush the Doctor, still stooping, off the stage.*]

PHINEUS: You can let them go now.

[CRAPE *and* GOLIGHTLY *release the Visitors who still stand where they have been forced, in stunned amazement.*]

This must be a most astonishing moment for you, Sir Frederick, must it not . . .

[*They open their mouths and gasp.*]

Please don't call out.

CRAPE: There's nobody to hear you. I've locked 'em all away. We're all in this together.

GOLIGHTLY: United we stand. Divided we – you know. I am not a worm. My name is Henry Golightly and I walk upon legs.

PHINEUS: But it should also be a beautiful moment because you will see how much, how very very much, we owe to you and to poor Lady Hapgood and to the kind ladies and gentlemen in the Government and in this beautiful countryside around us who take so much delight and interest in our welfare, and who always look after us like fathers and like mothers, to watch our every step and stumble, at a time in our lives when we are, as you know, no more than little children to wander and to cry and to need nothing more in life than to be continually looked after by kind fathers and mothers, who will watch our every step and stumble at a time in our lives when how few of us know what we want to do or where we want to go, or what possible good we are at all, being, as you see, like little children wandering and crying and in search once again of our fathers and our mothers –

[MRS LETOUZEL *and* HARDRADER *re-enter. leading the Doctor between them. He is now wearing a little boy's suit, with short pants, and wears a mask that entirely covers his face. It resembles the actor's*

own features closely, but is round, chubby, and childish. MRS LETOU-
ZEL *puts a lollipop into his hand and he sucks at it in a formal fashion.*]
Ah, here he is. My baby. Come little baby, come to your mama, sit
him on my knee, dear Mrs Letouzel, I'd like to sing him a song –
    [*They sit him on her knee.*]
Yes, baby, yes, baby, yes . . .
PHINEUS [*sings*]:
        Now mother holds her little boy
        And holds him to her heart
        Fall asleep, all you children, fall asleep.
        The rising up of sun or moon
        Shall never make us part.
        Fall asleep and dream the world is all safe and sound.
ALL OLD PEOPLE [*formally*]: Everybody, listen! Take warning from
us. Be cheerful in your old age. Find some useful hobby. Fretwork.
Rugmaking. Basketry. Make yourselves *needed*. Remember: a busy
pair of hands are worth ten thousand times the Crown of a Queen.
Go home, and remember: your lives too, will have their termina-
tion.
VISITORS: Help. Help. Help. Let us out. Let us out.
PHINEUS: Let them out.
    [CRAPE *opens the door and they all run out.*]
VISITORS [*cries disappearing offstage*]: Help! Help! Help! . . .
OLD PEOPLE [*bowing to the audience*]: Good night. Good night.
Good night.
    [*They all leave the stage. They carry with them the remains of the
    coffee and refreshments.* MRS PHINEUS *and* MRS LETOUZEL *carefully
    put the Doctor in the wheelchair, and* MRS PHINEUS *wheels him out.*]

CURTAIN

PETER SHAFFER

Five Finger Exercise

For Harry and Jean

FIVE FINGER EXERCISE

First produced at the Comedy Theatre, London, on 16 July 1958, with the following cast:

STANLEY HARRINGTON, *a furniture manufacturer; in his middle forties*	Roland Culver
LOUISE, *his wife; in her middle forties*	Adrianne Allen
CLIVE, *his son; nineteen*	Brian Bedford
PAMELA, *his daughter; fourteen*	Juliet Mills
WALTER LANGER, *a German boy; twenty-two; employed by Mrs Harrington as tutor to her daughter*	Michael Bryant

Produced by John Gielgud

The action of this play takes place in the Harringtons' week-end cottage in Suffolk. The time is the present.

ACT ONE
SCENE 1: A Saturday morning in early September. Breakfast
SCENE 2: A Saturday night two months later. After dinner

ACT TWO
SCENE 1: The following (Sunday) morning. Breakfast
SCENE 2: Sunday night. After dinner

THE SETTING

THE setting is the week-end cottage of the Harrington family in Suffolk. A multiple set enables us to see a fair amount of this house: the living-room, the hall, the landing, and the schoolroom where Pamela has her lessons.

The living-room occupies all of the stage on the ground floor. It is well furnished, and almost aggressively expresses Mrs Harrington's personality. We are let know by it that she is a Person of Taste; but also that she does not often let well alone. There is more here of the town, and of the expensive town, than is really acceptable in the country: the furnishings are sufficiently modish and chic to make her husband feel, and look, perpetually out of place. To the left – from *the viewpoint of the audience* – there is a sofa or banquette, and a coffee-table. To the left of the sofa and just downstage of the front door is a table with a lamp and their telephone. A comfortable armchair, with a round table to the right of it, bridges the gap between the social centre of the room and its eating centre. This last is to the right, and slightly more upstage is a dining-table with three matching chairs and an upholstered bench downstage of the table. The wall upstage, running parallel to the table, is made of brick and contains a large fireplace. Built into the wall is a brick bench, covered with a red cushion. Inside the fireplace, which actually begins at the height of the bench, we see polished andirons and a brass bowl of green leaves. The right wall contains the french window, through which comes all the light the room receives – autumn light from an old garden. Below the window is a built-in window-seat – high enough for Mrs Harrington to use it as a sideboard. There is a lamp there, also a decorative bowl of grapes and leaves. The door to the garden is downstage of the window-seat. Left of the window, and on the same wall as the fireplace, is the kitchen door. Up centre against the back wall, stands a commode bearing a crystal candelabra, a tray with whisky decanter, pitcher of water, and glasses, and a lamp. Under the stairway, left of the commode, is a china umbrella-stand filled with green leaves.

The hall can be seen behind the sofa. It is quite small and contains the usual paraphernalia of cottage halls: a mirror on the wall, a hall tree with hats and coats on the pegs. The front door opens into it, left, and the staircase of the cottage leads out of it, right, on to –

The landing. This occupies a fairly small but important central area upstage and above the living-room. Walter's bedroom door opens on to it, right: the door must be recessed and not too prominent. On the left of this, a corridor leads off to two bedrooms (Clive's and his parents') and the bathroom, all of which are invisible. We do, however, see a window on the upstage wall. On the extreme left, a further short flight of steps leads up to a doorway into –

The schoolroom, which is directly above the sofa area of the living-room. This is very much Pamela's room, it is littered with her possessions, her books, and old toys. Down centre is an oval table where her studies are done, and two chairs. The upstage wall contains the door to her bedroom, a bookcase, and a gas-fire. The left wall has the window, gaily framed in curtains, a wall lamp, and an old school desk. To the right of the desk is an old wooden stool.

The whole stage shows a compact dwelling, disposed with feminine care.

Light switches are located at the following points:

The double switch on the pillar, at the centre edge of the sofa, contains switches for the living-room.

A switch just left of the kitchen door turns on and off the lamp on the sideboard.

A switch left of Walter's door on the landing controls the lights for the landing.

The switch for Pamela's schoolroom is right of the schoolroom door.

ACT ONE

SCENE ONE

A bright Saturday morning in early September.

STANLEY *and* LOUISE *are seen at rise;* STANLEY *in the armchair smoking his pipe and reading the newspaper;* LOUISE *is seated at the table finishing her coffee.*

Stanley is a forceful man in middle age, well built and self-possessed, though there is something deeply insecure about his assertiveness. Louise is a smart woman in her forties, dressed stylishly, even ostentatiously, for a country week-end. Her whole manner bespeaks a constant preoccupation with style, though without apparent insincerity or affection. She is very good looking, with attractive features, which are reflected – though with greater instability – in her son.

> [STANLEY *looks at his watch.*]

STANLEY: Is Clive coming down at all today?

LOUISE: I've left him to sleep. He was very late last night.

STANLEY: What time did he get in?

LOUISE: I haven't the faintest idea. I didn't wait up for him.

STANLEY: That's a wonder.

> [*She looks at him with irritaton and returns to her coffee. Upstairs,* CLIVE *appears on the landing. He is a boy of nineteen, quick, nervous, taut, and likeable. There is something about him oddly and disturbingly young for his age, the nakedness of someone in whom intellectual development has outstripped the emotional. He calls up towards the schoolroom.*]

CLIVE: Pam! [*There is no answer. He goes on downstairs. He enters hesitantly, conscious of being very late.*] Good morning.

STANLEY: Good afternoon. What do you think this place is – a hotel?

CLIVE: I'm sorry.

LOUISE [*being extra friendly and welcoming for Stanley's benefit*]: Good morning, Jou-Jou! How did you sleep, darling?

CLIVE [*crossing and sitting above the table*]: Very well, thank you.

LOUISE: Don't I get a kiss this morning? [*He kisses her.*] That's better. . . . [*looking at the plate of eggs she has placed before him*] I'm afraid those eggs are quite horrid now. Let me make you some more.

CLIVE: No, these are all right. Really.

LOUISE: It's no trouble, darling.

CLIVE: They are fine, thank you, mother. . . . Where's Pam?

LOUISE [*knowing this is going to come as a surprise*]: She's out walking, with her tutor.

CLIVE: What on earth do you mean?

LOUISE [*mischievously as she pours Clive's coffee*]: Her tutor, dear. You know – the German boy I engaged in London to come in every morning and give Pamela her lessons. Well, he's going to live with us. As part of the family.

CLIVE: You mean . . . he's here? Now?

LOUISE [*delighted with her effect*]: Yes. Isn't it amusing? He came down with us last night on the 6.30 train! It's my big surprise. Don't you like it? Pamela's mad about the idea and I thought you would be too.

CLIVE: Why should I be? I hardly know him.

LOUISE: Well, you will now. He's terribly nice. And anyway, it's time you had some well-bred friends for a change. He's marvellously educated and has the most divine manners. I always say it takes a Continental to show us just how ignorant we really are. [*She exits into the kitchen.*]

CLIVE [*dumbfounded*]: Well ! ! ! And when was all this decided?

STANLEY: Yesterday morning in London – after you left the house. You like the idea, I suppose?

CLIVE: No . . . as a matter of fact, I think it's ridiculous . . . I mean, unnecessary. . . .

STANLEY: Your mother thinks different. Apparently the Best People have private tutors, and since we're going to be the Best People whether we like it or not, we're going to have a tutor too. We don't send our daughter to anything so common as a school. Oh, I can afford it. What's money after all? We have a town place, so we've simply got to have a country place.

[LOUISE *enters from the kitchen with toast for Clive.*]

LOUISE: You always said you wanted a country place!

STANLEY: I meant a little week-end cottage. Not a damn great fancy place like this. [*Rises. To Clive again.*] However, now we've got a country place, we've simply got to have a tutor.

LOUISE [*seated – L. of dining-table*]: Now look, Stanley. This is Walter's first day down here and I want everyone to be very sweet to him. So just keep your ideas to yourself. We don't want to hear them.

STANLEY: We? Clive agrees with me.

LOUISE: Do you, Clive?

CLIVE: Well, yes, I mean, well, no. Isn't it a bit early for this kind of conversation?

STANLEY: You just said you thought a tutor was ridiculous.

CLIVE [*unhappily*]: Well, not really ridiculous. . . .

LOUISE: Just get on with your breakfast, darling.

STANLEY [*irritated, rounding on his son*]: Why were you so late last night?

CLIVE [*made nervous*]: I – I got involved. In London. I had some work to do.

STANLEY [*sits R. of dining-table*]: Work?

CLIVE: I promised to review something. It's going to be printed.

STANLEY: Oh? In *The Times*, I suppose?

CLIVE: No, it's more of a magazine actually. It's not really famous.

STANLEY: Well, why did they ask you to do it?

CLIVE: It was more me did the asking. Anyway, it was two free tickets.

STANLEY: What for?

CLIVE: A play.

STANLEY [*aloofly*]: Was it any good?

CLIVE: Yes . . . It was splendid, as a matter of fact.

LOUISE: What was it, dear?

CLIVE: *Electra*.

STANLEY: What's that?

LOUISE [*with exaggerated surprise*]: You can't mean it! You just can't mean it.

STANLEY: Mean what?

LOUISE: Really, Stanley, there are times when I have to remind myself about you – actually remind myself.

STANLEY [*quietly*]: Suppose you tell me, then. Go on . . . Educate me.

LOUISE [*loftily*]: Clive dear, you explain it to your father, will you?

[CLIVE *sits eating*.]

STANLEY [*to him*]: Well, go on.

CLIVE [*low*]: It's Greek.

STANLEY: Oh, one of those.

LOUISE [*brightly, putting her husband in his place*]: Who was in it, dear? Laurence Olivier? I always think he's best for those Greek things, don't you? . . . I'll never forget that wonderful night when they put out his eyes – I could hear that scream for weeks and weeks afterwards, everywhere I went. There was something so *farouche* about it. You know the word, dear: *farouche*? Like animals in the jungle.

STANLEY [*to Clive*]: And that's supposed to be cultured?

CLIVE: What?

STANLEY: People having their eyes put out.

CLIVE: I don't know what 'cultured' means. I always thought it had something to do with pearls.

LOUISE: Nonsense, you know perfectly well what your father means. It's not people's eyes, Stanley: it's the *poetry*. Of course I don't expect *you* to understand.

STANLEY [*to Clive*]: And this is what you want to study at Cambridge, when you get up there next month?

CLIVE: Yes it is, more or less.

STANLEY: May I ask why?

CLIVE: Well, poetry's its own reward, actually – Like virtue. All Art is, I should think.

STANLEY: And this is the most useful thing you can find to do with your time?

CLIVE: It's not a question of useful.

STANLEY: Isn't it?

CLIVE: Not really.

STANLEY [*staring at him gravely*]: You don't seem to realize the world you're living in, my boy. [LOUISE *gives Clive the lighted cigarette from her cigarette holder.*] When you finish at this university which your mother insists you're to go to, you'll have to earn your living. I won't always be here to pay for everything, you know. All this culture stuff's very fine for those who can afford it; for the nobs and snobs we're always hearing about from that end of the table . . . [*Indicating Louise. He rises and takes a few steps upstage.*] But look here . . . if you can't stand on your own two feet you don't amount to anything. And not one of that pansy set of spongers you're going around with will ever help you do that.

CLIVE: You know nothing about my friends.

STANLEY: Oh yes I do. I've seen them. Arty-tarty boys. Going around London, giggling and drinking and talking dirty; wearing Bohemian clothes . . . Who did you go with last night, for instance?

CLIVE: Chuck.

STANLEY: Chuck? Oh yes, the fellow that never washes. Sings in cafés and wants to stay in school till he's thirty, living on government grants. Such a dignified way to go on. [STANLEY *crosses to the centre table and re-lights his pipe.*]

LOUISE [*sharply. Crosses to her purse which is on the centre table*]: I should have thought it was a sign of maturity to want to become more educated. Unfortunately, my dear, we were not all born orphans; we didn't all go to grammar schools or build up a furniture factory on our own by sheer will-power. [*Takes handkerchief from purse.*] We can never hope to live down these shortcomings, of course, but don't you think you might learn to tolerate them? We just didn't have the advantage of your healthy upbringing in the tough world outside. [*She is holding the chafing dish in one hand, the coffee-pot in the other, and standing to the left of the kitchen door.*] Jou-jou! *La porte.*

> [LOUISE *exits after* CLIVE *opens the door for her.* CLIVE *then crosses left of the dining-table to the bench. Picks up the newspaper and sits on the bench.*]

STANLEY [*gets the golf club from left of the commode*]: Well, I'll see you later. That is, unless you want to walk around with me and Joe Benton. [*Pause.*] No, of course not. [*Pause.*] You'd better get out in the air. I didn't take this place so you could lounge about indoors all week-end. [*He contemplates his son.*] You know, Clive – I don't understand you. . . .

> [LOUISE *re-enters from the kitchen. Closes the door.*]

I don't understand you at all. Not at all. [*He goes out through the front door.*]

CLIVE: Breakfast as usual.

LOUISE [*crossing right to above chair R. of dining-table*]: It was just one of his moods, dear.

CLIVE: Oh yes.

LOUISE: Oh, Jou-Jou, I want you to be very happy down here, darling. Really happy, not pretending. After all, it's why I made Daddy buy this place – to get away from London and all the squabbling. To come into the country and relax in our own little retreat . . . So you see, you've just got to be happy. You can't let me down. Can you? [LOUISE *sits in armchair.*]

CLIVE [*rises, salutes, crosses to his mother, and kneels to her left*]: *Votre Majesté.* My empress!

LOUISE [*permitting her hand to be kissed*]: *Levez-vous!*

CLIVE: The Empress Louise, ill-fated, tragic, dark-eyed Queen from beyond the seas! What is your wish, Madame? I am yours to command.

LOUISE: I've told you already, my little Cossack. *Sois content.* Be happy.

CLIVE: *Bien.* On my honour as a guardsman, and on my beautiful hat of genuine black sheepskin, I promise to you six big laughs a day, and twelve little giggles.

LOUISE: Darling. My darling Jou-Jou!

CLIVE: *Maman!*

[*They embrace very fondly.*]

LOUISE: Now that's a promise, you know. To be happy. Then I can be happy too. Because I can tell when you're not, you know; and that makes me miserable also. So remember; no complexes.

CLIVE: No complexes, *Majesté.*

[*She kisses his forehead.*]

LOUISE [*rises*]: Come on. I'll wash and you dry. It won't take five minutes.

CLIVE: It'll take at least twenty. I can't think why you don't get a maid in.

LOUISE [*crossing to dining-table, where she removes her watch, rings, bracelets, etc. and leaves them on the table*]: You know we've tried all that. Their bicycles break down or there's illness at home; they're always late or they don't come at all. And anyway, dear, housework's all in the fun. Everyone does it these days.

[CLIVE *allows himself to be coaxed and follows his mother into the kitchen. The kitchen door is left open.*]

PAMELA [*running through the front door and calling back to Walter*]: Hurry up, Walter. . . . [*running up the stairs*] You're the slowest runner I've ever met. You must be in dreadful condition.

[PAMELA *is a girl of fourteen, as quick as her brother and wholly without his melancholy.*]

WALTER [*hanging his coat and cap on the hat rack in the hall*]: I'm older than you are.

[WALTER *is a slim German of twenty-two, handsome, secret, diffident, but happily at ease with his young student.*]

PAMELA [*rushing up to the schoolroom*]: If I get up there first, no French today.

WALTER: Oh, no you don't . . . you're not going to get out of it as easy as that. [PAMELA *closes the schoolroom door and stands against it.* WALTER *tries to open it.*] Hey!

PAMELA [*from the schoolroom*]: What?

WALTER: French.

PAMELA: You are invading my privacy, sir.

WALTER: Open the door.

PAMELA: What for?

WALTER: French . . . Come on now.

[*Reluctantly* PAMELA *opens the schoolroom door and exits into her bedroom.*]

PAMELA [*from off*]: But it's too cold to think in French, Walter.

WALTER: Is it? Well, I'll light the gas-fire then. Where are the matches?

PAMELA: They're on the window-sill.

[WALTER *gets the matches from the window-sill and lights the fire.* PAMELA *enters from the bedroom with her essay book.*]

WALTER: *Parler*: to talk. Future tense. Now think hard.

PAMELA [*concentrating*] *Je parlerai?*

WALTER: Good.

PAMELA: *Je parlerai, tu parleras, il parlera, nous parlerons?* [*Nods.*] *Vous parlerez, ils parleront.*

WALTER: Good. That's the first time you have had it right.

PAMELA: Oh phooey to French! I hate it really.

WALTER: Why?

PAMELA: Because the French are a decadent nation. Personally I think we all ought to study Russian and American.

WALTER: But American is the same as English.

PAMELA: Oh, no it isn't . . . When they say 'dame' they mean young girl, and when we say 'dame' we mean old girl. But when we call someone 'old girl' we really mean what they call a dame. So you see . . .

WALTER: No.

PAMELA: Well, of course. I know all about America from Mary. You've still to meet her. She's my only friend here.

WALTER: Where does she live?

PAMELA: Over the stables in Craven Lane. You'll just fall when you see her.

WALTER: How? In love?

PAMELA: Of course. Mummy says she's common, but that's just because she wears shocking pink socks and says 'Drop dead' all the time. I know her mother drinks and has lovers and things. But her husband's dead and so you really can't blame her, can you? Just like Clive says. There-but-for-the-Grace-of-God Department.

WALTER: And she knows all about America because she says 'drop dead'?

PAMELA [loftily]: Of course not. How can you be so brutish? For one thing, she's got an American boy friend in the Air Force.

WALTER: How old is she?

PAMELA [airily]: Sixteen. But that's all right; they like them young. I don't think they actually . . . well, you know . . . Sometimes, she gets decked up in her black jeans and goes off to some sexy club in Ipswich under a Polish restaurant. But her mother doesn't like her going round the streets looking like that, so she has to sneak off when no one's looking.

WALTER: Like witches.

PAMELA: Witches?

WALTER: Going to their Sabbath.

PAMELA: What's that?

WALTER: When they used to worship the Devil. They used to sneak off just like that. It was the same thing like your English Teddy Boys. You make yourself very excited, then people give you a bad name and start being afraid of you. That's when you really do start worshipping the Devil.

PAMELA: Oh, phooey.

WALTER [*more gravely*]: Not phooey.

PAMELA: You talk as if you'd seen him.

WALTER: The Devil? I have.

PAMELA: Where?

WALTER: Where he lives.

PAMELA: Where's that?

WALTER: Where I was born.

PAMELA: And what was he doing?

WALTER: Sitting down.

PAMELA: Where?

WALTER: Behind people's eyes ... [*Seeing her confusion.*] Well, isn't that a good place to sit?

PAMELA: D'you miss it?

WALTER: What?

PAMELA: Your home.

WALTER: It's not my home.

PAMELA: Still, there must be things you miss. Birthdays or Christmases or something.

WALTER: Christmas, yes ... Where I was born it was better. It's called Mühlbach. The stars are more clear there.

PAMELA: Just the stars?

WALTER [*with a small spurt of excitement*]: No, ice too. Ice grows all down the river, and at night you go skating all alone, all alone for miles in the black, and it's terribly cold and fast – and suddenly you see torches coming towards you, and voices come, and there's a crowd of happy people with nuts and fruit and hot rum, kissing you a good New Year.

PAMELA: Oh, wonderful!

WALTER [*with reservation*]: Yes, it is for that ...

PAMELA: Let's go! [*Rises.*] Just for Christmas, you and me. You can teach me enough German in twelve weeks so I can understand everyone – Oh, I'm sorry. I forgot. You don't teach German.

WALTER: No.

PAMELA: Walter, I never asked before – but why not? I mean you'd make more money doing that than anything else.

[WALTER *shakes his head slowly* 'No'. PAMELA *crosses above table to stool L. of desk.*]

You're really a very strange young man.

WALTER: Am I?

PAMELA [*kindly*]: I suppose part of it's living in a foreign country all the time.

WALTER: It's not foreign. I've been here five years, and soon I get my citizenship.

PAMELA: Then you'll be English?

[WALTER *nods* 'Yes'.]

Then you'll like Christmas here too, because this'll be home and you'll spend it with us here in the country. Don't you have any family at all?

[WALTER *shakes his head.*]

No one?

WALTER: No.

PAMELA: But that's the wrong answer now. When I say 'Have you got no family?' you must say: 'Yes, of course I have a family, and a very fine one too.' Now repeat after me. 'My family lives at 22, Elton Square, London and The Retreat, Lower Orford, Suffolk.' Come on.

WALTER: My family lives at 22, Elton Square, London and The Retreat', Lower Orford, Suffolk.

PAMELA [*crossing above Walter*]: Good. Ten out of ten. Now you look much happier ... you should wear a high collar and one of those floppy ties. Then you'd look like Metternich or someone. And wear your hair very sleek and romantic. [*She smooths his hair.*] Like this ...

WALTER: Stop that!

PAMELA [*going to the schoolroom door*]: No, it's terribly becoming ... [*Opens the door.*] Count Walter Langer, Knight of the Holy Golden Soup-ladle!

WALTER [*picking up the wild flowers from the table and crossing to the door*]: Pamela, no! [*He runs down the stairs on to the landing. She chases him. The schoolroom door is left open.*] Stop it! You're not to –

PAMELA: Pompous, pompous, pompous!

LOUISE [*at the kitchen door, wearing apron and carrying a dish towel*]: Walter!

WALTER: There's your mother calling me.

LOUISE: Walter! [*Returns to the kitchen.*]

WALTER: I go now. You go and get on with your history. What's that in French – 'I go?'

PAMELA [*at the schoolroom door*]: Je allez?

WALTER: No, I've told you one million times. Je vais.

PAMELA: Je vais. [*She climbs the stairs to the schoolroom. Stops at the door.*] Hey!

WALTER: Yes?

PAMELA: See you anon, Mastodon.

WALTER: Quarter to four, Dinosaur!

[*He goes downstairs to the living-room.* PAMELA *enters the schoolroom, closes the door, and applies herself to the history book. She sits at the table.* CLIVE *comes in from the kitchen and goes to the dining-table.*]

CLIVE [*to Walter, as he enters*]: Hello.

WALTER: Hello.

CLIVE: Welcome to the family.

WALTER: Thank you.

CLIVE: What do you think of our house?

WALTER: Oh, it's wonderful. Very elegant.

CLIVE [*dryly*]: It's certainly that.

WALTER: I think your mother was calling me.

CLIVE: She's in the music room. Through there.

WALTER: You have a music room here?

CLIVE: Oh, yes. It used to be an outside privy. But mother wasn't daunted by that. She bought a baby grand for fifteen pounds and knocked down a wall to get it in. It's lucky it's at the back because His Godship doesn't care for music.

WALTER: Oh . . . I brought my record-player down with me. I was playing it in my room last night. I'm sorry.

CLIVE: He'll soon let you know if he minds.

[WALTER *puts the wild flowers on the centre table.*]

How do you like being tutor to our little hepcat?

WALTER: Oh, she's delightful. When your mother first met me, and engaged me to teach her, I was so pleased. My last job was not so easy . . . and now that I have been invited to live with you, I am very happy. [*He is very shy at saying this.* CLIVE *reacts kindly to this. He starts to fold the table-cloth.*] Let me help you.

CLIVE [*folding cloth with Walter*]: Have you never lived with a family before?

WALTER: No. I had a flat in North London.

CLIVE: Did you?

WALTER: Well, it was more of a basement, really.

CLIVE: I can imagine.

WALTER: This is my first family.

CLIVE: Yes? [*Crossing to the commode to put the table-cloth in the top drawer.*] Well, let me give you a word of warning. This *isn't* a family. It's a tribe of wild cannibals. Between us we eat everyone we can. You think I'm joking?

WALTER [*putting the bowl of flowers back on the table*]: I think you are very lucky to have a family.

CLIVE: And I think you're very lucky to be without one . . . I'm sorry. [*Crosses to the coffee-table.*] Actually we're very choosey in our victims. We only eat other members of the family.

WALTER [*crossing to above the armchair*]: Then I must watch out. Your sister thinks I'm almost a member already.

CLIVE: Pam? [*Offers Walter a cigarette.* WALTER *declines.*] You know, I don't like the way she's growing up at all. She wants to include people all the time. She doesn't seem to want to exclude or demolish anybody.

WALTER: Perhaps that's because she takes after her mother.

CLIVE [*sits on sofa*]: Well, of course, a girl who took after my father would be almost unthinkable . . .

[WALTER *starts to cross L.*]

You're not at all like a German.

WALTER: Am I not?

[*Enter* LOUISE, *holding music album.*]

LOUISE: Walter, my dear, I do hope I didn't disturb your lesson. But I'm longing for us to start ours. [*She gives album to Walter.*] Actually I thought this morning *you* could do the playing and I'd just watch. I mean, you could try my little piano – see what it's capable of . . . [*She sits in chair R. of dining-table.*]

WALTER: I'd be delighted, Mrs Harrington.

LOUISE: You have such beautiful hands. [*She takes one of his hands.*] I remember once shaking hands with Paderewski. Of course it was many years ago, and I was only a girl, but I've never forgotten it. He had hands almost exactly like yours, my dear boy. Much older of course – but the same bone formation, the same delicacy . . . This was my Mother's album.

WALTER: It's charming.

LOUISE: What are you going to play for me? Something Viennese, of course.

WALTER [*sits on bench below dining-table*]: What would you like? Beethoven? – Brahms?

LOUISE: Wonderful! And you can explain to me all about it. I mean where it was written and who for. I always think it so much increases one's enjoyment if you know about things like that. Take the 'Moonlight', for example. Now what was the true story about that?

CLIVE: Well, it wasn't really moonlight at all, Mother. Moonlight was the name of the brothel where Beethoven actually was when he started writing it.

LOUISE [*rises, shocked*]: Jou-Jou!

CLIVE: He got one of the girls to crouch on all fours so he could use her back for a table. It's in one of the biographies, I forget which.

LOUISE [*to Walter*]: He's being very naughty, isn't he? Really, Jou-Jou!

WALTER [*going to centre table and picking up posy of wild flowers*]: I found these in the lane. They're quite rare for this time of year – I thought you might be interested –

LOUISE [*taking posy*]: How charming! I am very touched. Thank you, my dear. [*Pause.*] You know, I must give you a nickname. Walter is much too formal. Wait. Of course! Clive's Jou-Jou so you can be Hibou. Perfect. Hibou, the owl. [*To Clive.*] He looks rather like a little owl, doesn't he?

CLIVE: Why not Pou? That's better still.

LOUISE: Oh, he's impossible this morning. Your father's right, a walk in the fresh air would do you a lot of good.

[*PAMELA snaps her book shut and comes bounding out of the schoolroom and down the stairs.*]

PAMELA [*running downstairs*]: Mother! Mother . . .!

LOUISE: Good heavens, what a noise that girl makes. [*To Walter.*] I'm afraid you're going to have to teach her some etiquette as well.

[*PAMELA comes bursting into the living-room.*]

PAMELA: Mother!

LOUISE: Quietly, dear. Quietly.

[WALTER *crosses to kitchen door.*]

PAMELA [*breathless*]: Sorry. Mother, will you test me on my history?

LOUISE: Ask Clive, will you dear? I'm busy now. [*Picks up glass of wild flowers.*] We're going to *our* lesson. Walter's going to play for me.

PAMELA: Are you, Walter? How lovely!

LOUISE [*to Walter*]: Come along, my dear.

[LOUISE *goes out with* WALTER *into the kitchen.* CLIVE *lies down on the sofa and covers his face with his handkerchief.* PAMELA *studies her brother, then knocks on the commode.*]

PAMELA: General Harrington.

CLIVE [*as if deaf. Sits up*]: Eh? ... Eh? ... What's that? ... Who's there? ...

PAMELA: It's only me, General. May I come in?

CLIVE: What? [*He uses the rolled up magazine as a telescope and studies her. He speaks broadly and heavily.*] Well, bless my soul! ... If it isn't little Daphne. Spike my cannon! Come in, me dear. Come in.

PAMELA [*sits to the left of Clive*]: Thank you.

CLIVE: That's the way. Don't be afraid. I must say it's damned decent of you to call on a boring old soldier like me.

PAMELA [*coyly*]: Oh, it's nothing.

CLIVE [*putting his hand on her knee*]: Well, how are you, me dear? Eh?

PAMELA [*removing it*]: Fine, thank you. And how's the – [*Whispers.*] you-know-what?

CLIVE [*normal voice*]: Do I?

PAMELA [*normal voice*]: Gout.

CLIVE [*General's voice*]: Oh, it comes and goes, y'know. Comes and goes.

PAMELA [*Daphne's voice again, gushing*]: I think it's wonderful of you to take it so well. I'm sure I'd be complaining all the time. I'm a real silly-billy about pain.

CLIVE: Nonsense, me dear. Lord, though, how yer remind me of yer dear mother. Hair just like hers.

PAMELA: Ow?

CLIVE: Yellow as a cornflower, I always used to say.

PAMELA [*normal voice*]: There's something wrong about that.

CLIVE [*normal voice*]: Is there? What?

PAMELA: Cornflowers are blue.

CLIVE: Well, your mother certainly didn't have blue hair.

PAMELA [*archly*]: That's all you know ... Anyway, you've got to test my history. Come on.

CLIVE [*beckoning*]: Your bow.

[*Automatically she leans to him for it to be tied. The sound of piano music from the music room. Brahms – 'Capriccio in B minor.'*]

PAMELA [*listening*]: He's the best, isn't he?

CLIVE: Is he?

PAMELA: Oh, you can tell. I knew just as soon as he came in the door. [*They listen for a moment.*]

CLIVE: How d'you get on together?

PAMELA [*rises. Crosses to armchair. Sits*]: Oh, we simply adore each other.

CLIVE: Is he going to teach you anything?

PAMELA: Everything, my dear. Just wait and see, I'll be the most erudine girl for my age in London.

CLIVE: Dite.

PAMELA: What?

CLIVE: Eru*dite*. Come on, let's make a start. [CLIVE *studies the list earnestly for a moment.*] Which was the most uncertain dynasty in Europe.

PAMELA: I haven't the faintest.

CLIVE [*as if reading*]: The Perhapsburgs.

PAMELA: Who?

CLIVE: The Perhapsburgs.

PAMELA: Now, Clive, really –

CLIVE [*enthusiastically*]: I don't know much about them yet, but I'm working on it. So far there's just Thomas the Tentative – a successor of Doubting Thomas, of course – and Vladimir – the Vague.

PAMELA: That's marvellous! How about a woman?

CLIVE: By all means.

PAMELA: Dorothea.

CLIVE: Nice.

PAMELA: Dorothea the – the Downright.

CLIVE: But that's just the opposite. There's nothing Perhaps about her.

PAMELA: Well, she could be the black sheep of the family. [*Music stops.*]

CLIVE: We'll see . . . Now. [*He consults the list.*] Pay attention. Who was known as the Crying Cavalier?

PAMELA [*protesting*]: Now, Clive, really . . .

CLIVE: Answer me. Who?

PAMELA: I don't know.

CLIVE: Who was the Unknown Civilian?

PAMELA: I don't know.

CLIVE: Who was the Curable Romantic?

PAMELA: I don't know. I don't know . . .! [*She throws herself at Clive.*]

CLIVE: Really, you are the most impossibly ignorant child . . . [*Struggling with her happily.*] Hepcat! Hepcat! Hepcat . . .

PAMELA: Clive!

CLIVE: What?

PAMELA [*springing away from Clive*]: Tell me a story!

CLIVE: Sweet or sour?

PAMELA: Sour.

CLIVE [*sitting R. of dining-table*]: All right. Once upon a time there was a little girl who lived all by herself in a prison.

PAMELA: Why? What had she done?

CLIVE: Nothing: that's just the point. They took away all her clothes and made her wear blankets instead.

[*WALTER enters from the kitchen.*]

WALTER: Excuse me. Mrs Harrington was asking for her handbag.

PAMELA: Here it is. [*Takes handbag from centre table and hands it to Walter.*] Stay with us. Clive's telling me a story.

WALTER: A story? About history?

PAMELA: About a prison.

CLIVE [*showing off to Walter*]: Yes, it's going to be brilliant! [*Rises and goes to Walter.*] All Gothic darkness and calamities. It's called the 'Black Hole of East Suffolk'. [*Mock grave.*] Sit down and I'll unfold.

WALTER: No, excuse me. Mrs Harrington is waiting.

[*He gives Clive a short bow and leaves.* CLIVE *stares after him.*]

PAMELA: What's wrong?

CLIVE: Nothing.

PAMELA: What about the little girl in prison?

CLIVE [*turns and looks at her. He speaks with sudden energy, rather bitterly*]: It wasn't a girl. It was a little boy. A little German boy with blond hair, who played the piano rather well. He walked straight into the prison of his own free will and shut the door behind him.

[CLIVE *leaves through the front door. We hear the piano again playing the same piece as the gramophone.*]

SCENE TWO

A Saturday night two months later.

The family has finished dinner and is taking coffee, at least STANLEY *and* LOUISE *are.* CLIVE *is at the sideboard up centre, pouring himself a whisky. We hear* PAMELA *practising the piano – first scales, then plays Bach's 'Preludio XI'.*

LOUISE [*to Clive*]: Don't you want any coffee?

CLIVE: No, thanks.

LOUISE: I do think you might have caught an earlier train from Cambridge. I cooked a special dinner for you to welcome you home. All your favourite things.

CLIVE [*crosses to sofa. Sits R. of Louise*]: I'm sorry. Actually, I had a perfectly good sandwich from British Railways.

LOUISE [*to Clive as he sits next to her*]: I think you've got into some rather bad habits in Cambridge. Isn't that your third drink already?

CLIVE: No, I don't think so.

LOUISE: Well, what if it is? It's a special week-end, isn't it?

[*She smiles at him lovingly.* STANLEY *watches this with irritation.* WALTER *comes out of the kitchen and picks up the record from the commode.*]

STANLEY [*referring to the piano practising*] : How much longer is that row going on, may I ask?

LOUISE: For another half hour, I hope. [*To Walter.*] How's she getting on, dear?

WALTER: Oh, very well, Mrs Harrington. [*To Stanley.*] We've only been working for six weeks, you know, sir.

LOUISE: Yes, it's amazing, isn't it? Oh, Walter, would you mind taking Clive's suitcase upstairs as you go?

WALTER: No, of course not, Mrs Harrington. [*He goes up the stairs and takes the suitcase into the hall.*]

LOUISE: Thank you so much. [*To Clive.*] I don't know why you can't put your own things away.

STANLEY [*to Clive*] : And that's what you call great music? Is that right? Great music?

CLIVE [*with an attempt at humour*] : Let's say it's a little distorted at the moment.

STANLEY: Distorted? It's driving me mad.

CLIVE [*unhappily*] : I suppose we can't expect her to be an expert in two months. Run-before-you-walk Department.

LOUISE [*rises and picks up tray from coffee-table. Starts to the kitchen*] : Your father imagines that everything can be done without hard work. Everything except making money out of the furniture business.

[WALTER *re-enters from the hall and goes into his room, where he turns on the lights.*]

[*To Stanley.*] Really you are absurd. How do you think Paderewski sounded when he was practising? What is that piece she's learning, dear? Mozart? [*He shrugs, embarrassed.*] Jou-jou, I'm talking to you.

CLIVE [*low*] : Bach.

LOUISE: You could play too if you wanted to. You've got the hands for it.

[LOUISE *goes out to kitchen.* CLIVE *smiles faintly. There is a pause.*]

STANLEY [*carefully*]: Clive, do you remember coming to the factory for your allowance the day you went up to Cambridge?

CLIVE: Yes, I do.

STANLEY: Did you have a talk to my Manager while you were waiting?

CLIVE: Did I . . . I suppose I did.

STANLEY: Is it true you told him you thought the furniture we make was – what was it – 'shoddy and vulgar'? [*Pause.*] Well?

CLIVE: I think I said it – it lacked . . .

STANLEY: What?

CLIVE: Well, that it didn't use materials as well as it might. Wood, for example. [*He smiles hopefully.*]

STANLEY: And the design was shoddy and vulgar?

CLIVE: Well, yes, I suppose I gave that impression. Not all of it, of course – just some things . . .

STANLEY: What things?

CLIVE [*plucking up a little courage*]: Well, those terrible oak cupboards, for example. I think you call it the Jacobean line. And those three-piece suites in mauve plush. Things like that . . .

STANLEY [*impassive as ever*]: Mr Clark said you called them 'grotesque'.

[CLIVE *lowers his eyes.*]

Is that right – grotesque?

CLIVE [*rises, crosses to commode for book, takes it to chair R. of dining-table*]: I think they are, rather.

STANLEY: And I suppose you think that's clever. That's being educated, I suppose; to go up to my manager

[LOUISE *enters.*]

in my own factory and tell him you think the stuff I'm turning out is shoddy and vulgar . . . Is it?

LOUISE [*crossing to the sofa*]: Just because *you've* got no taste, it doesn't mean we all have to follow suit.

[STANLEY *gives her a look which silences her, then turns again to his son.* CLIVE *continues to sit rigid at the table.*]

STANLEY: Now you listen to me, my boy. You get this through your head once and for all; I'm in business to make money. I give people what they want. I mean ordinary people. Maybe they haven't got such wonderful taste as you and your mother; perhaps they don't read such good books – what is it? – *Homes and Gardens*? – but they know what they want. If they didn't want it, they wouldn't buy it, and I'd be out of business.

[*Piano stops.*]

Before you start sneering again, young man, just remember something – you've always had enough to eat.

[*The explosive opening of the Brahms Third Symphony is heard from Walter's room.*]

[*Looking up, dangerously.*] One stops, the other starts. I'm going out. [STANLEY *stands up.*]

LOUISE: Where to – Mr Benton?

STANLEY: And if I am, at least I can get some peace there.

LOUISE: Ssh.

STANLEY: Don't you ssh me.

LOUISE: This is the first week-end we've all been here together since Clive went up to Cambridge. I think the least you can do is stay home, the first evening. Why must you be so disagreeable? [*She goes to the landing and calls.*] Walter! Walter! [*She turns on the landing lights.*]

WALTER [*coming from his room*]: Did you call, Mrs Harrington?

LOUISE: Do you think you could play your records another time, dear? Mr Harrington has got a slight headache.

WALTER: Of course, Mrs Harrington. I'm so sorry. So very sorry. [*He reaches into his room and turns off the machine.*]

LOUISE: That's quite all right, dear. I hate to disturb your concentration.

WALTER: Oh, no.

LOUISE: Come down when you want to. I've got some delicious petits fours and I'll make you some fresh coffee. [*She turns off the landing lights.*]

WALTER: Thank you, Mrs Harrington. [*He goes into his room.*]

LOUISE [*coming down the stairs and into the living-room.* STANLEY *is again in the armchair*]: I don't know! You say you can't stand London. I go to all the trouble fixing this place for you, and you can't stay in it a single minute. Now try and be a bit more pleasant will you. [*To Clive as she removes jewellery at the commode.*] Jou-jou, it's washing-up time. Are you going to help me?

CLIVE: Can't we leave it for once?

LOUISE: It's all right. I can manage perfectly well without you. [*She goes into the kitchen.*]

CLIVE: I'm sorry I said that about the furniture, Father. I suppose it was tactless of me.

STANLEY: Never mind. How are you settling down at Cambridge? What about the other boys, do you get on with them?

CLIVE: It's not exactly like prep school, you know. You rather pick your own friends.

STANLEY: Yes, I suppose you do. Well, what do they do there? I mean apart from lessons.

CLIVE: Anything you like. There are all sorts of clubs and societies.

STANLEY: Do you belong to any?

CLIVE: Yes, I joined a Dramatic Society as a matter of fact.

STANLEY: You mean for acting?

CLIVE: It's quite professional, you know. They have their own theatre and get reviews in *The Times*.

STANLEY: Don't any of your friends play games?

CLIVE: Yes, but – the cricket and football are sort of professional standards. I thought of taking up fencing, it's not as odd as it sounds. It's meant to be very good for co-ordination –

STANLEY: What's that?

CLIVE: Muscles, I think.

STANLEY: Clive, as you know your mother and I didn't see eye-to-eye about sending you to University. But that's past history now. The point is what use are you going to make of it? Well?

CLIVE: That's rather as it turns out, I should have thought. I mean you can't judge things in advance, can you?

STANLEY: Ah now, that's just what I mean. If you don't know where you're going you might just as well pack up.

CLIVE: Why?

STANLEY: It's quite simple, I should have thought.

CLIVE: It isn't. It just isn't like that. I mean if I knew where I was going I wouldn't have to go there would I? I'd be there already.

STANLEY: What kind of silly quibble is that?

CLIVE: It's not a quibble. Look, education – being educated – you just can't talk about it in that way. It's something quite different – like setting off on an expedition into the jungle. Gradually all the things you know disappear. The old birds fly out of the sky, new ones fly in you've never seen before, and everything surprises you too. Trees you expected to be a few feet high grow right up overhead, like the nave of Wells Cathedral. Anyway if you had seen all this before, you wouldn't have to go looking. I think education is simply the process of being taken by surprise, do you see?

STANLEY: Be that as it may.

CLIVE: You don't see.

STANLEY [rises – crosses to above dining-table]: Clive, I'm not talking about education. By all means, take advantage of your lessons. Look here boy, let's not pretend. Everyone doesn't get to Cambridge, you know it and I know it. You're in a privileged position and you must make the most of it. What you do now will influence the rest of your life. You know that, don't you?

CLIVE: Yes, I suppose it will.

STANLEY: Take your friends for example. What kind of friends do you have?

CLIVE: Do you want a list?

STANLEY: Now don't start getting on any high-horse. I'm simply saying this ... [Sits above the dining-table. Leans toward Clive.] People still judge a man by the company he keeps. You go around with a lot of drifters and arty boys, and you'll be judged as one of them.

CLIVE: I don't . . .

STANLEY [*cuts him off immediately and closes his book*]: I don't say you do, and you're old enough to decide for yourself anyway. Right?

[CLIVE *nods.*]

Number two is this. Now's the time for you to be making contacts with the right people, I mean people who will be useful to you later on. I don't mean the smart people or the fancy la-de-da people your mother's always on about. I mean the people that matter. The people who will have influence. Get in with them now and you won't go far wrong. I never had your opportunities, the contacts I made I had to work up myself. So I know what I'm talking about. Do you understand?

CLIVE: Yes, I do.

STANLEY: Good. Now you've got a good brain and I'll see to it you've got enough money. There's no harm in having a few pounds in your pocket, you know.

[LOUISE *enters. Closes kitchen door.*]

Never be so foolish as to look down on money. It's the one thing that counts in the end.

LOUISE [*at the commode putting on her jewellery*]: Money! Is that all you ever think about? Money!

STANLEY: You don't have any difficulty spending it, I notice. [*To Clive.*] Now let's see, how long have you been at Cambridge? Is this your half-term holiday?

LOUISE [*crossing to the sofa above the armchair*]: Half-term! You talk about it as if it were a grammar school instead of our leading University. Really, Stanley, I don't know how one can even begin to talk to you.

STANLEY [*rises, crosses R. a few steps as if to answer Louise. Then turns to Clive*]: Would you like to walk with me over to Benton's?

CLIVE: I – I've got some reading to do actually.

STANLEY: We can stop in at the Red Lion for a quick one.

CLIVE: No. I don't think so really.

STANLEY: Very well.

CLIVE: It's important, or I would.

[STANLEY *nods and goes out of the front door.*]

LOUISE: Are you going to be intense?

CLIVE: No.

LOUISE [*rises. Crosses to armchair – sits*]: Oh, Jou-jou! *Mon petit Cossack. Embrasse-moi . . . Non? . . .* It's your Empress.

[WALTER *comes from his room and turns the light off there.*]

CLIVE: Your *Majesté.*

LOUISE: Oh, come on, every family has its rows, you know.

[WALTER *enters the living-room carrying a book.*]

Oh, here you are, Hibou! I'm so sorry about your music.

WALTER: Oh, it's me to be sorry . . . How is Mr Harrington?

LOUISE: It's nothing serious, my dear. He's gone out to clear his head. I'll get the fresh coffee. It must be ready. [*To Clive as she goes to the kitchen.*] Don't sulk, Jou-Jou. There's no need to take everything as if it were one of your Greek tragedies. [*She exits.*]

WALTER: I'm so sorry about the noise. If I had known I would not have played the machine.

CLIVE [*rises. Goes to the commode*]: Yes, it's a pity. Music always affects him that way. The better the music the stronger the headaches. Do you want a drink?

WALTER: No, thank you.

CLIVE: Was that your new record?

WALTER [*crossing to the sofa and sitting*]: Yes. It's 'high fidelity' sound . . . more bright and clear.

CLIVE [*crossing to the R. of the armchair and then sitting*]: It sounds like the motto of a matrimonial agency. 'High Fidelity Guaranteed.'

WALTER: It's nice to see you back, Clive. Tell me, how are you liking Cambridge?

CLIVE: It's all right, I suppose.

WALTER: Is that all? Just all right?

CLIVE: No, it's wonderful, really. Like going to a new country. I suppose one of the thrills of travel is hearing people speak a foreign language. But the marvellous thing about this is hearing them speak my own for the first time.

WALTER: I know.

CLIVE: Pam speaks a few words of it, of course, but it isn't quite enough. Where is she?

WALTER: I don't know.

CLIVE: I suppose she's gone for a walk.

WALTER: It's a beautiful night.

CLIVE: Oh yes. A night for walks. Pam tripping along so gaily . . . Father marching along so . . . rightly. And I should be by his side. Or better still, a pace or two behind. 'Clive, to heel, sir. Heel!' Let me introduce myself: [*raises his glass in a toast*] 'Spaniel Harrington.' [*Drinks.*] What's the matter?

WALTER: Nothing.

CLIVE: Fathers should not be spoken to like that . . . is that it?

WALTER: I think, if you forgive me . . .

CLIVE: Well?

WALTER: I think you have a duty to your father.

CLIVE: A duty? What a very German thing to say. I'm sorry, I'm not quite sober.

WALTER: I did not mean duty in that sense. I meant that it seems to me . . . Clever children have a duty – to protect their parents who are not so clever.

CLIVE: Protect?

WALTER: I do not put it very well perhaps.

CLIVE: You know when I was on the train tonight, I was so looking forward to seeing them again. I know I've only been away a few weeks, but so much has happened to me . . . and I thought, I don't know why, they would have changed as much as I have. But everything's exactly the same.

[*LOUISE enters with tray holding pot of coffee, plate of petit fours, cups and saucers. WALTER meets her and takes the tray to the coffee-table. LOUISE turns off the lamp on the window-seat. Then she crosses to the sofa.*]

LOUISE: Isn't this nice? Well now, we seem to have the hour to ourselves. What are we going to do? I know! Walter shall recite some beautiful poetry for us in German.

CLIVE: You don't understand German.

LOUISE: It's not the meaning, it's the sound that counts, dear. And I'm sure this boy will speak it adorably. Most people make it sound like a soda syphon, but when you speak it I'm sure I'll feel exactly what the poet wanted to say – [gives cup to Walter] even more than if I actually knew the language and had to cope with all those miller's daughters and woodcutters and little people. It's difficult to explain – but you know what I mean.

CLIVE [takes his empty glass to the commode]: I don't – I'm going out.

LOUISE: Where?

CLIVE: To the pub.

LOUISE: You can't be serious.

CLIVE: Too vulgar?

LOUISE: Don't be silly, Clive. No, it's just so ... uncivil, dear. There's plenty of drink in the house if you really need it, though I think you've had quite enough already.

CLIVE [gravely]: You're right, I have. [To Walter.] Excuse me. I'm sure you recite beautifully. [He makes for the french windows.]

LOUISE [with a resurgence of desperation]: But your father asked you if you wanted to go to the pub and you said no.

CLIVE: True. [He goes out. WALTER stands stiffly, very uncomfortable.]

LOUISE: Poor boy. I'm afraid he gets rather upset down here. He's essentially a town person, really, like me. And I get it from my mother. Being French, of course. Like all Parisians she detested the country. She used to say: 'Fields are for cows. Drawing-rooms are for ladies.' Of course, it sounds better in French. If I had my way I'd never stir from London. I did all this [indicating the cottage] for Mr Harrington. He's what we call here an open-air type, you know.

WALTER [smiling]: Yes. I know this word.

LOUISE: And for Clive's sake, too. We'd all been a little restless in town, and I thought it would be amusing if we could have a little retreat ... Calm ourselves with country air ... And really, it's been quite successful, I think ... On the whole ...

[WALTER *sits on the sofa. She drinks some coffee.*]

A very clever boy I was recommended to did it up for us. Bunny Baily – d'you know him?

WALTER: No, I'm afraid not.

LOUISE [*lightly and rapidly*]: Well you will, I'm sure. He's very up and coming. Not just chic; I mean really *original*. He wanted to make us entirely early Medieval: stone flagging and rushes strewn on the floor. But my husband didn't quite see eye to eye with us on that. [*Drinks more coffee.*] Mr Harrington's very conservative, you know. Well, most men are, aren't they, essentially? ... Englishmen, anyway. The French are different ... And the Germans too. I'm sure. [*She smiles at him and points to the cigarettes on the coffee-table.*] Would you like to smoke?

WALTER [*reaching for the cigarette-box*]: Thank you.

LOUISE: You look a little upset too, Hibou. What's the matter?

WALTER: Oh, it's nothing.

LOUISE: It must be something. Has Clive been teasing you? He can be very naughty sometimes.

WALTER: Oh, no. You know, Mrs Harrington, I think he is not very happy.

LOUISE [*putting cup on table next to armchair*]: He gets that from me too.

WALTER [*impulsively*]: Is there anything that I can do? Anything at all?

LOUISE [*regardless*]: I'm not a very happy person either, you know. [*Rises. Crosses L. to below armchair.*] Well, you can see for yourself. Whatever you do, my dear boy, marry a girl who's your equal. If you can find one. I'm sure it'll be hard. When I married I was a very young girl. Believe it or not [*puts cup on table L. of armchair*] I'd hardly met anyone outside Bournemouth. [*Sits in the armchair.*] My parents didn't consider it proper for me to run about on my own. And when I met Stanley, they did everything in their power to encourage the match. You see they weren't very dependable people. My mother was an aristocratic little lady from France who had never learnt to do a thing for herself all her life. And helplessly extravagant as well. Of course, highborn people so often seem to have extravagance as a sort of inherited characteristic, don't they? My father was more stable, at least he was conscious of money though he never made very much. [*Drinks more coffee.*] And when he actually inherited something, he lost it all in speculation. Do you understand that word, dear? Speculation?

WALTER: Oh yes . . . he was a stockbroker.

LOUISE: Heavens, no – a lawyer. Both my parents came from professional people, so naturally they had reservations about marrying me into the furniture business. [*Gives her cup to Walter, who puts it on the tray.*] Still, I was attracted to Stanley. I won't deny it. He had sort of rugged charm, as they say. Obviously I was interested in all kinds of things like art and music and poetry which he, poor man, had never had time for. But when you're young, those things don't seem to matter. It's only later when the first excitement's gone, you start looking a little closer. [*An audible sigh.*] Walter, these past few years have been intolerable. [*Rises and goes towards Walter.*] There are times when I listen to you playing when I go almost mad with sheer pleasure. Year after year I've had to kill that side of myself. Smother it. Stamp it out. Heaven knows I've tried to be interested in his bridge and his golf and his terrible business friends. I can't do it – I just can't do it. I'm sorry. I didn't mean to talk like this. I'm embarrassing you.

WALTER: No.

LOUISE: I'm being vulgar, aren't I?

WALTER: You could never be.

LOUISE: Dear Hibou . . . you know, don't you? You of all people must know. You understand why I stayed. [*Sits in armchair.*] The children. At least I could see that they weren't stifled too . . . Do you condemn me?

WALTER [*puts out cigarette*]: How could I condemn – in your house?

LOUISE [*wryly*]: I think we can leave hospitality to one side.

WALTER [*pursuing his own thought*]: No, no. In the house you have given me also to live in, so I can sit here and talk to you as if always I had the right.

LOUISE [*sympathetically*]: Dear Walter . . .

WALTER: Where I worked before, I taught the children for two or three hours. I was paid by their mothers and back always to my small room – [*a faint smile*] – with my cooking which is not so good. You will never know how much I owe to you.

LOUISE: My dear boy . . . Tell me about your family. Your people in Germany.

[WALTER *stiffens perceptibly into withdrawal.*]

WALTER: There is nothing to tell.

LOUISE: There must be something.

WALTER: I was an orphan.

LOUISE: Like Stanley.

WALTER [*rises and goes R. to dining-table*]: My parents died when I was too young to remember them. I was brought up by my uncle and his wife.

LOUISE: Were they good to you?

WALTER [*noncommittal*]: Very good, yes.

LOUISE: And – that's all you want to say?

WALTER: There is nothing else.

LOUISE: Don't think I'm being inquisitive . . . It's only that you've come to mean so much to us all in this past two months.

WALTER: I do not deserve it.

LOUISE [*warmly. Rises*]: You deserve far more. Far, far more. I knew as soon as I saw you at that terrible cocktail party in London, standing all by yourself in the corner pretending to study the pictures. Do you remember – before even I spoke to you I knew you were something quite exceptional. I remember thinking: such delicate hands . . . and that fair hair – [*touching it*] – it's the hair of a poet. And when he speaks he'll have a soft voice that stammers a little from nervousness, and a lovely Viennese accent . . .

WALTER [*stiffly*]: I am not Viennese, you know. I am German.

LOUISE: Well, it's not so very different . . .

WALTER [*dogged*]: I am German. This is not so poetic. [*He crosses below Louise to the L. end of sofa.*]

LOUISE [*a little intimidated by the darkness in him*]: But Hibou, there's good and bad in all countries – surely?

WALTER [*gently. Crosses below Louise and the armchair to the left edge of the sofa*]: You are too good to understand. I know how they seem to you, the Germans: so kind and quaint. Like you yourself said: miller's daughters and woodcutters . . . But they can be monsters.

LOUISE [*prepared to mock him as she breaks down stage – left of armchair*]: Really now . . .

WALTER: Yes! . . . [*He is plainly distressed.* LOUISE *looks at him curiously.*]

LOUISE: Even in England we're not all angels.

WALTER: Angels to me! Because this to me is Paradise.

LOUISE: How charming you are.

WALTER [*with increasing heat*]: No, I am sincere. You see . . . here in England most people want to do what's good. Where I come from this is not true. They want only power . . . They are a people that is enraged by equality. They need always to feel ashamed, to breathe in shame – like oxygen – to go on living. Because deeper than everything else they want to be hated. From this they can believe they are giants, even in chains . . . [*Recovering as he sits on the sofa.*] I'm sorry. It's difficult to talk about.

LOUISE: Anything one feels deeply is hard to speak of, my dear.

WALTER: One thing I do know. I will never go back. Soon I'll be a British subject.

LOUISE [*crossing right a few steps*]: You really want to stay here.

WALTER: If you had seen what I have, you would know why I call it Paradise.

LOUISE: I can see for myself how you've suffered. It's in your face . . .

[*Extending her hand to him.*] Walter... You musn't torment yourself like this. [*She takes Walter's hand.*] It's not good for you. You're among friends now. People who want to help you. People who love you ... Doesn't that make a difference?

WALTER: You are so good to me! So good, good. ... [*Impulsively he bends and kisses her hands.*]

LOUISE [*suddenly she takes his head in her hands and holds it close to her. Tenderly*]: Oh, my dear ... you make me feel ashamed.

[CLIVE *comes in abruptly through the garden door. He stares at them fascinated.*]

It's been so long since anyone has talked like this to me.

[CLIVE *bangs the door.*]

Jou-Jou ... [*Trying to recover her composure.*] Did you have a nice talk? Did you see Pam?

[CLIVE *remains where he is, still staring at his mother. She rises and crosses to above armchair.*]

It's absurdly late for her to be walking alone. Are you sure you didn't see her? She's probably gone over to that terrible friend of hers, Mary whatever-her-name-is. I think it's high time she found another friend, don't you? [*As* CLIVE *goes on staring, her last remnant of poise deserts her.*] She may be upstairs after all. I'll just go up and see ...

[*She leaves the room and goes quickly upstairs to her own room.* WALTER *rises.* CLIVE *stays still by the chair left of the dining-table. Now* CLIVE *goes slowly over to Walter. He is evidently fairly drunk, but alcohol does not impair his speech. Rather it gives it energy, and turns of speed. Now it is more disturbed than he himself is aware.*]

WALTER: Clive, what's the matter? Why are you looking at me like that?

CLIVE: ... Hair is being worn dishevelled this year. The Medusa style. What would have happened if Medusa had looked in a mirror? Are monsters immune against their own fatal charms? Observe, please, the subtle and dialectical nature of my mind. It's the French in me, you understand. An inheritance from my very French, very aristocratic ancestors. Perhaps you've been hearing about them. In actuality, I regret to say, they weren't as aristocratic as all that. My great-grandpa, [*sinks on to sofa*] despite any impression to the contrary, did not actually grant humble petitions from his bedside – merely industrial patents from a run-down little office near the Louvre. The salary was so small that the family would have died of starvation if Hélène, my grandmother hadn't met an English lawyer on a cycling tour of the Loire Valley, married him, and exchanged Brunoy for Bournemouth. Let us therefore not gasp too excitedly at the loftiness of Mother's family tree. Unbeknownst to Father it has, as you see, roots of clay.

[CLIVE *pours himself some coffee.* WALTER *stares at him in silence, as he gets into his stride.*]

Still, they *are* French roots. I even have them in me. For example – my Mother's name for me – Jou-Jou. Toy. More accurately in this case, ornament.

[WALTER *remains silent.*]

Being French, Mother imagines she's real ormolu in a sitting-room of plaster gilt. She suffers from what I might call a plaster-gilt complex,

[WALTER *sits in armchair.*]

if you see what I mean. To her the whole world is irredeemably plebeian – especially Father. The rift you may detect between them is the difference between the Salon and the Saloon. At least that's what she'd have you believe . . . I won't deny that she's only really at home in the Salon; but then where else can you be so continuously dishonest?

WALTER [*stung into speech*]: Please –

CLIVE: Yes?

WALTER [*rises. Takes a few steps to Clive*]: I do not wish to hear this.

CLIVE: The young, charming tutor does not wish . . . So delicate; so old-world. A tutor and his employer by the fireside. Paris calls to Vienna. The waltz plays on the deserted boulevard; the leaf falls in-to the empty wine glass; Europe crumbles. Oh, the charm of it . . .

[*He lights a cigarette, then grabs pillows on the sofa, piles them up in the corner, and leans back on them.* WALTER *turns left – away from Clive.*]

Do let's salvage what we can. If we can't afford a château in Brittany, then we can afford a country place in Suffolk, a simple little farm-house which we can decorate out of all existence. If we can't install scholars in our library because we haven't got a library, since nobody reads in our house, then the least we can do is get in a young charming tutor for the girl, someone with tone, of course; nothing grubby out of Night School . . . You see, we're specialists in delicacy.

WALTER [*turns to Clive*]: Clive, why do you talk like this?

CLIVE [*rises – crosses to above armchair*]: Because I'm not so damned delicate after all. Because actually, if you want to know, I'm getting less bloody delicate all the time.

WALTER [*crosses right*]: I do not want to hear any more.

CLIVE: Where are you going?

WALTER [*gravely*]: If you had come from Europe, if you had been taken in, as I was – alone – then perhaps.

CLIVE: Taken in! Taken in is right!

WALTER: Excuse me.

CLIVE [*pushes Walter down on the centre table*]: Oh no – taken up! Like a fashion. Or an ornament; a piece of Dresden, a dear little Dresden owl . . . and believe me, like any other valuable possession, sooner or later you will be used. I know this family, let me tell you.

[*The front door slams.* PAMELA *comes in and runs upstairs.*]

LOUISE [*calling from the U.R. hall*]: Pam, is that you? [*She appears on the landing.*]

PAMELA [*running up the stairs, breathlessly*]: Yes. It's all me!

[*She turns on the light to the schoolroom and then goes into the bedroom where she also turns on the light.* WALTER *crosses to the L. of the dining-table –* CLIVE *goes R.*]

LOUISE [*in the schoolroom*]: Where've you been? It's very late. I wish you'd take your walks earlier.

PAMELA [*coming back into the schoolroom*] : I'm sorry.

LOUISE: Where did you go?

PAMELA: Over to Mary's. She's the funniest person in the world. Last week she went to the ballet for the first time. Well, she watched all these girls going up on their toes and dancing about and do you know what she said at the end? 'Mother, why don't they just get taller girls?' [LOUISE *is unamused.*] Don't you think that's funny?

LOUISE: Yes, dear, very funny. Good night, dear.

PAMELA: Good night, Mother.

LOUISE: Don't read tonight. It's too late.

> [LOUISE *returns to her room.* PAMELA *closes the schoolroom door, goes to the bookcase, selects a book, and crosses to turn out the schoolroom lights. She then exits to her bedroom.*]

CLIVE [*keeping still and quiet; to himself, as he crosses centre*] : Hepcat – she's the only one who's free with her private star of Grace ... [*Louder.*] It's a wonderful dispensation; to escape one's inheritance. Oh, I don't mean you. Walter, you're one of the best people who ever came into our house ...

> [WALTER *slowly crosses to the right end of sofa.*]

You think I don't know how lonely you were before you came here. I can smell your loneliness ... You see, I've only one real talent; being able to see what's true and just what isn't. And that's an awful thing to have. [*With sudden animation after a pause.*] Come away with me.

WALTER [*startled*] : Come away?

CLIVE [*rises and crosses below the armchair to the left end of the sofa. Kneels on it – facing Walter*] : Look – in four weeks my term ends. We could go somewhere ... anywhere ... to the West Country ... Wells Cathedral is the most astonishing thing in England. It's like walking down the throat of a whale: a great skeleton whale, with the vertebrae showing. No one will be there at Christmas. The Wye Valley without a single charabanc! That's a bus, you know.

WALTER: I know.

CLIVE: Please say yes ... You'd love it.

WALTER [*sits on the sofa. With a shy smile*]: I'm sorry. Christmas is a family time. For so long I have missed it. This year I wish very much to spend it here.

CLIVE [*insistently. Sits left of Walter*]: Well, afterwards. I could wait.

WALTER [*awkwardly; his whole stance awkward*]: I'm afraid it's not possible. My lessons, you see. I have been paid already to the end of January.

CLIVE: So what? Everyone takes Christmas off.

WALTER: I do not think I can go away.

CLIVE: Because you've been paid?

WALTER: No ...

CLIVE: Then why?

WALTER: I ... I have an ... [*searches for the right word*] obligation.

CLIVE: To my mother?

WALTER: Yes. An obligation.

CLIVE: Is that what you call it – obligation? [*Rises and crosses to above the armchair.*] Well, doff my plumed hat! Gallant Walter Langer ... The Cavalier Tutor to his Mistress! Or do I mean the Cavalier Teuton? ... Don't look so startled. Proper cavaliers have only figurative mistresses. Department of Old World Charm! [*He crosses to the right end of the fireplace, swept into frantic remorse.*] This is quite beyond anything, isn't it?

[WALTER *rises and crosses to the hall.*]

If you came away with me, it would be for my sake – not yours. I need a friend so badly.

WALTER: You are unhappy. [*Crosses left a few steps*]: I am sorry. I really ...

CLIVE [*the bitterness returning*]: Is that all you can say? 'I'm sorry.' Such an awkward position I put you in, don't I? The poor little immigrant, careful not to offend. So very sensitive. [*With sudden fury.*] When in hell are you going to stop trading on your helplessness – offering yourself all day to be petted and stroked? [*Sits in chair above dining-table.*] Just like I do. O.K., you're a pet. You've got an irresistible accent. You make me sick.

WALTER: Excuse me. [*He makes for the stairs.* CLIVE *seeks to detain him clumsily.*]

CLIVE: Walter, Walter, I didn't – please –

[WALTER *leaves the room and goes up to his own.*]

[*dully*] Please. . . . [*Slowly he goes to the bottle of whisky.* WALTER *reaches the landing, goes to his door, opens it, and turns on his light.* PAMELA *comes out of her room, leaves the door open, in her night clothes on her way to the bathroom.*]

PAMELA [*to Walter*]: Hullo! [*Turns on the landing lights.*]

[*She stops speaking when she notices the troubled expression on his face.*] What's the matter? You look as if they were going to cut off your head in the morning!

[WALTER *doesn't answer. Pulling open her dressing-gown and revealing her pyjamas.*]

Are you shocked because I'm in my this?

WALTER: Yes, I am. Very.

PAMELA: Then you'd better leave, sir. I'm on my way to the bathroom and I've no wish to cause you embarrassment.

[*He bows. She curtsies and turns off the landing lights.*]

Good night.

WALTER: Good night.

[*He goes into his own room and closes the door. She exits into the up right hall, after turning off the lights. Downstairs* CLIVE *is pouring out another drink.* STANLEY *comes in through the front door, takes off his hat, hangs it on the hat-rack, and comes into the living-room.* CLIVE *puts down the glass guiltily and leaves it on the sideboard.*]

STANLEY: What are you doing?

CLIVE [*breaks downstage*]: Stealing your drink.

STANLEY [*crossing centre*]: Stealing? You don't have to steal from me, Clive. You're old enough to take a drink if you want one. I don't keep it locked up. [*At commode.*] Where's your mother?

CLIVE [*crosses to sofa and sits*]: I don't know – upstairs . . .

STANLEY: You ought to have come with me to Benton's. We went over to the Golf Club. Jolly nice crowd there. [*Crosses to Clive.*] The sort of fellows *you* ought to be mixing with. There was a chap there in publishing. You'd have been interested . . . Clive, I've told you before, in this world you want to get in with the people that matter. But you've got to make an effort, my boy. Make yourself a bit popular. And you're not going to do that sitting here drinking by yourself. Are you?

CLIVE [*still low*]: No, I suppose not.

STANLEY: What d'you want to do it for anyway?

CLIVE [*shrugging*]: I don't know.

STANLEY [*crosses to armchair*]: Well, it's damn silly and it's not normal. [*Sits.*] If you want to drink—drink with others. Everyone likes a drink. You come over to the Golf Club with me, you'll soon find that out. I'll make you a member. You'll get in with them in a jiffy if you'll only try.

CLIVE [*rises and goes to stairs*]: Yes. Well . . . I think I'll go to bed now.

STANLEY: Just a minute. What's the matter? Aren't they good enough for you? Is that it?

CLIVE: No, of course it isn't.

STANLEY: Then what?

CLIVE [*gaining courage and coming back into the room*]: Well, all this stuff – right people, wrong people – people who matter. It's all so meaningless.

STANLEY: It's not a bit meaningless.

CLIVE: Well, all right, they matter! But what can I say to them if they don't matter to me? Look, you just can't talk about people in that way. It's idiotic. As far as I'm concerned one of the few people who really matters to me in Cambridge is an Indian.

STANLEY: Well, there's nothing wrong in that. What's his father? A rajah or something?

CLIVE: His father runs a pastry shop in Bombay. [*He sits on sofa.*]

STANLEY: Well, what about him?

CLIVE: He's completely still. I don't mean he doesn't move – I mean that deep down inside him there's this happy stillness, that makes all our family rows and raised voices here like a kind of – blasphemy almost. That's why he matters – because he loves living so much. Because he understands birds and makes shadow puppets out of cardboard, and loves Ella Fitzgerald and Vivaldi, and Lewis Carroll; and because he plays chess like a devil and makes the best prawn curry in the world. And this is him.

STANLEY: Do you want to be a cook?

CLIVE: No. I don't want to be a cook.

STANLEY [*bewildered and impatient*]: Well, Clive, I'm glad to know you've got some nice friends.

CLIVE [*sharp*]: Don't. Don't do that.

STANLEY: What?

CLIVE [*rises and crosses left a few steps*]: Patronize. It's just too much.

STANLEY: I'm not patronizing you, Clive.

CLIVE: Oh yes, you are. That's precisely what you're doing.

STANLEY: That's very unfair.

CLIVE [*working himself into a deep rage*]: Precisely. Precisely! [*Goes to the commode.*] 'I'm glad you have some nice chums, Clive. I had too at your age.' . . . These aren't my play-pals; they're important people. Important to me. [*He breaks down stage, left of the armchair with the glass of whisky he poured earlier.*]

STANLEY: Did I say they weren't?

[*PAMELA returns from the bathroom. She listens for a brief moment at the top of the stairs, then goes into the schoolroom, closes the door, and on into her bedroom.*]

CLIVE [*frantic*]: Important! It's important they should be alive. Every person they meet should be altered by them, or at least remember them with terrific – terrific excitement. That's an important person. Can't you understand?

STANLEY [*rises, crosses to the commode. Crushingly*]: No, Clive. I told you: I don't understand you at all. Not at all.

[*A slight pause.* CLIVE *subsides. When he speaks again it is to renew the attack in a colder and more accusing voice.*]

CLIVE: You're proud of it too.

STANLEY [*getting angry*]: What now?

CLIVE: That you don't understand me at all. Almost as if it defined you. 'I'm the Man Who Doesn't Understand.' [*Directly, his voice shaking with resentment.*] Has it ever occurred to you that *I* don't understand *you*? No. Of course not. Because you're the one who does the understanding around here – or rather fails to. [*Furiously.*] What work did you put in to being able to understand anybody?

STANLEY: I think you'd better go to bed.

CLIVE [*he puts his glass on the commode*]: I'll go to bed when I'm good and ready! . . . [*Breaks down stage to Stanley.*] D'you think it falls into your lap – some sort of a grace that enters you when you become a father?

STANLEY: You're drunk.

CLIVE: Yes, you think you can treat me like a child – but you don't even know the right way to treat a child. Because a child is private and important and itself. Not an extension of you. Any more than I am. [*He falls quiet, dead quiet – as if explaining something very difficult. His speech slows and his face betrays an almost obessed sincerity as he sits in the chair right of the dining-table.*] I am myself. Myself. Myself. You think of me only as what I might become. What I might make of myself. But I am myself now – with every breath I take, every blink of the eyelash. The taste of a chestnut or a strawberry on my tongue is me. The smell of my skin is me, the trees and tables that I see with my own eyes are me. You should want to become me and see them as I see them, but we can never exchange. Feelings don't unite us, don't you see? They keep us apart. [*Rises and goes to sofa.*] And words are no good because they're unreal. We live away in our skins from minute to minute, feeling everything quite differently, and any one minute's just as true about us as any other. That's why a question like 'What are you going to be?' just doesn't mean anything at all – [*Sits during pause.*] Yes, I'm drunk. You make me drunk.

STANLEY: I do?

CLIVE [*losing heart*]: You and everything . . .

STANLEY [*a little afraid now*]: . . . You've given me something to think about, old boy. It's getting a bit late. Don't you think you'd better go upstairs . . . we'll talk about it in the morning. Well, I'll say good night. [*He steps upstage.*] Clive . . . I said good night.

[*Still* CLIVE *takes no notice.* STANLEY *shrugs and goes up the stairs. On the landing,* STANLEY, *conscious of failure, hesitates to go into the hall.* CLIVE *picks up Walter's spectacles from the coffee-table and puts them on; he begins to cry terribly, almost silently. Presently* STANLEY *returns and stands left of the sofa, looking on with a helpless gesture.*]

Clive, don't forget to turn out the lights. [*He notices the boy's sobbing.*] What's the matter, boy? [*He sits on the sofa next to Clive.*] What? Come on, now. Out with it. What's the matter – can't you tell me? That's a stupid attitude to take, isn't it? After all, I'm your father. It's what I'm here for.

[CLIVE *shies away from the thought of contact as* STANLEY *makes to touch his shoulder.*]

I say, there's something really wrong, isn't there?

CLIVE [*whispering*]: No. [CLIVE *goes on shaking his head.*]

STANLEY: Did something happen while I was out?

CLIVE: No . . .

STANLEY: Well, what was it? . . . Did your mother say something? [*Taking spectacles from Clive's hand.*] Is it something to do with Walter?

[CLIVE *rises and crosses below Stanley. Sits on the right arm of the armchair.*]

That's it, Walter . . .

[*Then* CLIVE'S *wretched silence goads* STANLEY *beyond control. He grabs the boy's wrists and stares into his face.*]

STANLEY: Clive! What happened with Walter? . . .

CLIVE [*frightened*]: I don't know. I don't know . . .

STANLEY: Tell me! What happened with Walter?

[CLIVE *crosses away from Stanley and goes towards the stairs.* STANLEY *throws Walter's glasses into the armchair.*]

CLIVE [*slowly turning to face his father*]: It was Mother!

STANLEY: What?

CLIVE: I came in and they were there. [*He points to the sofa.*] He was kissing her. She was half undressed. And he was kissing her, on the mouth. On the breasts. Kissing . . .

[STANLEY *hits him,* CLIVE *falls on sofa.*]

Department of Just Deserts. . . .

ACT TWO

SCENE ONE

The following morning. Sunday. A bright, cold day.

PAMELA, *in her riding clothes, is sitting at the breakfast table finishing her coffee and reading one of the better Sunday papers.* WALTER *is sitting on the right end of the fireplace bench, drinking coffee and having a cigarette.*

PAMELA: Walter, what does 'salacious' mean?

WALTER: What word?

PAMELA: 'Salacious' – it's in this article.

WALTER [*rises and looks about for his glasses. He sees them in the armchair where Stanley dropped them the evening before. Puts them on and takes the paper from Pamela*]: Where? Ah, now, 'salacious'. [*Pause.*] Yes, it means wise. [*Returns the paper to Pamela and goes back to the fireplace.*]

PAMELA: Does it? I suppose I should have guessed. You ought to teach English.

WALTER: I wouldn't dare.

PAMELA: Oh, phooey. I'm sure you'd be miles better than the man at my last school. Anyway, he was a Dutchman. . . . Mother says this is the only Sunday paper she'll have in the house. I think it's mean of her. Everyone else has the popular ones with pictures of rapes. . . .

[LOUISE *comes from the kitchen.* WALTER *immediately stands.*]

LOUISE: Did you enjoy your kippers?

WALTER: Yes, they were splendid, thank you.

LOUISE: Do sit down, my dear.

[*He does so.*]

PAMELA: Mother, why can't we have Sunday papers with sexy pictures in?

LOUISE: Because they're vulgar, and give you a distorted view of life.

PAMELA: I don't mind.

LOUISE: Well, I do. Where's Clive?

PAMELA: Not down yet.

LOUISE: Really, you children are the limit. [*Goes to the kitchen door with coffee-pot.*] I don't see why you can't all have your breakfast together. It's late enough, heaven knows. Pamela, you'd better hurry up and finish dressing if you're going riding.

[*She goes back to the kitchen, leaving the door open.*]

PAMELA [*rises and goes to chair left of dining-table. Sits*]: Have you ever gone riding?

WALTER: No.

PAMELA: It's the best, absolutely. What games did you play in Germany?

WALTER: I – I used to walk.

PAMELA: You mean on hiking parties, all dressed up in those leather shorts?

WALTER [*sits in chair R. of dining-table*]: No. By myself. I liked it better.

PAMELA [*impulsively*]: Are you happy here? Are you really, really happy?

WALTER: Of course.

PAMELA: Who do you like best?

WALTER: You.

PAMELA: No, seriously.

WALTER: I like you all. You and your mother . . .

PAMELA: And Clive?

WALTER: Of course and Clive. I like him very much. I'm only sorry he is so unhappy.

PAMELA: Unhappy?

WALTER: I think so, yes.

PAMELA: That's because he was spoilt when he was young.

WALTER: Spoilt? I don't know that.

PAMELA: You know – to spoil someone. Like damage.

WALTER: Oh, damage; yes! . . .

PAMELA [*down right; drinking her coffee*]: I'm sure he ought to get married.

WALTER: Oh, he's so young!

PAMELA: For some people it's the best thing. You must help him find a girl.

WALTER: Why? Has he not had friendships with girls before?

PAMELA [*in her 'affected' voice*]: Not even acquaintanceships, my dear. [*Normal.*] Except for one; a girl called Peggy-Ann who worked in the tobacconist's when we were at the seaside. She used to wear tight leopard skin trousers and great sort of brass bells in her ears. Clive said they used to go down on the beach and neck, but I bet he was just bragging. So you see, you've got to help him. I'm sure you know hundreds of girls. [*Takes cup to window seat.*]

WALTER [*amused*]: Oh, yes. What kind would you suggest?

PAMELA [*leans on back of straight chair*]: Someone who'll pay him lots of attention. At home, everyone keeps on at him but no one really takes any notice of him. [*Brightly.*] Clive spends his whole time not being listened to.

WALTER: His mother listens, doesn't she?

PAMELA [*closes kitchen door*]: Not really listens, no . . . Well of course you can't expect her to. No mother ever really listens to her children. It's not done.

WALTER: You seem to know a lot about it.

PAMELA: Yes, I do. [*Sits in chair above dining-table.*] Poor Clive. You know, they really only use him to help them when they're rowing. [*Directly.*] Can you understand why they row?

WALTER: I think everyone has quarrels.

PAMELA: Yes, but this is different. With Mother and Daddy the row is never really *about* – well, what they're quarrelling about. mean . . . well, behind what they say you can feel – well, that Mother did this in the past, and Daddy did that. I don't mean any thing *particular* . . . [*She stops, confused.*] Oh, dear . . . marriage is a very difficult subject, isn't it?

WALTER [*humorously ; he is a little uncomfortable*] : You don't take your exam in it until you're a little older.

PAMELA [*pursuing her own thought*] : I mean, who begins things? Do you see?

WALTER : Please, Pamela –

PAMELA : I know Mother's frightful to him about Culture, and uses music and things to keep him out – which is terrible. But isn't that just because *he* made *her* keep out of things when they were first married? You know he wouldn't even let her go to concerts and theatres although she was dying to, and once he threw a picture she'd bought into the dustbin; one of those modern things, all squiggles and blobs. [*Gestures.*] . . . But then, mightn't *that* just have been because being brought up by himself he was afraid of making a fool of himself. Oh, poor Daddy . . . Poor Mother, too. [*To him, brightly.*] You know, I shouldn't wonder if parents don't turn out to be my hobby when I grow up.

[STANLEY *appears on the landing and descends the stairs.*]

WALTER [*warmly*] : You know something? You have a wonderful mother. Did you know that?

PAMELA : Yes, I suppose so.

WALTER : Is that all? Only suppose?

PAMELA : People who make you feel stupid are always called wonderful.

[STANLEY *comes into the living-room. He looks tired and strained.* PAMELA *crosses to him.*]

Good morning, Daddy.

[WALTER *rises.*]

STANLEY [*kissing her*] : Morning, dear. [*He stares at Walter with a curious unwilling stare.* WALTER *rises rather awkwardly.*]

WALTER : Good morning, sir.

[LOUISE *comes in from the kitchen with the coffee-pot, which she puts on the window-seat.*]

LOUISE: Stanley ...? You might let me know when you come down. Walter, dear, will you come and get Mr Harrington's cereal for me?

WALTER [*eager to help, he takes a used plate, cup, and saucer from the table and starts for the kitchen*]: Of course, Mrs Harrington.

[*She goes into the kitchen again.*]

I hope your headache is better this morning, sir. [*He exits to the kitchen and closes the door.* STANLEY *nods, apparently unable to speak. He sits right of the dining-table.*]

PAMELA [*going to the window-seat and pours a cup of coffee for Stanley*]: Aren't you playing golf today, Daddy? It's late.

STANLEY: No, not today.

PAMELA: Why? Aren't you feeling well?

STANLEY: Oh, I'm all right ...

PAMELA: Why not come riding with me then?

STANLEY [*wrapped in himself*]: No ... not today. I ... just want to take things easy today.

PAMELA [*mischievously as she gives him the coffee*]: You must be getting old.

[*He looks at her searchingly.*]

STANLEY: When are you going to learn to fix that bow. Come here. [*She kneels to his right. He fixes the ribbon.*] Has Clive come down yet?

PAMELA: No, the lazy pig. You were talking to him late last night, weren't you? I could hear you from upstairs. [*Crosses to centre table.*] Well, really, it seemed more like Clive was talking to you.

[*He stiffens, but she doesn't notice.* WALTER *reappears with porridge.* PAMELA *sits on C. table.*]

WALTER [*placing it before Stanley*]: Mrs Harrington asks would you prefer eggs or kippers?

STANLEY [*quietly*]: Nothing.

PAMELA: Daddy, you must have something.

STANLEY: Don't fuss, Pam. [*Curtly, to Walter.*] Nothing.

WALTER [*with a half bow*]: Yes, sir. [*He goes back to the kitchen, deflated.*]

PAMELA: He'd make a wonderful waiter, wouldn't he?

[STANLEY *gets newspaper from bench. Sits there and opens paper.*]

How did you like Clive talking to you man to man? [*Brightly.*] He must have been drunk.

STANLEY: Why do you say that?

PAMELA: Because if he wasn't, he never would have. Not properly, anyway. He'd be too nervous.

[*He looks at her sharply.*]

That's because you like him to answer questions all the time, and he hates to.

STANLEY: Why?

PAMELA: I don't know. I suppose he's just not the answering type. D'you know he even has a dream about you?

STANLEY: Clive does?

PAMELA: Yes. He gets it quite often, so he must think an awful lot about you. You ought to be flattered, though it's not exactly what I'd call a flattering dream ... [*Recounting it carefully, with increasing drama. She sits R. of table.*] Apparently, he's always in bed lying down under thick blankets; and there is a window and he can see into a big garden all covered in snow. It's freezing so hard outside he can hear twigs snapping on the trees. Then suddenly you appear, coming slowly over the snow towards him – crunch ... crunch ... crunch. You disappear inside the house and he can hear you coming upstairs – crunch ... crunch ... and along the passage to his room. Then the door slowly opens and you come in, and cross the room to see if he's asleep. So while you stand there he pretends to be asleep, as asleep as can be, except that sometimes he starts shivering, which spoils the effect. Then you start taking off the blankets one by one. Clive says there must be about ten blankets on the bed, and with each one you take off he gets colder and colder. Usually he wakes up with all his bedclothes on the floor. Isn't that the silliest dream you ever heard ...? I told him

the next time he heard you coming upstairs he was to wait till you
came up to the bed, then sit bolt upright and shout 'Go to hell!'

[STANLEY *has listened to this impassively but with the greatest*
attention. He still sits involved in his own silent conflict as LOUISE
returns from the kitchen. WALTER *follows carrying the picnic basket.*]

LOUISE [*to Pamela*]: Pamela! Are you still here?

[PAMELA *rises.*]

You're going to be very late for your ride. And I've told you
before, unpunctuality is just bad breeding.

PAMELA [*to Walter, who crosses right below the table*]: I've decided
you'd make the most wonderful waiter.

LOUISE [*shocked*]: Pamela! What a thing to say.

PAMELA: Well, he would. Can't you just see him bowing to old
ladies with Pekineses.

LOUISE: Stóp it, Pamela. That's very rude. A waiter! Can't you
think of anything else for Walter to be? I only hope one day you'll
have a tiny part of his education, and a few of his manners. [*To*
Pamela.] Now hurry up and get dressed.

[WALTER *goes upstairs and into schoolroom to change a book.*]

Your picnic's all ready.

PAMELA [*goes to dining-table. Picks up basket*]: Daddy, can I borrow
your lumber jacket? Please say yes.

STANLEY [*quiet*]: Of course – it'll be a bit big for you, won't it?

PAMELA: Oh, yes, but I'll wear it as a cape. Of course I won't look
half so good in it as you.

STANLEY: Enjoy the ride.

PAMELA [*intimately*]: You bet.

LOUISE: And tell Clive from me, if he's not down right away he
won't get any breakfast.

[PAMELA *goes upstairs and into the hall.* LOUISE *crosses left.*]

Stanley, what are you sitting there for? Walter says you don't
want any cooked breakfast. And you haven't even touched your
cereal. That's absurd. You must have something to eat.

[*He stares now at her, puts paper on bench.*]

What's the matter? Did you have too much to drink last night or something?

[*He rises and goes to french window.*]

Stanley . . .

[*Abruptly he goes into the garden,* LOUISE *stares after him in astonishment. She sits down at the table.* PAMELA *emerges on the landing with Stanley's lumber jacket.*]

PAMELA [*knocks on his door*]: Walter!

WALTER [*coming from his room*]: Yes?

PAMELA: I wasn't really rude just now, was I?

WALTER: Rude? No, of course not. As a matter of fact, I was a waiter once, for a short time in Berlin. But they threw me out.

PAMELA: Why?

WALTER: They said I had no dignity.

PAMELA: How ridiculous. You're the most dignified man I ever met. [*Running off into the hall and knocking on Clive's door.*] Clive! Wake up, wake up, whoever you are! Get into your slippers, go down for your kippers . . .! Wake up, wake up . . .

[*She reappears and goes to the schoolroom, then to her bedroom.* CLIVE *follows in a jacket and trousers, with a slight hangover.*]

WALTER [*at his door*]: Good morning.

CLIVE: Good morning.

WALTER: Excuse me. I think I'll do a little work. [*He exits into his room.* CLIVE *goes up to the schoolroom.* PAMELA *reappears with riding-cap and riding-crop.*]

PAMELA: Salaams. A thousand welcomes, my handsome slave boy. Mine eyes rejoice in the sight of you! [*She whirls Clive around.*] Dance with me, my little pomegranate! Madden me with desire!

CLIVE: Drop dead! Where is everybody?

PAMELA: Downstairs. You'd better go down. You look a bit green. Do you want a fizzy?

CLIVE: No.

PAMELA: Well, salaams.

[*She runs off into her room.* CLIVE *goes slowly downstairs, where* LOUISE *still sits at the table. He is clearly reluctant to go.*]

LOUISE: You slept late. Perhaps you had a little too much to drink last night, too.

CLIVE: What do you mean?

LOUISE [*at window seat*]: There's kippers or eggs.

CLIVE [*crossing left*]: No, thank you. Is there any coffee?

LOUISE: Now what is this? First your father and now you.

CLIVE: Where is he?

LOUISE: Outside.

CLIVE [*perplexed. Crosses to the french door*]: Where?

LOUISE: In the garden. [*Pouring Clive's coffee.*] Well – isn't he?

CLIVE [*looking out*]: Yes. He's sitting down under the apple tree.

LOUISE: *Sitting?* In this weather! Without an overcoat? He'll catch his death. Tell him to come in at once.

CLIVE: Perhaps he prefers it outside.

LOUISE: Don't be ridiculous, Clive. The man must be mad, sitting out there on a freezing morning like this. [*Advancing to the french window.*] What on earth he thinks he's doing, I can't imagine.

CLIVE [*sharply*]: Leave him alone!

LOUISE [*amazed*]: Are you talking to me?

CLIVE [*firmly; almost surprised at himself*]: Leave him alone.

LOUISE: Are you sure you're feeling all right?

CLIVE: I – I'm sorry.

LOUISE: So you should be. That was very, very ill bred.

CLIVE [*whispering*]: Not really done.

LOUISE [*crosses above and to the right of table*]: Clive, I don't understand you this morning. I really don't.

CLIVE [*French accent*]: *Votre Majesté* should not worry 'erself about eet. It makes, as the French say, no nevaire mind. Your *Majesté*.

[*He extends his hand in salutation. At the same moment the slow movement of the Brahms Third Symphony is heard from Walter's room. Suddenly she draws him to her – he allows himself to be drawn – and embraces him. A brief instant of great intimacy recurs, as it happened in the first scene.*]

LOUISE [*sits R. of table*]: Jou-Jou . . . !

CLIVE [*kneels to her*]: Maman . . . !

LOUISE: *Mon petit Cossack.* . . . Silly boy. [*She holds him tenderly, in the position of subservience he took up before his Empress – only now very close to her. His back is to the audience, and from his inclined posture she can fondle his head.*] D'you think I'm so stupid that I don't know what's wrong? D'you think I can't see for myself . . .? We're a little bit jealous, aren't we? As if you didn't always come first. You know that. Don't you?

[*He nods, stiff now with reluctance.*]

Then it's ridiculous, isn't it, to be jealous? And of whom? A poor lonely boy with no people of his own to care for him, all by himself in a foreign country. Really, Jou-Jou, you ought to be ashamed. Let's say no more about it. I want you always to be happy – remember? Very, very happy.

[*He nods again.*]

There. [*She kisses his forehead.*] Now, let me cook you some breakfast. You could eat an egg, couldn't you? [*She rises.*]

CLIVE [*sits on bench below table*]: I suppose so.

LOUISE: You finish your coffee while I get started. [*She looks at him tenderly.*] Silly boy . . . [*She goes out into the kitchen.*]

CLIVE [*with a sort of bitter disgust; to himself. Rises and crosses U.C.*]: On waves of sympathy. On waves . . . !

[STANLEY *comes in from the garden. He crosses the stage, goes out, and leaves the house through the front door, which he bangs behind him.*]

[*The door of Pamela's bedroom opens after a moment and she comes into the schoolroom. She goes out of the schoolroom wearing the lumber jacket as a cape, and her riding-cap, and starts downstairs with her picnic basket and riding-crop. She misses her footing and falls in an undignified heap on the landing.*]

PAMELA: Damn! Damn! Damn!

[*Music stops.* WALTER *comes rushing out, startled by the great crash.*]

WALTER: What's the matter? . . . I'll help you. Are you hurt?

PAMELA: Of course not. Walter, put me down. Walter, put me down.

CLIVE [*who has reached the landing*]: Pam, are you all right?

[LOUISE *enters from the kitchen.*]

PAMELA: Yes, of course I am all right.

[CLIVE *goes back downstairs and into the kitchen.*]

LOUISE: What happened? What on earth was that noise?

PAMELA: It's all right, Mother. Don't fuss. Anyone would think I was dying. [*Feeling her head.*] Ow!

[WALTER *picks up Pam's jacket, cap, crop, and basket.*]

WALTER: See? You bumped your head.

PAMELA [*witheringly*]: When you fall down, you must bump something.

LOUISE: What happened, Walter?

WALTER [*concerned*]: She fell. I think you should look on her head, Mrs Harrington.

LOUISE [*with a faint touch of hauteur*]: Thank you, Walter. You can leave her to me now. [*She takes Pamela's things from Walter.*]

WALTER: Yes, Mrs Harrington. Of course. [*He gives his half bow and goes back into his own room.*]

LOUISE: Go on upstairs. . . .

[*They both go up to the schoolroom.*]

PAMELA: Fuss, fuss, fuss.

LOUISE [*Pamela sits in chair left of the schoolroom table. Louise puts the clothes on the table. Examining her daughter's head*]: Let me look. Does it hurt?

PAMELA: No, it doesn't.

LOUISE: You say that as if you wanted it to. What on earth were you doing?

PAMELA [*exasperated*]: Nothing. I just tripped. And that stupid Walter has to come in and pick me up as if I was a chandelier or something. Holding me that way.

LOUISE [*carefully*]: What way, darling?

PAMELA [*crossing above Louise to her left*]: Well, trying to carry me as if I was a baby.

LOUISE: But wasn't he only trying to help?

PAMELA [*angrily*]: I think he's just plain soppy.

LOUISE: Because he was worried about you?

PAMELA: Oh, Mother. [*She rises and crosses to the chair right of the table. Puts her foot on the chair and rubs her ankle.*] You don't understand anything . . . It's just so *undignified*, can't you see? It shows no *respect* for you. I mean, if you're two years old it's all right to pick you off floors that way, and even then it's an invasion of your privacy. If children of two could speak, you know what they'd say? 'Why can't you keep your filthy hands to yourself?'

LOUISE [*picks up lumber jacket*]: You'd better be off on your ride before you get into any more trouble. [*Gives the lumber jacket, to* PAMELA *who puts it over her shoulders.*] Here, take this. [*Picks up Pamela's riding-crop and basket from the table; the brown sweater from the back of the left chair.*]

PAMELA [*crossing to the door*]: Oh, it's one of those days.

[*They leave schoolroom. The Symphony starts again in Walter's room.* PAMELA *crosses to his door and listens.* LOUISE *closes the schoolroom door.*]

I bet you anything the horse breaks its legs. D'you think Walter heard me just now?

LOUISE: Well, you weren't exactly whispering, were you?

[*Both go downstairs and into sitting-room. While they are on their way, the record off stage sticks. The passage is repeated several times, then the needle is moved on.*]

PAMELA: I think I'm the most impossible person I know. . . But then I suppose wonderful people always make you feel like that. Sort of ashamed all the time.

LOUISE: He makes you feel ashamed?

PAMELA [*takes cap from her mother*]: Not exactly ashamed but, well, like in those advertisements. I always feel like the grubby shirt next

to the dazzling white one. [*Puts on cap.*] He's so fresh! Fresh and
beautiful . . . [*Brightly.*] Don't you think he's beautiful?

LOUISE [*confused*]: I hadn't thought.

PAMELA [*takes basket and riding crop from Louise*]: It's just exactly
what he is. [*Crosses L. to the right end of the bench.*] He should wear a
frock coat and have consumption.

LOUISE: What nonsense.

PAMELA: Why? There *are* people like that.

LOUISE [*with sudden irritation*]: Well, Walter certainly isn't one of
them. He's obviously quite a happy, normal young man. [*Crosses
to Pam.*] There's simply no reason for you to weave any romantic
ideas about him being tragic or different in any way.

PAMELA [*grandly*]: I'm afraid it's obvious you don't know him very
well.

[*But* LOUISE *is unamused. Instead, she is making an effort at self-
control.*]

LOUISE: If you're going, you'd better go. You'd better put on a
sweater.

PAMELA: Oh, phooey.

LOUISE: Darling, it's cold out.

PAMELA: It isn't really.

LOUISE: Pam, it's very cold. Now do be sensible.

PAMELA: But Mother, I've got Daddy's big jacket on.

LOUISE [*snapping*]: Do as I say! Put on your sweater!

[*She leaves the room abruptly and goes up into the schoolroom.*
PAMELA *looks after her in surprise.*]

PAMELA [*puzzled*]: 'Bye.

CLIVE [*off in the kitchen*]: Pam, is that you?

PAMELA: Yes, I'm just off.

[CLIVE *comes in, carrying a plate of eggs.*]

CLIVE [*sits above table*]: What were you playing at just now? Being
the walls of Jericho?

PAMELA: Oh, shut up!

CLIVE: Have a nice time.

PAMELA: You should come with me.

CLIVE: I know. It does you good to get in the air.

[LOUISE *exits into Pam's bedroom with the clean bedclothes which were on the school desk.*]

PAMELA [*in a wildly affected, cheerful voice*]: Well then, bye-bye, darling. You're sure there's nothing I can get you from the village? A barrel of beer? Harris tweed?

CLIVE [*matching her accent*]: No, thanks, old girl. Just bring back the usual papers. The *Hunting Gazette* and the *Shooting Gazette*.

PAMELA: Righty-ho!

CLIVE: And the *Fishing Gazette* – and some wax for the old moustache.

PAMELA: Certainly, dear.

CLIVE: I say, Pamela – you are a brick!

PAMELA: Then I'll say . . . [*Blowing him a kiss.*] Cheeribye, darling.

[*She shimmies out through the french window.* WALTER *emerges from his room with a book of piano pieces. He comes downstairs.*]

CLIVE: Hullo.

WALTER: Hullo.

CLIVE: What's the matter with your record?

WALTER: It's not the record. The needle keeps jumping. I think the table's not quite level.

CLIVE: Oh, really? It must be one of Father's.

[WALTER *gets a cigarette from the table next to the centre armchair.*]

Do you know that a judge trying a copyright case in this country once asked learned counsel: 'What exactly *are* Brahms . . .?'

[WALTER *smiles in appreciation, sits on back of armchair.*]

Well, how are you? Clearly unwell, I should say. Only the sick and corrupt would spend a bright Sunday morning listening to music. In all decent English homes this time is reserved for sport. Staying still is the absolute proof of decadence.

WALTER: Yes. This is familiar to me. Where I was born – to sit reading was an offence too.

CLIVE: Why? You had to be out playing games?

WALTER: Games. Yes, but in small uniforms.

CLIVE [*scenting difficulty*]: I suppose every kid wants to be a soldier?

WALTER: Oh yes. [*Pause.*] But in England they are not told it is a good thing to be.

CLIVE: Why? Did your uncle believe it was?

[WALTER *does not reply.*]

Parents and guardians are desperately unreliable.

WALTER [*turning, smiling*]: Maybe we expect too much of them. After all, they are only us, a little older.

CLIVE: A little older and a little more depended on.

WALTER: Exactly.

CLIVE: So not a bit like us.

WALTER [*mischievously*]: Do you think *you're* going to make a very good father?

CLIVE [*takes plate to window-seat*]: I don't see why not. I was a complete success as a baby. [*Cross to R. of dining-table.*] I was so demanding, I gave my parents the idea they were indispensable.

WALTER: I wish I had known you then.

CLIVE: What on earth for?

WALTER: It would have been nice when I was a child.

CLIVE: Sometimes you make me wonder if you ever were ... But you're such an excluded person. It's the thing about you.

WALTER [*softly*]: No, not any more. ... Clive, I'm sorry I ran out on you last night.

CLIVE [*stiffly. Crosses to bench – sits*]: Oh, let's forget it.

WALTER: It was kind of you to suggest a holiday together.

[CLIVE *looks at him woodenly.*]

I know you're not happy here ... I would be most honoured if you could talk to me about it. If there were things you want to say – like last night I felt there were things.

CLIVE [*darker*]: Look I think we'll forget it.

[*In difficulty.*]

Walter, don't take me wrong ... but are you sure you did the right thing when you left Germany?

WALTER [*in amazement*]: You sound as if you wanted me to go back.

CLIVE [*very quiet*]: Yes.

WALTER: Why . . .?

　[CLIVE *does not reply.*]

　Last night you did not want it.

CLIVE [*with sudden desperate anger*]: Last night . . .! I want it now. I want you to go. [*Modifying his tone with effort.*] For your sake. Only for your sake, believe me . . . You've got a crush on our family that's almost pathetic. Can't you see how lucky you are to be on your own? Just because you never had a family you think they're the most wonderful things in the world.

WALTER: Clive . . .

CLIVE: Why have you got to depend all the time? It's so damned weak!

WALTER: You know nothing!

CLIVE: I can see.

WALTER: What can you see? My parents? My father – can you see him, in his Nazi uniform?

CLIVE: But – you told me your parents were dead.

WALTER [*crosses up to commode*]: Yes, I know. They are alive. In Muhlbach. Alive. There was no uncle.

CLIVE: Your father was a Nazi?

WALTER [*crosses to back of armchair*]: Oh, yes. He was a great man in the town. Everybody was afraid of him, so was I . . . When war broke out he went off to fight and we did not see him for almost six years. When he came back, he was still a Nazi. Everybody else was saying, 'We never liked them. We never supported them.' But not him! 'I've supported them,' he said. 'Hitler was the greatest man our country has seen since Bismarck. Even now we are defeated, we are the greatest country in Europe. And one day we will win, because we have to win . . .' [*He crosses and sits in the chair R. of the dining-table.*] Every night he used to make me recite the old slogans against Jews and Catholics and the Liberals. When I forgot, he would hit me – so many mistakes, so many hits.

CLIVE: But your mother?

WALTER: My mother . . . she worshipped him. Even after we found out.

CLIVE: What?

WALTER: That during the war . . . he worked at Auschwitz concentration camp . . . He was one of their most efficient officers. [*A slight pause.*] Once he told me how many. . . . [*He stops in distress. His voice dead with loathing.*] I could have killed him. I could have killed him till he was dead. And she worshipped him – my mother. She used to smile at him, stare at him – as though he owned her. And when he used to hit me, she would just – just look away as though what he was doing was difficult, yes – but unavoidable, like training a puppy. That was my mother.

CLIVE: I'm sorry.

WALTER [*recovering*]: So you see, Clive, I do know what is is like to have a family. And what I look for is somewhere . . . where now and then good spirits can sit on the roof.

CLIVE: And you think you've found it here? Do you?

[WALTER *does not answer.*]

[*Rises – cross R. a few steps.*] You're fooling yourself every minute.

WALTER [*gravely*]: Don't you think I should find that out for myself?

CLIVE: Oh, for God's sake! If that horrible story was meant to change my mind, it didn't.

WALTER: I did not tell it for that.

CLIVE: Then go. Just get the hell away from here.

WALTER [*rises*]: Clive. . . .

CLIVE: For my sake – I want it.

WALTER: But why?

CLIVE: Because I can't bear to watch.

WALTER: Watch? I don't understand you.

CLIVE: Well, then, just *because.*

[LOUISE *comes out of Pamela's bedroom, goes through the schoolroom and on to the landing.*]

LOUISE [*calling downstairs*]: Walter . . .?

[WALTER *looks at Clive inquiringly, unwilling to court interruption.*]

CLIVE [*hard*]: Go on. Answer her. It's your duty, isn't it?

WALTER [*low, appealing*]: Clive ...

LOUISE: Walter!

CLIVE [*turning on him ferociously*]: Answer her!

[*As* WALTER *stands irresolutely,* CLIVE *turns again and goes out abruptly through the front door.* LOUISE *descends the stairs.*]

LOUISE [*coming into the living-room*]: Ah, there you are, my dear boy, all alone ...? [*Going to coffee-table.*] Come and talk to me, it's not good for you to be on your own too much.

WALTER: I was not alone. Clive was here. He's just gone out.

LOUISE [*takes cigarette and holder*]: Where?

WALTER: I don't know – Mrs Harrington, I'm most worried for him.

LOUISE [*smiling*]: Poor Hibou, you worry about everybody, don't you? But you mustn't about Clive, really. It's just a tiny case of old-fashioned jealousy, that's all.

[WALTER *lights her cigarette.*]

Well, it's only to be expected, isn't it? [*Crosses to armchair.*] We've always been so wonderfully close, he and I.

WALTER [*courteously*]: Of course.

LOUISE: He'll get over it. One day he'll understand about women. At the moment, of course, he thinks there must only be room in my heart for one boy. So silly ... [*She sits. Warmly.*] I don't believe you can ration love, do you?

WALTER [*sits, sofa. Admiringly*]: With someone like you it is not possible.

LOUISE: Nor with you, my dear. You know, last night held the most beautiful moments I've known for many years. I felt – well, that you and I could have a really warm friendship. Even with the difference ... I mean in – in our ages.

WALTER: Between friends there are no ages, I think.

LOUISE [*tenderly*]: I like to think that, too.

WALTER: Oh, it's true. Like in a family – you don't notice how old people are, because you keep growing together.

LOUISE: Yes. Dear little owl ... What's the matter ... Are you embarrassed?

[*He shakes his head 'No'.*]

It's the last thing you must ever be with me.

[WALTER *smiles.*]

What are you thinking? Come on: tell me.

WALTER: Some things grow more when they are not talked about

LOUISE: Try, anyway. I want you to.

WALTER [*looking away from her*]: It is only that you have made me wonder –

LOUISE [*prompting eagerly*]: Tell me.

WALTER [*lowering his voice still more as he walks toward Louise*] Mrs Harrington, forgive me for asking this, but do you think it's possible for someone to find a new mother?

[LOUISE *sits very still. The expression of eagerness fades, and its rennant hardens on her face. She stares at him.*]

Have I offended you?

LOUISE [*smiles, without joy*]: Of course not. I am ... very touched

WALTER [*moved. Kneels*]: I'm so glad. [*Eagerly.*] That is why I feel I can talk to you about Clive, for example. I am most worried for him. He is not happy now. And I do not think it is jealousy. It is something else – more deep in him – trying to explode. Like the beginning of an earthquake or so.

LOUISE [*with increasing coolness. Rises. Crosses to coffee-table*]: Really, my dear, don't you think you're being a little over-dramatic?

WALTER [*dogged. Rises*]: No. I mean exactly this. You see ... that boy ... It is very difficult for me to explain.

LOUISE [*wryly*]: I appreciate your attempt ... [*crosses to centre table.*] But really, I'm sure I know my children a little better than you.

WALTER [*persisting*]: Of course. But just in this case – with Clive – I feel something which frightens me – I don't know why –

LOUISE [*her temper breaking*]: Oh, for heaven's sake!

[WALTER *recoils.*]

[*Recovering quickly. Crosses to dining-table with dirty ashtray.*] I mean

... after all, as you admit yourself, you *are* only a newcomer to the family, remember. [*Sweetly.*] Now why don't you go and play me some of your nice music?

[WALTER *looks confused, and lowers his eyes before her strained smile. He exits into kitchen.* LOUISE *starts to pick up dishes and silverware, but puts them down with a big crash.*]

SCENE TWO

The same night, after supper.

The living-room is empty. Up in the schoolroom, WALTER *is hearing* PAMELA *in her irregular verbs. They are sitting in their usual position at the table.*

PAMELA: *Je meurs, tu meurs, il meurt, nous meurons –*

WALTER: No.

PAMELA: It must be.

WALTER: It's not. It's *mourons.*

PAMELA: *Mourons.* Oh, phooey ... you know, this is the perfect way to end today. It's been a stinker, hasn't it?

WALTER: Has it? I thought you had a good ride this morning.

PAMELA: Oh, that ... I mean the atmosphere since I got back. What Mother calls the *aura.* And Clive not coming in for lunch or dinner. D'you think he's run away?

WALTER: I think we'll do more French.

PAMELA: Mother was livid tonight when he didn't turn up. That's funny, too. I'd have thought Daddy would have been the one to explode, but he didn't say a word ... Do you think Clive's lost his memory or something?

WALTER: What is the future of '*mourir*'?

PAMELA: Perhaps he's been kidnapped. Just think of Daddy paying ransom. I wonder if he would.

WALTER: I think Clive can take care of himself. Now, *please*, Pamela –

PAMELA: Oh, I'm sick of French! Anyway, it's Sunday and that's supposed to be a Day of Rest.

WALTER: Yesterday you said you felt Jewish and Saturday was your day of rest.

PAMELA: That was Saturday – not Sunday. Tonight I'm going to have a hot bath and go straight to bed and read. Mary gave me a most important scientific book last week and I just haven't had a moment to glance at it.

WALTER [*suspiciously*]: What kind of science?

PAMELA: Actually it's a kind of story.

WALTER [*resigned*]: Ah-ha.

PAMELA: But completely scientific. It tells what would happen if the earth got invaded by Venus. The people are just sweeties. They're all ten foot high and covered with blue jelly.

WALTER: Very educational.

[LOUISE *comes from the hall wearing a light blue sweater over her shoulders. She turns the lights on in the landing. We can now see that she is very strained and anxious.*]

LOUISE: Pamela –

PAMELA: There you are. You can't even have a scientific discussion any more without being interrupted by the world of triviality.

[LOUISE *comes into the schoolroom and goes to the right of Pamela.* WALTER *rises.*]

LOUISE: How's the bruise, darling?

PAMELA: It's all right, thank you.

LOUISE: I've turned on your bath.

PAMELA: Has Clive turned up yet?

LOUISE [*wearily, but with a vestige of deep anger*]: No. Not yet . . . [*Softening.*] Now get into your bath and don't dawdle, will you? [*She goes to the door. Having virtually ignored Walter, who has stood uncomfortably by the table, she just notices him on the way out.*] Good night, Walter.

WALTER: Good night, Mrs Harrington.

PAMELA [*whispering*]: She looks as if she needs a fizzy.

WALTER: Pamela, that's very naughty.

PAMELA: Well, she does. Mother always looks like that when she's lost an argument. It's meant to mean she's been misunderstood.

WALTER: I think she is worried about Clive.

PAMELA [*rises*]: Phooey! Anyone would think he was still a child the way she goes on. [*Wickedly.*] I hope he stays out all night. Wouldn't it be wonderful if he was giving babies to all the schoolgirls in Ipswich . . .?

[PAMELA *goes to her bedroom for her robe and slippers. Re-enters.* LOUISE *enters through front door. She turns on the living-room lamps at the switch on the pillar.*]

[*Affected voice again*] Well, I'd better go and have my bath, dear boy. Oh Lord, Sunday night. London tomorrow. Breakfast at half past seven for that rotten train. I think Mondays stink . . .

[LOUISE *exits through french door – L.*]

Is there any religion with its Day of Rest on Mondays?

WALTER: Yes. There is the religion of Lazy Girls.

PAMELA: Oh, you are brutish!

[PAMELA *goes down the stairs, turns off the landing-lights and exits into the hall. Presently the front door opens.* STANLEY *comes in and walks into the living-room, taking off his overcoat.* LOUISE *enters through french window.*]

LOUISE [*hearing the noise of his entry*]: Clive? Oh, it's you . . .

STANLEY [*coming in*]: Isn't he back yet?

LOUISE: No.

STANLEY: Well, no one's seen him in the village. He hasn't been in any of the pubs.

LOUISE [*bitterly*]: The pubs. Always the pubs.

STANLEY [*goes to left end of sofa*]: Well, where else would he be likely to go? You know what the trouble is? Your son's turning into a drunkard.

LOUISE: . . . The way you've been behaving lately's enough to make anyone drink. No one would think he's your son. You treat him abominably. [*Takes off sweater, leaves it on chair above dining-table.*]

STANLEY [*sits on sofa*]: Do I?

LOUISE: You haven't the faintest idea how to deal with sensitive people. If I was Clive, I'd have run away from home long ago.

STANLEY [*bitterly*]: If it weren't for the saving grace of his mother. His sensitive mother.

LOUISE [*crosses to armchair*]: At least I understand him. I make an effort. Just because you can't see beyond the end of your stupid, commonplace nose – [*Sits.*]

STANLEY [*savage. Rises. Crosses to commode. Pours himself a drink.*]: Shut up!

LOUISE: Charming.

STANLEY [*his pain also becoming rage*]: And what have you ever done for him that's so wonderful, may I ask? I'll tell you. Turned him into a snivelling little neurotic. A mother's boy.

LOUISE [*trying to recover poise*]: That's not true.

STANLEY [*crosses down stage – left of chair*]: And I'll tell you something else. He's going peculiar. Yes: looney, if you want to know. He talked to me last night and I didn't understand one word he said.

LOUISE [*loftily*]: That doesn't surprise me.

STANLEY: It was like listening to a lunatic.

LOUISE: And that's my fault too? Just because I take an interest in our son, which you've never bothered to do in all these years, I'm driving him insane.

STANLEY [*with wild demand in his tone. Crosses above chair to her right*]: And when I tried to teach him things, what happened?

LOUISE: What things?

STANLEY [*crosses to sofa*]: Golf – swimming – I don't know, I can't remember. Who was it said, 'Clive's too delicate'? 'Clive can't waste his time on silly games. He's got his reading to do ...' [*Sits.*]

LOUISE: So it was wrong of me to encourage his reading?

STANLEY: He was my son as much as yours!

LOUISE: Yes, and what did you want to do for him? Push him straight into your third-rate furniture business for the rest of his life. That's not good enough for me, Stanley.

STANLEY: Well, he was my son.

LOUISE: He still *is*, my dear.

STANLEY [*hard*]: No. Not any more. You've seen to that.
　　[LOUISE *looks away from him sharply.*]

LOUISE [*collected*]: That's the nastiest thing you've ever said to me.

STANLEY: I didn't mean it.

LOUISE: Yes, you did.

STANLEY [*wearily*]: I don't know what I mean any more . . . It's all so bloody mixed up.

LOUISE: Must you swear?

STANLEY: I don't know . . .

LOUISE: I can't stand much more. I just can't.

STANLEY [*dead*]: What?

LOUISE [*rises and crosses left of armchair*]: It's no good, Stanley. My life was never meant to be like this – limited in this way . . . I know I'm unpredictable sometimes. I say things I don't mean. But don't you see . . . I don't know what I'm doing half the time, I'm so frustrated. I'm sorry, but it's the only word, Stanley. There are times when I feel I'm being choked to death – suffocated under piles of English blankets. Yes, my dear, I'm not English at heart and never will be, no matter how I try. I've never been able to take your boring world of shops and business seriously. Can't you understand? Can't you understand anything? [*She sits in the armchair again.*]

STANLEY [*flat*]: What do you want me to do, Louise? Louise, I'm asking you a question. D'you want a divorce . . . ? Well?

LOUISE: Oh, it's all so vulgar.

STANLEY [*tired*]: I'm a vulgar man.

LOUISE: Do *you*? Do *you* want one?

STANLEY [*plainly*]: I'm too old to start again. And, besides, there's Pam. It wouldn't do her any good.

LOUISE: I notice you don't mention Clive.

STANLEY: Clive's no longer a child. Much as it may upset you to think of it, my dear, he's nearly twenty years old.

LOUISE: I think it's you who haven't gathered that.

STANLEY: Don't start – just don't start.

LOUISE: I didn't begin it.

STANLEY: Louise . . . I know I'm not the easiest man in the world to live with . . . I don't know what it is you want: but anyway I don't seem to have been able to give it to you . . . [*After a moment, in an altered voice, rises and goes to her.*] Look here . . . suppose we went away somewhere – alone together? Just the two of us. Do you think it would help? We could go to Monte Carlo.

LOUISE: You know I can't stand the place.

[*PAMELA comes from the U.R. hall on the landing in her dressing-gown and goes downstairs into the living-room.*]

STANLEY [*controlling himself*]: Well, somewhere else then . . . any-where . . .

[*PAMELA enters the living-room. STANLEY goes up to commode and leaves his glass there.*]

PAMELA: Mother, isn't Clive back yet?

LOUISE: Good night, dear. Sleep well and don't read too late.

PAMELA: No. [*She crosses to Stanley and kisses him.*] Good night, Daddy. [*She goes out and upstairs to the schoolroom.*]

STANLEY [*goes to sofa. Sits*]: Well . . . it's worth a try, isn't it, Louise?

LOUISE: Yes, Stanley, it's worth a try.

PAMELA [*to Walter, in the schoolroom*]: Good night.

WALTER: Sleep tight.

PAMELA: Mind the bugs don't bite.

[*She goes into her bedroom.*]

LOUISE [*after a pause*]: Stanley, I want to ask you to do something for me – something rather difficult. [*She rises and crosses above sofa.*]

STANLEY: What's that?

LOUISE: It's to do with Pamela. I feel it's something you can manage better than I can.

STANLEY: Pam?

LOUISE [*crosses left to above armchair*]: Actually, it's about Walter. I'm afraid he's having rather a bad effect on her. She's just at that stage, you know – impressionable, romantic – long walks in the moonlight. I'm afraid she's got a bit of a crush. Nothing serious of course – she'll get over it.

STANLEY: You want me to talk to her?

LOUISE: No. Something rather more drastic, I'm afraid. I think we must let Walter go. In the most tactful way, of course. Actually the sooner the better.

STANLEY: I see.

LOUISE: I think he's upstairs now – shall I send him down to you? I'll make myself scarce and you will be tactful, won't you?

[*She starts up the stairs.* CLIVE *blunders in through the front door – leaves the door open. He is drunk, but, as on the previous evening, perfectly coherent.* LOUISE *comes back down the steps.*]

LOUISE: Clive!

CLIVE: Good evening, all.

LOUISE [*closes the front door*]: Oh, Clive.

STANLEY: Would you mind telling me where you've been? You've been out since twelve.

CLIVE: Like the tide. But we're back, you see.

STANLEY: Answer me!

CLIVE: Why do we always have to ask expected questions?

STANLEY [*rises*]: Now listen, my boy . . .

LOUISE [*crossing down stage to the left of Stanley*]: Why don't you go upstairs, dear, and do what I asked you to?

STANLEY: Very well. I'll leave you to take care of your sensitive son.

[*He looks at Clive angrily for a moment, then he goes out of the room and up the stairs. He knocks at Walter's door, receives no answer, and less resolutely approaches schoolroom door.*]

LOUISE [*bitterly*]: Your father and I have been worried to death.

CLIVE [*insolently*]: Do I detect a new note in the air? Your father and I. How splendid.

[LOUISE *sits on sofa.*]

The birth of a new moral being. Your-father-and-I . . . When did you last see your-father-and-I? Or is it just a new alliance . . . ? All the same, I congratulate you. I always thought you two ought to get married.

LOUISE [*rises*]: You're drunk! And disgusting! [*Crosses to kitchen.*] I'll get you something to eat.

CLIVE [*coldly*]: Your-father-and-I will now get your supper.

[LOUISE *goes into the kitchen. The lightness of the room troubles* CLIVE. *He shuffles clumsily across the room and turns off the lights so that only the glow from the fire remains in the sitting-room. He sinks wearily into the armchair and covers his eyes.* STANLEY *enters the schoolroom.*]

STANLEY: Are you busy?

WALTER [*standing up; as always, made nervous by his appearance*]: Of course not, Mr Harrington. Is Clive back yet?

STANLEY: He just came in – drunk. Do you drink? I don't remember seeing you.

WALTER: Not very much, no.

STANLEY: Sensible. [*Pause.*] My son drinks. A lot. Doesn't he?

[WALTER *says nothing.*]

Can you think of any good reason for it?

WALTER: I do not think people drink for good reasons.

STANLEY: Sit down.

[WALTER *sits uneasily.* STANLEY *stands left of table facing him.*]

You don't think much of me, do you? Why?

WALTER: Mr Harrington –

STANLEY: Because I'm not educated. Is that it?

WALTER: Of course not.

STANLEY: Then why? Because the children say things?

WALTER: Mr Harrington, please, I –

STANLEY [*crosses to window*]: And what do they know? People say parents are selfish. They've got nothing on children. [*Crosses back to table.*] Do they ever think about anything but themselves? *Their* troubles . . .? As if nobody ever had 'em before. Well . . .? You ought to know. You teach 'em.

WALTER [*softly*]: I think children are less able to deal with their own troubles.

STANLEY [*not really listening*]: I tell you, children are the most selfish things in the world . . . So he drinks. Did you know it was my fault? I drive him to it. So I hear.

[WALTER *says nothing.*]

Well, have you lost your tongue?

WALTER [*very low*]: No.

STANLEY [*sits left of table*]: I'll tell you why he drinks. He drinks so he can get over being with me. Have you noticed how this family never gets together in this house? Are you afraid of me?

WALTER [*straight*]: No.

STANLEY: Well, that's a wonder. My son is. That's something else I hear. What do you think?

WALTER: I . . . I think . . . yes.

STANLEY [*blankly*]: Do you?

WALTER [*with difficulty*]: I think he feels you do not love him, and yet all the time you are expecting him to love you.

STANLEY: Rubbish.

WALTER [*retreating at once*]: I'm sorry. You did ask me.

STANLEY: He's my *son*. How can he think that?

WALTER: He feels always that you are judging him. When you look at him, he feels you are thinking – 'How useless he is.'

STANLEY: And when he looks at me – what's *he* thinking? That's a different story, isn't it? [*Bitterly.*] 'How common he is.'

WALTER: Oh, no –

STANLEY: Don't tell me. I've seen it too often. Common.

WALTER [*gently*]: You are wrong about him. With you always he feels that he has to justify his life. His Greek, maybe, or because he loves an opera. When a boy must apologize for ears and eyes, it is very bad.

STANLEY: Apologize? When have I asked him to apologize?

WALTER: That's not what I meant.

STANLEY: Then why use such ridiculous words? I can see where he gets them from.

WALTER [*gravely*]: Your son has got nothing from me, Mr Harrington. I wish he had. Look, sir. Clive needs help. Will he get it?

STANLEY: He can always come to me. He knows that.

WALTER [*raising his voice slightly*]: And will he come? *Does* he come?

STANLEY [*gathering dignity about him*]: As a matter of fact, we had a very frank talk last night. You didn't know that, did you?

[WALTER *shakes his head.*]

What are you thinking?

WALTER: I was thinking that you are very like your son, Mr Harrington.

STANLEY [*sarcastic*]: Oh yes. In education, I suppose.

WALTER: I say too much always . . .

STANLEY [*he shrugs. Suddenly he begins to talk more or less to himself*]: You needn't apologize . . . What's it matter? You start a family, work and plan. Suddenly you turn round that there's nothing there. Probably never was. What's a family anyway? Just kids with your blood in them. There's no reason why they should like you. You go on expecting it, of course, but it's silly really. There's just nothing. Bloody nothing . . .

[*Unseen by him,* WALTER *gestures towards him in a futile attempt at communication. He goes on staring into space, not heeding the tutor at all.*]

All the time you're saying: It'll be better next year. Next year it'll be all right. The children going to prep school, leaving it. Short trousers, long trousers. Perhaps he'll make the rugger fifteen or the cricket team or something – anything – and then his first girl friend and bringing her home – or perhaps just keeping her to himself till

he's sure ... [*Frankly.*] But nothing ... Nothing ... and now he
hates me.

WALTER: No ...

STANLEY: D'you think I don't know? How sensitive do you have to
be for that? Tell me, because I don't know too much about that
sort of thing ... [*His bitterness rises again.*] I'm always too busy
making money. [*Violently.*] Go on, tell me. Sensitive people have
deep feelings, don't they? They suffer a lot.

WALTER: Please, Mr Harrington.

STANLEY [*violently*]: I don't want to hear.

WALTER: Excuse me.

[*He rises, goes to the door, opens it, and goes down the stairs.
STANLEY is left staring into space. He then goes to the bedroom door,
opens it a little to see if Pamela is asleep. Convinced that she has heard
nothing, he closes the door, reaches down, and turns off the gas fire.
He turns off the schoolroom lights, closes the door, and exits down the
stairs into the hall. WALTER reaches the living-room where CLIVE
has been lying inert in the armchair in a strange awkward position
suggesting acute depression.*]

WALTER: Clive? Are you all right? What are you doing sitting here
in the dark? [*He goes to the commode and turns on the lamp.*] I've been
talking to your father. He thinks you hate him.

[CLIVE *does not appear to hear.*]

Clive ... The kings of Egypt were gods. Everything they did was
right; everything they said was true; everyone they loved became
important. When they died, they were given faces of gold.
[*Pause.*]

You must learn to forgive your parents for being average and
wrong when you worshipped them once ... [*Crosses R. to the edge
of the sofa.*] Why are you so afraid? Is it – because you have no girl
friend? Oh, you are so silly. Do you think sex will change you?
Put you into a different world where everything will mean more
to you. [*Sits – sofa.*] I thought so too once. I thought it would
change me into a man so my father could never touch me again.

I didn't know what it would be like, but I thought it would burn me and bring me terrible pain. But afterwards, I'd be strong and very wise ... There was a girl in Muhlbach. She worked in her mother's grocery shop. One night I had a few drinks and just for a joke, I broke into her bedroom through the window. I stayed with her all night. And I entered heaven. I really did. Between her arms was the only place in the world that mattered. When daylight came, I felt I had changed for ever. A little later I got up. I looked around, but the room was exactly the same. This was incomprehensible. It should have been huge now and filled with air, but no, it was small and stuffy and outside it was raining ... I remember I hated the soap for lying there in the dish just exactly as it had done the night before. I watched her putting on her clothes. I thought: 'We're tied together now by an invisible thread.' And then she said, 'It's nine o'clock; I must be off' – and went downstairs to open the shop. Then I looked into the mirror: at least my eyes would be different. [*Ironically.*] They were a little red, yes – but I was exactly the same – still a boy. The rain was still here and all the problems of yesterday were still waiting. [WALTER *rises and crosses to the right of Clive. He kneels.*] Clive, sex by itself is nothing, believe me. Just like breathing – only important when it goes wrong, and this only happens if you're afraid of it. What's the matter, Clive? Why don't you talk to me?

CLIVE [*very low*]: Walter ... What's wrong with me?

WALTER: There's nothing wrong with you. Nothing.

CLIVE: Don't fool me. I know.

WALTER: There's nothing wrong but in your mind. What you think about.

CLIVE [*despairingly*]: What is it? What have they done to me?

WALTER: Clive, your parents love you. Everything they have done has been from love. I am sure of this.

CLIVE: Then God save me from love.

WALTER: He will not ... You have more in you than any man I've ever met.

CLIVE: Stop it . . .

WALTER: Please, let me help you.

CLIVE: Cut that out!

WALTER: What?

CLIVE: Pity.

WALTER [*gently. Rises and crosses above chair to Clive's left*]: I don't pity you, Clive. And you mustn't pity yourself. You can end this and you must. You must go away from here. [*Crosses.*] You – not me. At the moment you are – [*Gestures.*] – on your family. I don't know the word. Like a butterfly on a pin.

CLIVE [*with distaste*]: Impaled.

WALTER: Yes, that's it . . . and you must get off the pin. [*Sits on centre table.*] At the end of term in Cambridge, don't come back here. Go anywhere else you like. Join your friend singing. Go into a factory. The important thing is this – the moment you get out of here, people will start telling you who you are. Clive, what is it you want from life? I could tell you what *I* want. To live in England. To be happy teaching. One day to marry. To have children, and many English friends . . . And what about you, Clive?

CLIVE [*intimately*]: I think I want . . . to achieve something that only I could do. I want to fall in love with just one person. To know what it is to bless and be blessed. And to serve a great cause with devotion. [*Appealing.*] I want to be *involved*.

WALTER: Then break the glass! Get out of the coffin! Trust everything, not because it's wise, but because not to trust will kill you. Trust me, for instance. I'll see you often. But you must go away from here. Now please, say yes – you will go.

[STANLEY *enters from the hall. He is stopped by the conversation in the living-room. He stands at the top of the stairs listening.*]

CLIVE [*nodding*]: Yes. I'll go.

WALTER: The next vacation?

CLIVE: The next vacation.

WALTER: Good!

[STANLEY *starts coming down the stairs.*]

CLIVE: Isn't it silly? We seem to spend all the time ordering each other out of the house!

WALTER: A very friendly way to spend the time.

[STANLEY *has reached the pillar. The light switch he turns on lights the lamp R. of the sofa.*]

STANLEY: Clive – don't you think you'd better go to bed?

[CLIVE *rises and starts to the stairs.*]

WALTER [*gently to Clive*]: Are you all right now?

CLIVE: Yes, I'm all right. Good night, Father.

[CLIVE *goes upstairs and into the hall.* WALTER *gives his half-bow and crosses below the armchair. He is stopped by Stanley before he reaches the hall area.*]

STANLEY [*raging*]: Just who the hell do you think you are? [*Breaks down stage.*] So the world owes you a living; is that it?

WALTER [*comes down stage*]: Mr Harrington –

STANLEY [*brutally*]: Don't 'Mr Harrington' me, with your smarmy voice and bowing from the waist. You had the gall to patronize me just now – tell me what's wrong with my home . . .

WALTER: You forget – you asked me for my opinion.

STANLEY: Oh, yes. And what else did I ask you to do? Turn my son into a sissy?

WALTER: Your son is a fine, intelligent boy.

STANLEY: He's a mess, that's what he is. And it's your fault.

WALTER: My fault –

STANLEY [*blindly*]: Yes. You, the arty boys. It's you who've taken him . . . [*Hurtling the names as if they were insults.*] Shakespeare! Beethoven! . . . All the time, till I can't touch him . . . Who gave you the right to steal my boy?

WALTER [*with pity*]: You will believe what you please.

STANLEY: I'm not blind you know – and I'm not deaf. I heard you telling him just now. 'Get away from here. Get out of this house,' you said.

WALTER: Yes, I did.

STANLEY: How dare you say a thing like that? What right have you got – in my house, working for me – to say a thing like that?

WALTER: My friendship for your son.

STANLEY: And your friendship with my daughter Pamela too, what about that?

WALTER: Pamela?

STANLEY [*crisply, with satisfaction*]: Your employer, Mrs Harrington, has asked me to dismiss you because she thinks you are having a bad effect upon our daughter.

WALTER: . . . Mrs Harrington said this?

STANLEY: Yes.

WALTER: But it's not true. Not true at all . . .

STANLEY [*carefully*]: No. I don't think it is.

[*Slight pause.* WALTER *looks in utter distress and bewilderment at Stanley.*]

WALTER: Then – why . . . ?

STANLEY [*crosses to Walter*]: Could it be because you've been trying to make love to my wife?

[WALTER *reacts sharply to protest.* STANLEY *goes on in the same quiet tone.*]

You filthy German bastard.

[*The boy winces as if he has been slapped.*]

Once a German, always a German. Take what you want and the hell with everyone else.

[WALTER *stands rigid, with face averted.*]

You're a fool, too. Did you really think she would ever risk anything for you? Oh, I know it's very cultured to look down on money, but that's a very different thing from giving it up. Well, now you've had your chips, and she's sent me to give them to you.

[STANLEY *crosses up to the commode . . . keeping his back to Walter.*] *A long pause. When* WALTER *speaks, it is very quietly, from the depth of his humiliation.*]

WALTER: You can't believe this . . . ? It's not possible . . .

STANLEY [*turns to Walter*]: Oh, yes – it's quite possible. We've got a perfect witness, 'unimpeachable' as we say in England.

[WALTER *looks at him.*]

Can't you guess . . .? No . . .? [*Hard.*] Your pal. Your good pal.

WALTER: Clive?

STANLEY: Of course Clive. Who else?

WALTER [*in disbelief*]: No !

STANLEY: He told me he saw you together last night in this room.

WALTER [*looks at sofa*]: No – no.

STANLEY: Do you know what we do with people like you in England? Chuck 'em out. [*Lowering his voice.*] I'm going to fix it so you never get your naturalization papers. I'm going to write to the immigration people. I'll write tonight. I'll say – let's see – 'Much as I dislike complaining about people behind their backs, I feel it is my duty in this case to warn you about this young German's standard of morality. Whilst under my roof, he tried to force his attentions on my young daughter, who is only fifteen.' Try and get your papers after that. They'll send you back to the place where you belong . . .

[LOUISE *enters the kitchen with tray holding a covered dish. She turns on the lamp on the window-seat.*]

LOUISE: Stanley, I thought you were upstairs – Walter ! What's the matter? [*Puts tray on dining-table.*]

STANLEY: I did what you asked me.

LOUISE Yes, but how did you do it? [*She crosses below Stanley to Walter.*] Was he very brutal, *mon cher*?

[WALTER *does not look at her.*]

But you know yourself it's for the best, don't you? So it's foolish to be upset . . .

WALTER [*grasps her hands, on his knees*]: Don't . . . I beg of you . . .

LOUISE [*trying to free herself, extremely ruffled*]: Walter, really . . .

WALTER: No . . .

LOUISE: Really, Walter . . . Get up at once.

WALTER: Please . . . don't . . .

[STANLEY *backs left a few steps not being able to take his eyes off the the scene.*]

LOUISE: Do you hear me? Walter! You're being embarrassing and ridiculous. [*She breaks loose from him and backs to the commode. She moderates her tone.*] Now, get up at once and stop making an exhibition of yourself.

[*He does so. He leans on the sofa with his back to the couple.*]

I'm sorry, but I'm afraid you deserved to be spoken to like that. I'm really very disappointed in you ... Both our children have been considerably disturbed by your presence in our house and you know I could never allow that. They've always come first with me. I'm sure you understand.

[*No reply. A few steps towards Stanley.*]

Now, about the financial arrangements, we will make it as easy for you as possible. You could manage an extra month's wages, I think, Stanley?

STANLEY: Oh ... yes.

LOUISE: There you are. A month's wages. I call that quite generous, don't you?

WALTER [*in a remote, disinterested voice*]: Yes, I do.

LOUISE: Good. [*Seeing his distress. A few steps right.*] Oh, Hibou, don't look so stricken. It makes it so much more difficult for everybody.

[*A pause.* WALTER *leaves the room and goes up to the landing.*]

LOUISE [*goes to the stairs*]: Walter ...

CLIVE [*appears from hall as* WALTER *reaches the landing*]: What on earth's the matter?

[WALTER *shakes him off and rushes into his room.*]

LOUISE: Well, of all the embarrassing, hysterical scenes ...! [*Rounding on Stanley.*] You seem to have handled it brilliantly, I must say.

[CLIVE *comes down the stairs into the living-room.*]

CLIVE: What's the matter with Walter?

LOUISE [*crosses below Stanley. Sits on bench below dining-table*]: He's a little upset. There's some supper here for you – you'd better eat it.

CLIVE: Why is he upset? What's been going on down here?

LOUISE: I think it's better if we don't talk about it.

CLIVE: Do you want to talk about it, Father? What have you done to Walter both of you? I'm only asking a simple question.

STANLEY: If you really want to know, I told him what you said last night about him and your mother.

LOUISE: Me?

STANLEY: You and your daughter's tutor, my dear – a pretty picture.

LOUISE: What did he tell you? Clive, what did you say?

STANLEY: Never mind – I didn't believe it.

LOUISE: I want to know what Clive said to you.

STANLEY: What's it matter? It never matters what he says.

CLIVE [*looks at Stanley*]: So you didn't believe me?

STANLEY: Do you really think I would?

CLIVE: Then why did you pretend to Walter just now as if you did? – Well?

[STANLEY *goes upstairs.*]

LOUISE: Jou-Jou, you didn't suggest ... but this is horrible. You couldn't have said such things about me, surely?

CLIVE: Yes – I said them.

LOUISE: But why?

CLIVE: I don't know.

LOUISE: Jou-Jou!

CLIVE [*crosses below sofa*]: I don't know why. I do something terrible that I'll remember all my life, that'll make me sick whenever I think of it – and I don't know why.

LOUISE [*crosses to above chair*]: You're ill. You must be.

CLIVE: Oh no. It just means that I can damage people too. I can dish it out just like everybody else.

LOUISE: But it's not true. It's not true what you said!

CLIVE: True? I told a lie, yes. But what I felt under that lie, about you and Walter – was that so untrue? No, don't answer me, because whatever you say just won't be real. You've forgotten what it is to be honest about feeling. True? [*Sits, sofa.*] The only true thing I know is what's happened to him – my father!

LOUISE: You're out of your mind.

CLIVE: And you're so worried about me, aren't you?

LOUISE: Clive, you frighten me. Why are you being so terrible? What have I done?

CLIVE: Don't you know? Can't you see what you've done? There isn't a Stanley Harrington any more. We've broken him in bits between us.

LOUISE: I don't know what you're talking about. I really don't.

CLIVE: No, you don't. Poor man.

LOUISE [sits in armchair]: Clive ... You hate me.

CLIVE: I hate. Isn't that enough? Is the war in this house never going to end?

LOUISE: War?

CLIVE: The war you both declared when you married. The Culture War, with me as ammunition. 'Let's show him how small he is ...' 'Let's show her where she gets off ...' *And always through me!* He wasn't always a bully. You made him into one.

LOUISE [rises. Crosses to R. of dining-table]: I won't go on with this conversation another moment. It's obscene. Your father's upset, that's all. Simply upset.

CLIVE: But *why* is he upset?

LOUISE: About something I asked him to do.

CLIVE [rises. Crosses above armchair]: It was something to do with Walter, wasn't it? What have you done to Walter?

LOUISE: If you must know – he's been dismissed.

CLIVE: Mother – no !

LOUISE: I assure you there were excellent reasons.

CLIVE: But you can't dismiss him. You *can't*. Not even you – [In sudden despair.] He can't go away from here.
    [She looks at him curiously.]

LOUISE [calmly]: If you want to know, I did it for Pam. I'm afraid his influence over her was getting far stronger than I cared for.
    [A slight pause. She sits.]

CLIVE [also calm]: I see.

253

[*The Third Movement of Mahler's Fourth Symphony is heard from Walter's room.*]

LOUISE: Well, evidently the boy himself is not so shattered by the news as you are ... [*Sits right of table.*] Don't you think you'd better eat your supper?

CLIVE [*matter of fact*]: What was it? Jealousy? Shame, when you saw the innocent together? Or just the sheer vulgarity of competing with one's own daughter?

LOUISE [*turns to Clive*]: How dare you!

CLIVE: Dearest mother, who are you trying to fool? I know your rules. Don't give sympathy to a man if others are giving it too – he'll never see how unique you are. Besides, doing what everyone else does is just too vulgar. Like going to Monte Carlo, or falling in love.

[LOUISE *bursts into tears. Puts her arms and head on table.*]
[*Anguished.*] Mother!
[*She sobs helplessly for a moment with a wild, hopeless grief.*] Oh, it goes on and on. No meeting ... Never ... Why can't we be important to each other? Why can't we ever come into the room and be new to each other? Why doesn't a night's sleep, lying all those dark hours with ourselves forgotten and then coming alive again, why doesn't it give us new things to see – new things to say too: not just 'Eat your eggs', or 'You were in late' – the old dreariness. [*Desperately, crossing to his mother.*] I want to *know* you. But you wonderful – changed into yourself ... Don't you understand? So that you can change me.

[*She sits unmoving, no longer crying, giving no indication of having heard.* CLIVE *kneels to her and embraces her with desperate tenderness.*]
[*Tenderly.*] Maman ... Maman, chérie ...
[*For a moment she endures his embrace, then, with a gesture of hysteria, shakes him off.*]

LOUISE: Don't!

CLIVE [*falling back*]: Maman ...

LOUISE [*rounding on him, her face terrible*]: D'you think you're the only one can ask terrible questions? Supposing I ask a few. Supposing I ask them . . .! You ought to be glad Walter's going, but you're not. Why not? Why aren't you glad? You want him to stay, don't you? You want him to stay very much. Why?

CLIVE [*in panic, he rises from the floor*: LOUISE *drives him to the sofa*]: Maman!

LOUISE [*harsh, pitiless now*]: Why . . .? you said filthy things to your father about me. Filth and lies. Why? Can you think of an answer? . . . Why, Clive? Why about me and Walter? Why . . .? Why . . .? Why?

[*The record in Walter's room has stuck.*]

CLIVE: Stop it! You're killing. . . .

[*In the silence, they both become aware of a strange sound: the record playing in Walter's room has stuck. The same phrase is being played again and again. The needle is not moved on. The pause is held. A dawning alarm expresses itself in* LOUISE'S *face. She runs up the stairs to Walter's room. She tries to open his door, but can't.*]

LOUISE: Something's wrong! It's gas. [*Calling.*] Stanley. Stanley! Come quickly. [*She switches on the landing lights.*]

[STANLEY *enters up right. He rushes to Walter's room and turns the handle, but has to push the door hard to get it open. Walter's jacket is stuffed under the door. Both go into the room. The music stops.* STANLEY *drags out* WALTER *on to the landing.* LOUISE *follows, handkerchief to her face.*]

STANLEY [*kneeling over Walter*]: Louise, get a doctor.

[CLIVE *has moved slowly out of the living-room and is now on the landing.* LOUISE *goes down the stairs.*]

Oh God, let him live. Let him live!

CLIVE: Walter!

STANLEY [*to Clive*]: It's gas. Open the window.

[CLIVE *goes into the hall and opens the window.*]

LOUISE [*at the phone*]: 342 please.

WALTER: *Ich verlasse euch fur immer – immer.*

STANLEY: Thank God.

CLIVE: He's not going to die?

STANLEY: No . . . no . . . he's coming around.

[PAMELA, *hearing the noise, enters from her bedroom putting on her robe. She crosses to the schoolroom door, turns on the light, and opens the door.* CLIVE *rushes up to her.*]

LOUISE [*on the phone*]: The doctor, please. It's urgent.

PAMELA [*to Clive*]: What is it? What's the matter?

CLIVE [*closes the schoolroom door and takes* PAMELA *to the bedroom door*]: Nothing . . . it's all right. Walter fell down and hurt himself. Like you did. Now go back to bed. . . . Go on.

[PAMELA *returns to her bedroom. Closes the door.* CLIVE *crosses to the schoolroom door. Almost to himself. . . .*]

The courage . . . For all of us. Oh, God – give it.

[*He turns off the schoolroom light and opens the door. He starts down the stairs as*

THE CURTAIN FALLS